AF594693

Yesterday's News

Yesterday's News

—— MY OWN STORYLINE ——

Tony Ridder

with Steven M. L. Aronson

TidePool Press
Cambridge, Massachusetts

Published in the United States in 2025 by TidePool Press

Every reasonable effort has been made to identify and contact copyright holders for all images used in this book. All photographs not otherwise attributed are from private archives of Ridder and Delano family members.

TidePool Press, LLC
6 Maple Avenue, Cambridge, Massachusetts 02139
www.tidepoolpress.com

Printed in the United States

Library of Congress Cataloging-in-Publication Data

Tony Ridder, 1940–
Yesterday's News: My Own Storyline
with Steven M. L. Aronson

ISBN 978-8-9901334-1-9

1. Ridder, Tony 2. Biography/memoir
3. United States—Newspaper industry
I. Title

2025931245

TO MY FAMILY—PAST, PRESENT, AND FUTURE

Contents

Acknowledgments

I WISH TO THANK Connie, my beloved wife of fifty-one years who died untimely but whose spirit is everywhere in this book. And Dede, the wonderful wife who has lived my life backwards with me as I explored it for this book.

My son Par who has followed in the Ridder family's footsteps and now runs one of the most important newspapers in the country.

And my three daughters: Linda, who has devoted her life to helping disadvantaged boys and girls navigate the educational system; Susie, who is as committed to the legal profession and as devoted to gardening as her mother was; and Katie, who, with her incredible creativity, is one of America's top interior designers.

I remain grateful to Katie and her husband, Peter Pennoyer, for introducing me to the perfect collaborator—the prize-winning writer and editor Steven M.L. Aronson.

Introduction

In most households in America back in the thirties and forties, and into the fifties before the advent of television, the men would get up in the morning and go to work (there was typically one wage earner in a family), and when they came home, they would sit around before dinner and read the paper. The edition would have gone to press in the late morning and been either purchased on the street or delivered in the mid-afternoon by some sure-footed youth carrier, another thing of the distant past.

Newspapers (most cities had more than one) were the only game in town. They were the eagerly awaited primary deliverer—in fact, the sole mass-medium source—of credible information on what had happened overnight in the community and out there in the world, incorporating everything from sports scores, movie times, weather forecasts, and the comics, to tectonic geopolitical events.

If it was unadulterated entertainment you were after, you could turn on the radio and tune in to "Your Hit Parade" for the week's most popular songs, which is what I did, growing up in Duluth, Minnesota. (As an overly enthusiastic Boy Scout, I had gone and built myself a crystal radio.)

Then times changed, big time. Television got rolled out, with its capacity to deliver information in a new way. At six o'clock the family would gather around the set for the "Evening News." It was up-to-the-minute, while the afternoon paper's news was stale, passé—six hours old or even older.

Reading habits shifted to the morning newspaper, which became the industry's cash cow. By the time I got out of college and was ready to start a job in the "Fourth Estate," that's what was happening with dailies all around the country. My life's work auspiciously turned out to be running thirty-two of them.

Everyone predicted that radio and television would wreak havoc on the newspaper industry. Instead, we had a whole golden age of journalism. Right up to the millennium, the country's approximately 1,600 dailies continued to thrive, many of them operating at peak profitability.

Then, with the force of a Category 5 hurricane, came change: the disruptive technologies of cable and the internet—laptops, tablets, smart phones, smart TVs, social media, and other ways (other than newspapers) to access information and entertainment. Aided and abetted by the Great Recession of 2007, they ate ravenously into the advertising which had been supporting and propelling groundbreaking public-service journalism. Newspapers high and low, far and wide, folded left and right, or at any rate were severely weakened—pared down and degraded.

Those that managed to survive are but shadows of their former selves—many are owned by bean-counting hedge funds that have aggressively frozen hiring, slashed travel budgets, trimmed bonuses, and laid off reporters. With their resources curtailed, they are no longer able to do the original, independent, in-depth (often months-long) reporting necessary to fulfill their roles as watchdogs in their communities, holding politicians and other crooks accountable.

This has all been terrible for civic life in America. Downright disastrous.

I spent my entire forty-four-year career in and out of rhythm with the vicissitudes of the newspaper industry. But one thing for me will never change. First thing every morning, I sit down and read the printed versions of the *New York Times* and the *Wall Street Journal*, as well as the local newspaper wherever I happen to be. I hold those papers close, and I hold them dear.

Who was it who said life can only be understood backwards. Remembering—attempting to remember—myself has been a multifaceted experience: glancing back to the settings and defining events of my childhood, youth, and early manhood, and even further back to my Delano and Ridder forebears. And not only glancing but looking intently and from time to time even stopping to stare.

Well, as a poet once wrote, if I am the host at last to my own past, may others be at home in it.

Dad on the day I was born—September 22, 1940—
playing golf at the Northland Country Club in Duluth.

CHAPTER ONE

Par for the Course

RIDDERS WERE ALL born with the golf gene. My father, my uncles, my brother, you name it.

Dad—Bernard Herman Ridder Jr., universally known as Bernie—was the best of the golfing lot. The day I was born—September 22, 1940—he was playing in a tournament at the Northland Country Club in Duluth, Minnesota. Mummy—Jane Delano Ridder—was close at hand, following Dad, as she always did, down the decades till the day he died. When he was on the back nine, she went into labor and started to have me. A good friend volunteered to take her to the hospital so Dad could continue playing. He stayed the course, not only winning the tournament but shooting a par on all eighteen holes.

Thirteen months before, by a fluke, he had been playing golf at the same club, if in a bigger-deal tournament—the vaunted Northland Invitational, the longest running individual match play in the Midwest—when my mother had my sister Laura. That day Dad lost, but he went on to win the invitational on two subsequent occasions.

Now, getting back to little me. To par every single hole, all eighteen, not just a round of seventy-two, was a rare occurrence, and Dad wanted to commemorate it. Which he did by bestowing the initials P-A-R on his newborn son. The R for Ridder was preordained, and the A for Anthony was also a given because Mummy had always liked the name "Tony." All they needed now was to come up with the P, but together my parents decided not to have it stand for anything, to have it just be the initial. But when the minister at my christening was told that my name was to be simply "P. Anthony Ridder," he protested that every infant had to have a first name. My befuddled mother turned to my father, "Bernie, how about Peter or Paul?" Dad said he didn't care one way or the other, so my mother picked "Paul" on the spot.

For all that, my parents never once called me "Par," though I did my level best to live up to my unspoken nickname. I started playing golf at the age of ten and went on to win junior tournaments. In my early teens, some of my golfing pals occasionally called me "Par." But when I got to St. Paul's School, my classmates—typical prep school stuff—seemed to get a kick out of transposing the T and the R in my name, and I found myself having to answer to "Roney Tidder." One of my future wife's brothers picked up on this and called me Roney for years.

When Connie and I had *our* son, we named him Paul Anthony Ridder, Jr., and we've always called him "Par," and nobody has ever called him anything but. He's a golfer, too, naturally: a chip off the old block, off *all* the old blocks. My relationship with my own father was fostered on golf courses, and Par, for his part, plays every year with me in the "Father and Son" tournament at the Cypress Point Club in Pebble Beach, which is universally rated one of the world's best golf clubs and is arguably the most beautiful.

If the Ridders have all been good at golf (my brother Peter, for instance, won two senior and two super-senior club championships at Cypress Point), golf in turn has been good for the Ridders. We used the game to cultivate long-term relationships with advertisers, who represented eighty-five percent of the revenue of our newspapers back in the day. An outing of two or three days on some glorious golf course with major retailers or auto dealers was known to work wonders—call it customer relations to a tee.

Playing in the Bing Crosby Pro-Am Golf Championship, Pebble Beach, 1976. I competed in it for a good twenty-five years.

At the time that Ridder Publications merged with—more precisely, was bought by—the mammoth Knight newspaper chain in 1974, it was riddled with Ridder "nepos," because instead of picking the best man for whatever the job was, the Ridder powers-that-were would pick the best Ridder. And yet you would have been hard pressed to find anyone in the entire newspaper industry who foresaw the day a Ridder would get to run the combined company. That I rose successively to the positions of KR newspaper division president, company president, chairman, and CEO could in all fairness be counted a triumph *over* nepotism. I worked harder than any Ridder ever had (which admittedly is not saying much).

My grandfather, Bernard Herman Ridder, Sr., known to one and

My grandfather, Ben Ridder, in his hail-fellow-well-met prime.

all as Ben, was unabashedly less interested in news than in advertising and promotion, not to mention self-promotion—self-*celebration*—all of which he raised to an art. He was a near-genius at revitalizing retail in St. Paul, Minnesota, where he moved in 1938 to take the reins of the family's then flagship paper, the *Pioneer Press*. By all accounts, Ben Ridder was the best thing that ever happened to local business—he all but singlehandedly resuscitated it. "You can't run a live newspaper in a dead town," he lamented, and within a year of his hands-on involvement, St. Paul ranked fifth in the National Buying Index, and merchants could afford to advertise in his newspaper.

Ben originated the idea for, and begat, an entity designed to vigorously encourage the female citizenry of St. Paul to shop *there* rather than in its more cosmopolitan Twin City competitor, Minneapolis. The organization, christened the Women's Institute and underwritten by the *Pioneer Press*, initially set its sights on upgrading everything from the city's shop windows and merchandise to hotel and restaurant services; in time it would expand its horizons, functioning as the virtual engine of civic pride and undertaking projects such as municipal beautification, traffic control, and school safety.

With an eye to promoting local wares, the institute put on fashion-and-style shows wherein models strutted their stuff on a specially constructed forty-foot runway in the St. Paul auditorium. It offered a variety program as well, featuring nationally known speakers as well as top-tier entertainers such as the Trapp Family, Liberace, Guy Lombardo, and Benny Goodman. My grandfather was a past master of the personal touch, that indispensable staple of public relations, and would collect the visiting celebrities at the airport himself in his Cadillac. (In the case of Ed Sullivan, given that his eponymous Sunday-night television show was sponsored by Lincoln Mercury, Ben took care to show up in one of those.) The institute's first evening guest was the Metropolitan Opera's leading baritone Robert Merrill. (He would also turn out to be its last, bringing down the curtain, and indeed the house, with his rendition of "Auld Lang Syne," when, no longer able to compete with TV variety programs and Broadway roadshows, the Women's Institute ended its thirty-two-year run in 1971.)

When it came to speakers, the inaugural one was a showstopper: the then sitting First Lady of the United States, my grandmother's good friend and relative, Eleanor Roosevelt, who she always spoke of as "Cousin Eleanor." On September 20, 1939, a day that would live in homespun fame, "Mrs. R. with all her trimmin's" (as Cole Porter insolently styled her in *Anything Goes*) took in a "supper style show, my one and only style show for the year," as she noted in her syndicated newspaper column "My Day." That particular day's

Roy Rogers, "King of the Cowboys," holding my younger brother, Peter, at the Women's Institute in Duluth. I am on the lower right.

was headlined "Viewing Styles with 10,000 Women" (reputedly the largest gathering of females ever assembled in the Midwest). Cousin Eleanor earnestly saluted them for "showing what their own shops could produce, stimulating shopping at home and the development of industry."

Other speakers followed in short order, including the professional hostess and "personality" Elsa Maxwell, the iconic decorator Dorothy Draper, and the feminist novelist Fannie Hurst, who exhorted her audience to refrain from letting East Coast book critics regulate their reading habits.

The Women's Institute was where my grandfather first encountered the woman he would make his fourth and final wife in 1944: Agnes Kennedy, who was in turn the organization's treasurer, membership chairman, and executive director. Upon marrying her, he had discovered that his Nevada divorce from my grandmother, Nell Ridder, was invalid. At one problematic point he had two ex-wives suing him for alimony in New York (all three of his ex-wives would wind up living within a few blocks of one another on Manhattan's fashionable Upper East Side). His assets there had been frozen, and he dared not set foot in the state—not even to attend the quarterly board meetings of Ridder Publications—on penalty of being served with sundry judgments. In addition to his invidious habit of withholding alimony, Ben was a deadbeat dad, and my poor father, though only in his teens, was reduced to begging his rich uncles for child support.

My grandfather's twin brothers, Joseph and Victor, ribbed him mercilessly for the careless way he went through women ("left and right"). Ben was a chess addict, and the conceit was irresistible to his siblings, one of whom wrote to the other: "Ben 'The Marrying' Ridder had to give up playing chess because his mates required too many checks. Or did his checks go to too many mates?"

My grandfather was a portly man, with a belly so bulging we grandchildren would joke among ourselves that he looked like he was perpetually having a baby. He was pompous, to boot. There is no polite way to put it: Ben Ridder had this big line of bull, which extended to his reading aloud his endless stock of self-published poems—to the acute embarrassment of his sons and brothers. None of the little ditties he composed over the decades ever evinced a scintilla of self-awareness, with one evident exception:

A Ridder is a monotone
Whose voice is raw and raucous.
He's very loud when he's alone
But louder still in caucus ...
A Ridder is a monologue
No fact but plenty of fiction,
Defying contradiction.

For all his flamboyance, my grandfather's St. Paul house was nothing to write home about. It was a far cry from those enormous places out on the river or on Summit Avenue in town where folks like Garrison Keillor live now—it wasn't even in a fashionable section. But it boasted a nineteen-bed garden that foregrounded a vertiginous variety of tulips (he would have 15,000 bulbs planted at a time) that attracted thousands of visitors a year from all over the Midwest. He could often be seen conducting the garden tours himself.

Ben, to his credit, also conducted scholarly research on flowers, working in collaboration with the University of Minnesota physics department to develop new mutations of zinnias. The abiding grief of his horticultural life was that he was unable to write the garden off on his taxes. Speaking of which, he and Agnes wrote boundless travel columns for the *Pioneer Press* to justify their annual European *vagabondages* to the IRS, as well as to the newspaper's accounting department. These columns were all profusely illustrated with the color slides they took—mostly of works of art in museums and cathedrals—which synergistically became the subject of shows at the Women's Institute.

My grandfather was a stickler for the bottom line. Ben and his little black book! He had an actual one, and it was indeed full of numbers, though hardly those of available women. Every single dollar the company spent was recorded therein: the total lineage reports of all the Ridder newspapers, with the advertising broken down in terms of classified, retail, and national. He even kept records of the company's competitors.

Full of bull as Ben substantially was (his son Joe once playfully presented him with a small bronze statue of a man throwing a bull over his shoulder), the Ridder origin story that he imparted to me incrementally, as embellished as it inevitably came out sounding, turned out to be more or less accurate. I readily concede that the poor-boy-makes-good angle is in fact almost too good to be true, and yet my grandfather's version of the family history was corroborated over time in practically every particular by other, more generally reliable members, as well as attested to by the historical record.

CHAPTER TWO

The Ridders: Founders and Keepers

THE RIDDERS GO back in an unbroken line to at least a couple of centuries before Napoleon—they were farmers in Westphalia, a Prussian province on the Dutch-German border. My great-great-grandfather Herman Ridder—my grandfather Ben's grandfather—was born there in 1816. It took him twenty years to eke out enough for steerage passage on a ship to the New World, and then ten years in New York (doing God knows what, having arrived there without any wherewithal and with virtually no English-language skills) before he was able, in tried-and-true immigrant fashion, to send for his sweetheart back home. Gertrude was her name, and she was a prolific producer of progeny, starting with my great-grandfather, Herman, in 1851, and going on to deliver eight other offspring.

Young Herman dropped out of Grammar School No. 35 in Manhattan at the age of eleven to help the family proverbially make ends meet. He went to work for three dollars a week as an "odd-jobs boy" in a hat shop—the family joke was that he thereby began not at the bottom but at the top. His next job, and hats off to him, was a step up, to eight dollars a week, as janitor/handyman at the Tradesmen's Fire Insurance Company on Fulton Street downtown. Their offices were directly across from those of the *New-York Tribune*, which was where that ineffable thing called Providence kicked in. Herman took to stopping by the *Trib* offices every day after work—he drank in the atmosphere and managed to ingratiate himself with the editors and reporters by fetching beer and light snacks.

One Saturday night—November 9, 1872, a red-letter day as far as the Ridders went, and they were to go far indeed—he was walking past the teletype machine in the newsroom and registered out of the corner of his eye that there was a fire raging in Boston. At the time, the entire Northeast, not to mention Canada, was battling an epidemic of epizootic equine flu that rendered horses too weak to, among other essential things, haul fire engines. Many of the vulnerable buildings in Boston were too tall, anyway, for fire ladders to reach their uppermost levels, and on top of that, there was insufficient water pressure for the hoses to extinguish the flames that were leaping from rooftop to wooden mansard rooftop like, well, wildfire. In other words, Boston was a hot mess. As a last resort, buildings were blown up in an effort to create a fire break, but in the end, a staggering 776 structures, on sixty-five acres in the heart of the city, bit the dust.

Enter my enterprising great-grandfather. After getting a squint of that teletype report, he tore across the street to the closed insurance company and combed through its files for the names and addresses of its policy holders in Boston. Then he talked his way onto the mail car of the New Haven Railroad night train and, once in Beantown, contrived to get as close to the inferno as he could safely manage so he could estimate the relevant property damage. The next day he took the train back to New York, and early Monday morning, it was from the mouth of little Herman Ridder that the giant insurance company learned the details of what was already being described as the Great Boston Fire. It was literally one for the books—to this day, it ranks among the costliest property losses in American history.

Most of the incinerated buildings turned out to be insured at full or above value, and the information provided by Herman enabled the company to get a jump on activating the assets and reserves necessary to meet the crisis head-on. That its deliverer was a lowly employee barely out of his teens, a cipher they had probably never even deigned to notice, must have beggared belief. Herman's reward was an immediate promotion from janitor to insurance agent, his territory to consist of the German Catholic societies that were fast accruing in New York. From there, to shorten a long story, in true Horatio Alger fashion, he worked his way up to company officer.

Along the way, Herman married up, into a prominent German-American Catholic family: Mary Amend was the daughter of a New York Supreme Court justice (two of Herman's sisters would wind up marrying two of her brothers). She went on to bear Herman five children: Herman Bernard, who died in infancy; Bernard Herman (my grandfather Ben); twins Joseph Edward and Victor Frank; and William Joseph, who expired at the age of seven.

With the savings that Herman had husbanded during his fourteen years at the insurance company, he was eventually able to purchase a major interest in the oldest, largest, and most influential German-language—in fact, the largest foreign-language—daily in the country, the *New Yorker Staats-Zeitung und Herold*. Among New York City's miscellaneous dailies, it was exceeded in circulation only by the *New York World* and the *New-York Tribune*.

One fine day in the year 1890—again, Providence can be said to have been working overtime—Herman was having a haircut in the building occupied by the *Staats*, and the barber let slip that the paper's proprietor, the so-called "father of German Journalism in America," the Austrian émigré Oswald Ottendorfer, was in failing health.

A week or so later, greatly daring, Herman presented himself at the Ottendorfer residence and, according to the *New York Times*, "smiling with his eyes and being serious with his chin, as was his wont, said, 'Well, Mr. Ottendorfer, I've come to help you run your paper.'" With the considerable stake he was permitted to purchase, Herman became, at the age of forty, the general manager, treasurer, and a trustee of the *Staats*. At Ottendorfer's death a decade later, he

My great-grandfather, Herman Ridder, the family patriarch, circa 1900.

gained complete financial and editorial control of the most influential organ of public opinion among German Americans. The position provided a nonpareil bully pulpit: overnight, Herman Ridder became the de facto spokesman for the German community not only in New York but nationally and even internationally.

In 1904 he was appointed chairman of the relief committee in the wake of the *General Slocum* disaster (the pleasure boat had burst into flames while paddling up Manhattan's East River with 1,400 mostly German, and mostly women and children, passengers; with 1,000 casualties, it was the greatest municipal loss of life until 9/11).

And on extended trips to the Old Country in both 1906 and 1910, he was wined and dined by the Kaiser.

Herman also came to wield significant political influence at the city, state, national, and, again, international level. He was frequently mentioned as a strong candidate for New York mayor, lieutenant governor, and governor, as well as for United States senator and U.S. ambassador to Germany. Formally offered the spot of running mate by William Jennings Bryan on the 1908 Democratic ticket in the latter's third and final bid for the presidency (Herman and his sons had together made the largest donation to the Bryan campaign—more than a million dollars in today's currency), he declined the honor on the grounds that it would compromise his journalistic ethics: "I don't believe that a man can hold public office and be an unprejudiced journalist. If a man takes office, he is bound to have a feeling of gratitude toward those who put him in the position he occupies. That is human nature. I wanted to stay in the newspaper business. I like it. So, I didn't take office. But if the occasion had arisen where I was the one man that could beat the other fellow I might have acted otherwise. But I would have given up the newspaper business."

All that said, he went on to accept the position of treasurer of the Democratic National Committee, where in no time he distinguished himself as an early advocate and incorruptible enforcer of campaign-finance transparency. The *New York Times* proclaimed that "there isn't a more popular man in the Democratic National Headquarters than Herman Ridder. He is everybody's friend and, what counts for a great deal more in politics, everybody is his friend. Quiet and uneffusive; dignified, yet kindly to the extreme; patient and always anxious to do his very best for everyone, no matter whether it's a stenographer or a state committeeman; ever ready to listen and to give advice of the highest possible value; smiling, even when very weary with a day's work as newspaper proprietor, publicist, and National Committee treasurer; never angry and always optimistic—that's Herman Ridder." The *New-York Tribune* also weighed in fulsomely, describing Herman as "exceptionally tall, 6 foot 6, imposing, heavy-set, a young man of pronounced blond tendencies, with an outsize personality."

Herman was a founder of the American Newspaper Publishers Association (ANPA), where he helped to create national arbitration agreements with the major labor unions active in the newspaper business. In 1907 he was elected, and went on to serve for four years as, the group's president—a position that his great-grandson, an upstart by the name of Tony Ridder, would hold almost a century later, in 2003–2004, the organization having been renamed the Newspaper Association of America (NAA) in 1992. In the living room of my house in Pebble Beach I have the ornate silver bowl presented to my great-grandfather by ANPA in appreciation of his indispensable service. He had also helped found the cooperative newsgathering organization the Associated Press, of which he remained a director until his death. Again, in the fullness of time, the aforementioned upstart—that is, me, myself, and I—would be elected an AP director, serving three terms, from 1995 through 2003.

Herman's undoing was print technology. He became fixated on the manufacture of low-cost typesetting machines and, around 1911, founded, with two of his sons, a publicly traded corporation named the International Typesetting Machine Company or Intertype. Dependent as it was on European sales, which plummeted with the coming of World War I, and further stymied by litigation concerning patents, the company was placed in receivership in 1915 and then sold at auction.

Herman, who had borrowed heavily to keep it afloat, died that year, at the age of sixty-four—broke and broken. And yet, fifteen hundred mourners packed the funeral chapel, including publishing titans Joseph Pulitzer and William Randolph Hearst, and several thousand lesser mortals lined the surrounding streets. The first carriage in the procession from the church to the cemetery was occupied by my great-grandmother and my grandfather, her oldest son, who had recently succeeded his father as publisher of the *Staats*.

The silver bowl (inscription inset) presented to my great-grandfather, Herman Ridder, by the American Newspaper Publishers Association.

A standing-room-only memorial service was held a few months later in Carnegie Hall, with New York governor Charles Whitman presiding. U.S. Senator James O'Gorman delivered a stirring eulogy: "Herman Ridder reveled in the glorious memories of the people from which he sprang. Like millions of our most loyal and devoted citizens, he felt a worthy pride in his ancestry and cherished a love for the history, the language, the literature, and the traditions of the cradleland of his great race. But above all, as the nation understood, Herman Ridder was an American—an earnest, intense, ardent, patriotic American. He was the product of our civilization; he was born on our soil and reared beneath our flag. He rose to power from opportunities which the republic offers to all her children. He was impregnated with our spirit. He was a devotee of our institutions, a lover of our liberty and the champion of our flag."

During the last year of his life Herman and my grandfather collaborated on an English-language column chronicling the progress of the war in Europe that was published in the *Staats* and nationally syndicated. As America had yet to enter the fray, the Ridders felt free to propagate the German cause. But with the advent of war, anti-German sentiment in the U.S. escalated to the point where there was talk of eliminating the teaching of the German language in American high schools, of changing the name of the sleepy Hudson River Valley enclave of Germantown, and of discouraging the usage of "frankfurters" in favor of "hotdogs" and of "hamburgers" in favor of "burgers."

The *Staats* faced advertiser and newsdealer boycotts and came under increasing government scrutiny. There was even a movement afoot to subject it to censorship, compel it to publish in English, and deny it access to the U.S. mails, but it went on being successfully published by the Ridders until the early 1950s when it was sold.

It took Herman's three sons more than a decade to pay off the company's two-million-dollar debt, so that it wasn't until the late 1920s that they were in a position to expand. It was my grandfather who spearheaded the drive to begin acquiring English-language newspapers. He and his brothers were able to borrow sufficiently toward the $2.85 million purchase price of the *New York Journal of Commerce*, one of the leading financial papers in the country. The publication monitored the movements of the approximately 4,500 cargo ships that plied the seas from London to Cyprus and published their daily arrival and departure times, along with information pertaining to marine insurance, financing, and commodities (the company invested in a deep-water sailer that could speed past the slowpoke rowboats that the other papers employed and easily reach the vessels on the far horizon).

A year or so later, the brothers negotiated another loan, facilitating the acquisition of the evening *St. Paul Dispatch* for $5.25 million. And before long, they were borrowing again, this time to snap up the evening *St. Paul Daily News*, ultimately combining them with the morning paper, the *St. Paul Pioneer Press*, and renaming the whole shebang the *St. Paul Dispatch-Pioneer Press* (soon to be known simply as the *Pioneer Press*).

There followed in quick succession the purchase of majority stakes in the *Duluth News Tribune*, North Dakota's *Grand Forks Herald*, and South Dakota's *Aberdeen American News*, and a minority interest in the *Seattle Times* (the only newspaper that the Ridders ever heavily invested in without succeeding in acquiring control). Along the way, they also picked up the *Chicago Journal of Commerce*. And that was more or less the company until the early 1950s. Not too shabby, given that they had had the Great Depression and two World Wars to weather. (All eight of the second-generation Ridder sons served in the armed forces in World War II: three in the Marines, three on active sea duty with the Navy, one in the Coast Guard, and one in the Army. A newsletter, titled "The Fighting Ridders," was created to keep the family abreast of where the boys were and the boys apprised of developments in the company.)

By the end of World War II there were eleven male Ridders in my grandfather's and father's generations working for the company at strategic points. As Victor once explained, "We are Catholics, we have many children, and we have to buy a newspaper for every son." It was something of a standing joke in the industry.

Victor had declared, "If we are going to raise a race of publishers they have to be trained as publishers." To that end, each young male Ridder was assigned to work in various departments of the various newspapers (beginning at the smaller ones), from platemaking to the pressroom, which afforded them the opportunity to experience the full and integrated operation of a newspaper.

BJ and Eric were working for their father, Joseph, at the *New York Journal of Commerce* (never mind that three Ridders would have been a crowd in that relatively small operation). My father was working at the Duluth paper, where his uncle Victor held the title of publisher. In April 1949, my grandfather, taking care to retain the title of president, relinquished the publisher's job at the St. Paul paper to his forty-year-old oldest son, Hank, Dad's half-brother, in order to devote more time to the Women's Institute and other civic entities, as well as to his photography hobby and his blooming tulip bulbs and embryonic zinnias.

In St. Paul alone, there were four Ridders (they were practically bumping into each other): in addition to Ben and Hank, my uncles Dan and Joe, who were co-general managers. The company took pains to instill a sense of community responsibility in each of the boys—public service was held to be a professional obligation—and Hank lost no time immersing himself in community activities. He eagerly took on the chairmanship of both the St. Paul Open Golf Tournament and the wildly popular St. Paul Winter Carnival, which featured such competitions as snow-castle and ice-sculpture building.

Joe, for his part, came up with a sure-fire promotional idea of his own—a winter treasure hunt, with a first prize of a thousand dollars, the clues to be released daily in the newspaper as a circulation stimulator. He had the so-called treasure buried in a snowbank and stretched the hunt out as long as possible, building to a fever pitch.

The company had meanwhile embarked on a newspaper-buying spree. In 1952 they went Westward Ho! and in separate transactions acquired the *San Jose Mercury News* for $3.3 million, as well as the *Long Beach Independent* for $6.5 million, combining them into a single morning-evening-and-Sunday publication. Now they were operating coast to coast.

Hank was posted as publisher to Long Beach, where there was already a highly competent general manager in place, Sam Cameron (as a rule it was non-Ridders who served as general managers). Uncle Hank was a serious drinker, but he showed up at the office every day, none the worse for wear. He was especially cozy with Jesse "Big Daddy" Unruh, the all-powerful Speaker of the California State Assembly and, later, California State Treasurer. It was all very quid pro quo: for instance, to attract tourists, which was beneficial to both the city and the newspaper, they hatched a plan to develop the Long Beach waterfront, purchasing the retiring British ocean liner the *Queen Mary* from Cunard with municipal funds. They had a pier built for her, and within four years the ship was minting money as a first-class floating hotel.

In 1952 Dad was offered the publisher's job at the *San Jose Mercury News* by his father and two uncles. Once-in-a-lifetime opportunity that it was, Dad turned it down to remain in Duluth, one of the company's less important papers, where he had been general manager since 1947. The city, punishingly cold in winter, was otherwise a veritable Eden of lakes and trees and, in my parents' estimation, a "great place to raise kids." My mother gave birth to my sister Jill that year; my sister Robin was only two or three, and my brother Peter, only six. Mummy was comfortably established and popular in the community, and she found the idea of moving, of uprooting her brood, anathema. With the exception of the war years, she and Dad had been based in Duluth since the summer of '39, and the prospect of going out to San Jose seemed too much like having to start over. For Mummy, one of the most appealing aspects of life in Duluth was that it was not particularly social—certainly not as socially active as the Twin Cities. Her friends, as a whole, were not living in those gothic Duluth mansions, though some of them must have grown up in them as children of the folks who controlled the area's rich shipping industry and iron-ore mines.

Dad, looking back, described his years in Duluth as the happiest he had ever known in the newspaper industry. His uncle Victor, though billed as the publisher, was one in name only—he lived in Duluth only in the summer and exercised no responsibility for any part of the paper. Even when Victor was around, it was Dad who ran the paper, with the help of a general manager named Van Horn. Dad was elevated to publisher in 1952 and, with that, the paper became a highly ethical and egalitarian operation, endorsing Republicans and Democrats alike.

When Dad turned down San Jose, and his cousins BJ and Eric followed suit (they were too busy leading society kind of lives in

New York), that plum job (in a town where the farming consisted primarily of apricot trees) went to Dad's tall, slim-hipped thirty-two-year-old brother, my Uncle Joe, a William and Mary graduate. For him, it was a dream come true, being only a matter of miles from gay-friendly San Francisco. It wasn't long before he was spending so much time there that he was able to talk the company into renting him a fancy pied-à-terre.

Uncle Joe, who had earned his stripes as promotion manager in Duluth and then co-general manager in St. Paul, had inherited the self-promotion gene from his father. He talked a good game, vowing from the outset to make the *Mercury News* the best newspaper on the Pacific Coast, a promise that was left to yours truly to fulfill. He did, however, become a force in the development of the city of San Jose and its environs, aiding and abetting, for better and worse, its explosion in industrial growth.

In 1956, the company added the *Pasadena Star-News* to its roster for $2.5 million. Dad's first cousin, BJ, who had been working at the *New York Journal of Commerce* since '46, was transferred there as publisher. It was far from an onerous job, which was just as well, given that BJ's heart was in horse racing rather than newsprint. He was one of the leading thoroughbred breeders in the country, with several Kentucky Derby contenders under his belt. (At a horse sale at Hollywood Park racetrack, a panhandler he had just told to go to hell pulled out a switchblade and stabbed and robbed him. BJ was a feisty fellow, and it would have been just like him, when a stranger approached, to stick the program in the guy's face.)

BJ's brother, Eric, had succeeded him as publisher of the *New York Journal of Commerce*, but Eric's heart was elsewhere as well—in yachting and sailboat racing. He was co-skipper of the twelve-meter sloop *Constellation* during its successful defense of the America's Cup in 1964 and never let you forget it.

In 1958, practically overnight, my parents' lives changed dramatically, and all on account of Uncle Dan's marital issues. After serving in the Navy as a press officer with the Normandy invasion fleet, he apprenticed at the Ridder paper in North Dakota in the late '40s. He tarried there just long enough to get the publisher's daughter, Betty Oppegard, pregnant and have to marry her. Hustled out of town to St. Paul as business manager, he joined his half-brother Hank, the publisher there, and his brother Joe, the co-general manager. When Hank left for Long Beach, Dan succeeded him, but by 1958 he was carrying on so openly with a prominent married woman that the Ridder elders decided it would be too awkward for him to carry on as publisher. They relocated him as far afield as possible, creating an executive position for him in Long Beach, where, once again, he found himself working under Hank. (After Hank died in 1969, Uncle Dan would become the publisher. He was popular in Long Beach and useful to the community—on the boards of the United Way and the sprawling California university system—Long Beach State, San Jose State, Fresno State, L.A. State, San Diego State ...).

Dad was now needed urgently in St. Paul as his replacement, and he and Mummy had to sell their much-loved place in Duluth. In addition to being publisher in St. Paul, where he was now the fourth Ridder to hold the job, Dad retained the title of publisher of the Duluth paper, and for a while managed it from St. Paul (from then on, whenever he returned to Duluth, which was mostly to play golf, he stayed in a hotel). He and Mummy purchased a 200-acre non-working farm on Salem Church Road, just a twenty-minute drive from downtown St. Paul. It consisted of an updated farmhouse, a guesthouse, a barn where my sisters would keep their horses, and a large chicken coop that served as a dormitory where my own children and my nieces and nephews would all bunk when my parents hosted family reunions (the coop's screening kept sprouting holes, and the mosquitoes practically ate the lot of them alive). The British couple, Bill and Hilma Wheeler, who had come with the house in Duluth, moved with us to St. Paul—Bill took care of the property while Hilma did the housekeeping.

At the *Pioneer Press*, Dad operated in marked contrast to his father and brothers. He discouraged advertisers who were trying to influence copy or have stories killed. "If it's something advertisers don't want to get into the paper," he maintained, "the chances are it's news." He made sure that editorial policy was fair and balanced (he was friendly with both Hubert Humphrey and Walter Mondale).

Dad had started out as a Republican, and my mother followed his lead. From the time they got married in 1938, until maybe 1975 my parents were what I would call liberal Republicans, but after Dad retired there was a shift to the Democrats. He read the local paper wherever he lived, plus the *New York Times*, front to back and word for word. He rarely looked at *Forbes* or *Fortune* or *Business Week*. He subscribed to *Time* and *Sports Illustrated*, and that was it, while my mother took *Vogue* and *Town & Country*. He refused to subscribe to the *Minneapolis Star Tribune, t*he competition—but he would go out every day and buy it under-the-counter so he could follow his friend the sports columnist Jim Klobuchar (the father of the Democratic senator from Minnesota).

By the late 1950s my grandfather and his two brothers had succeeded in their grandly stated aim of providing or creating jobs for all their sons: every Ridder in Dad's generation was now the publisher of a newspaper (except for Victor's son Robert, who ran the company's radio and television interests). There's a name for that. The "N" word. Nepotism.

Then, suddenly, *my* generation of Ridders was starting to graduate from college. Barney, son of BJ, was the first out. After Yale, he went to Aberdeen, a stint he uncharitably characterized as "banishment to Siberia," and then on to St. Paul, and later to Long Beach as business manager. Meanwhile, his brother Mike, who graduated from Princeton the same year I graduated from Michigan, went to work at the *Grand Forks Herald* in production, followed by a stint in St. Paul as a classified ad salesman, eventually becoming business manager of the *St. Paul Pioneer Press* and, later, president of the Commodity News Service, the largest non-newspaper operation within Knight Ridder. Victor Ridder's grandson Mark Mattison went from the *Grand Forks Herald* to the *Post Tribune* in Gary,

Indiana, and Eric Ridder, Jr., went to San Jose and then back East to the *Journal of Commerce*. And down the road a piece, in 1971, my younger brother Peter began in Duluth as a trainee. That was the roundup.

"And now"—to invoke the slapstick last line of *Portnoy's Complaint*—"vee may perhaps to begin."

CHAPTER THREE

The Delano-Ridder Merger

My parents met in the prewar summer of 1938, on Nantucket. Dad had graduated from Princeton that spring and just started his first job, at the *Journal of Commerce* in New York. Mummy, for her part, was newly graduated from the Greenwood School near Baltimore and ensconced in her parents' townhouse on East 36th Street, in the Murray Hill section of Manhattan. She was visiting her classmate and lifelong friend Betsy Beinecke on the island (they and their coterie would go on referring to themselves and one another as the "Greenwood girls"), and Betsy had taken Mummy to a clambake on the beach, or maybe it was a lobster bake. In any case, there was Dad, the very definition of a catch—six foot five and handsome as hell. He struck her as a knight in bright and shining armor, and indeed it was a tournament that had brought him to Nantucket; he was on hand to defend the title he'd won the previous summer at Sankaty Head Golf Club. This contest he lost. But he won Mummy.

Dad was a born athlete—on the squash team at Canterbury, the elite Catholic boarding school in Connecticut; and then, at Princeton, on the golf team and the standout captain of the squash team. Heralded for his "mammoth pinwheel forehand and blindingly hard serve," he had gone on to win both the New York State Squash Rackets and the Metropolitan Squash Rackets championships as well as to be runner-up in the National Intercollegiate

Squash championship in both 1937 and '38. The only appreciable benefit of Dad's job, which paid him a niggling $15 a week for handling plates and mats for the *Journal's* advertising department, was that he was allowed to leave every afternoon at four for the University Club on 54th Street to keep his squash game honed.

My grandfather had a more ambitious job for Dad lined up at the Ridder newspaper in South Dakota, beginning April 1. His future seemed assured on all fronts. He and Mummy were deliriously in love, and she had accepted his marriage proposal. The only impediment—an immovable one, it would turn out—was Mummy's father. Lyman Delano considered Dad irredeemably beneath his daughter in the social order and opposed the union. Not going as far as to forbid it, he nonetheless declared his intention to abstain from any ceremony or reception.

Lyman was the first cousin, not to mention the Harvard classmate, of the sitting president of the United States, one Franklin Delano Roosevelt, and, as such, it would have been awkward to hold the wedding in New York and have him boycott it—the tabloids would have a field day. A convenient solution was for the couple to marry quietly in Chicago. Grandma Delano would take the train out from New York, accompanied by her son Fred, while Grandpa Ridder would fly from St. Paul (Dad's mother refused to attend, bemoaning the thought of being in the same city, let alone the same room, as her former husband). Both sides of the family would thus be covered.

Dad and Mummy buoyantly took out a marriage license, or rather, attempted to. The rub was that, unbeknownst to them, there was a mandatory three-day waiting period in Illinois. During that gap, the press got wind, or at least a whiff, of the toplofty name Delano, with its ineluctable connection to the White House. The *Chicago Daily News* ran with the story of the impending nuptials and the AP picked it up, to the consternation of those most intimately concerned.

They were married in due course in the chancery of Chicago's Holy Name Cathedral by a Catholic priest assisted by an Episcopalian minister. Grandpa Ridder had had a car delivered as a wedding

Jane Delano, Niece of F.D.R., Marries

Chicago, Feb. 24.—Jane Delano, 19, niece of President Roosevelt, and Bernard H. Ridder Jr., 23, son of a New York publisher, were married today in Holy Name Cathedral. The bridegroom came to Chicago recently to play in the National Squash Tournament. He was graduated from Princeton University. Miss Delano, daughter of Mr. and Mrs. Lyman Delano of New York, attended Greenwood School in Baltimore, Md.

Mrs. Bernard H. Ridder Jr.

Chicago Daily News article announcing the marriage of Jane Delano to Bernard Ridder Jr.

present and, jointly with Grandma Delano, staked the couple to a month-long honeymoon in California. Dad and Mummy proceeded to live it up, staying at the old Huntington Hotel in Pasadena and playing golf at Cypress Point, the club that would later play such an ongoing and exhilarating part in my own life.

My parents were hitched on February 23, 1939, and my sister Laura was hatched on August 13. I mean, do the math yourself. I, for one, was able to figure things out by simply counting. Whenever Mummy would say, "Laura was premature," my siblings and I

My father and mother on their honeymoon in California.
Photo by Acme Photo

would pipe up that she had weighed eight pounds when she was born. We joked about it with her—she knew we knew.

But getting back to my recalcitrant grandfather: Lyman Delano was the chairman of both the Atlantic Coast Line Railroad, at one point the longest in the world, which his maternal grandfather had organized and developed, and of the Louisville and Nashville Railroad, as well as a director of at least a dozen other railway and railroad-affiliated companies and of Pan American Airways. Staunch Republican that he was, he had declined to attend his cousin's two presidential inaugurations to date. As far back as 1920, the same day he learned of FDR's nomination as vice-president, he had written

Franklin to make his position known: "I regret that personal feelings and family pride cannot prevail on this occasion, but I feel most strongly that it would be prejudicial to the best interests of our country to entrust any longer the guidance of its affairs to the Democratic Party."

Lyman had furthermore forbidden my mother to attend the 1936 inauguration. But she was determined to go at all costs, and to

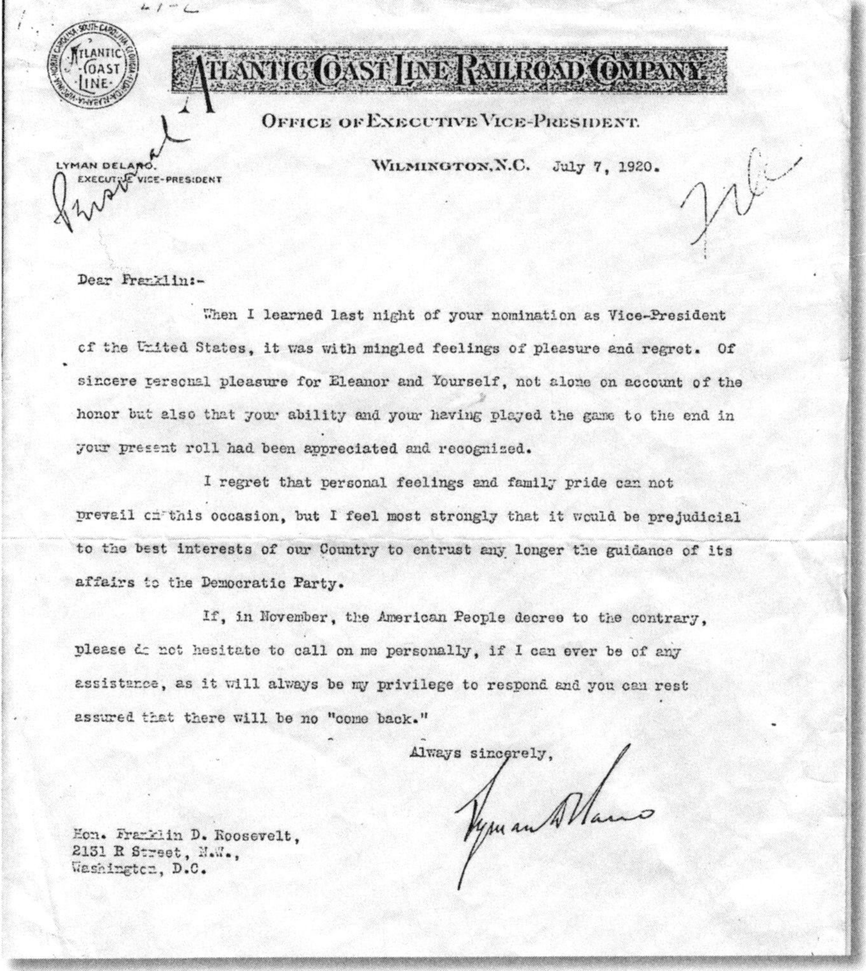

ATLANTIC COAST LINE
ATLANTIC COAST LINE RAILROAD COMPANY.
OFFICE OF EXECUTIVE VICE-PRESIDENT.

LYMAN DELANO.
EXECUTIVE VICE-PRESIDENT

WILMINGTON, N.C. July 7, 1920.

Dear Franklin:-

When I learned last night of your nomination as Vice-President of the United States, it was with mingled feelings of pleasure and regret. Of sincere personal pleasure for Eleanor and Yourself, not alone on account of the honor but also that your ability and your having played the game to the end in your present roll had been appreciated and recognized.

I regret that personal feelings and family pride can not prevail on this occasion, but I feel most strongly that it would be prejudicial to the best interests of our Country to entrust any longer the guidance of its affairs to the Democratic Party.

If, in November, the American People decree to the contrary, please do not hesitate to call on me personally, if I can ever be of any assistance, as it will always be my privilege to respond and you can rest assured that there will be no "come back."

Always sincerely,

Lyman Delano

Hon. Franklin D. Roosevelt,
2131 R Street, N.W.,
Washington, D.C.

Letter from Lyman Delano to FDR.

ensure her excusal from school she invited her headmistress, Miss Alcott, a Roosevelt devotee, to accompany her. ("Miss A" would remain a stellar figure in the Delano family constellation, as she also owned and ran a camp for girls on Squam Lake in New Hampshire, to which my three sisters would in due course be sent.) Mummy and Miss Alcott were ceremoniously put up at the White House—the thrill of a lifetime. The president was much taken with Mummy and would write to her from time to time on his presidential stationery. I don't know to this day if she ever dared confess to the father she was terrified of that she had defied him.

Born in 1919, Mummy was the youngest of Lyman's six children. Christened Jennie Walters Delano after his beloved mother, she was all of five when he told her she was no longer worthy of bearing her grandmother's name and that, from then on, she would be known as "Jane." Mummy, as you can imagine, was crushed.

Now, fifteen years later, her father had delivered another near-mortal blow by giving her wedding a wide berth. He had been fully and convivially present at her sisters' nuptials (according to a guest, "saying as he passed the bottle, 'Float your ice,' and he said it twice"), but when Mummy and Dad walked down the aisle in Chicago, he was secluded in his feudal Hudson River Valley redoubt, and doubtless fuming.

Steen Valetje, the estate was named—"little stone valley," in the Dutch of our Delano ancestors. The immense brick manor house had been constructed in 1851, with a Tuscan articulation, by workers imported from Italy, and later expanded by no less than the architect of the New York Public Library. It boasted towers, arches, bracketed roofs, and a wealth of round-topped windows that afforded matchless views of the Hudson River and the Catskill Mountain range beyond. There were frescoes and fretwork aplenty, loggias and porticoes galore, carved-marble fireplaces to spare (sixteen of them), and a profusion of French doors opening onto river terraces. There was a superb hand-carved staircase with a domed and frescoed skylight, and a bona-fide ballroom twenty-six by forty-two

Steen Valetje, the Delano estate on the Hudson, in all its original glory.

Three first cousins: my grandfather, Lyman Delano, Warren Delano Robbins, and FDR.
Franklin D. Roosevelt Presidential Library

feet that boasted a twenty-foot hand-painted tray ceiling and an oak-and-mahogany parquet floor.

The landholding eventually added up to some 800 acres of woods and fields; walking and bridle trails; lawns and lanes with stately oaks and other specimen trees; greenhouses, formal gardens, and ponds; and barns and paddocks. This bounty had been a wedding gift to merchant and diplomat Franklin Hughes Delano (FDR's great-uncle, for whom his favorite niece, Sara Delano Roosevelt, would name her exalted son) and his bride, Laura Astor, the favorite granddaughter of the original John Jacob Astor, the fur trader and real estate investor who was America's first multimillionaire.

Steen Valetje surpassed in splendor even *Ferncliff*, the neighboring Astor estate, and was appreciably larger and grander than *Springwood*, FDR's country seat, ten miles away in Hyde Park. From childhood unto death, the president regularly visited *Steen Valetje*, where he was often observed sitting on the west porch contemplating the river he so loved. (Again, everything connects: it was my Ridder great-grandfather, Herman, who, in 1909, along with J. P. Morgan and Andrew Carnegie, organized the elaborate Hudson-Fulton Celebration commemorating the 300th anniversary of Henry Hudson's discovery of the river, coupled with the 100th anniversary of Robert Fulton's invention of the first commercially successful steamboat.)

Franklin Delano, dying childless in 1894, left the estate to his nephew Warren, my great-grandfather, who would leave it in turn to his oldest surviving son, the thirty-seven-year-old Lyman. When my grandfather came up to *Steen Valetje* from the city, it was always in his private railroad car. The tracks ran through the estate, to Albany and the Midwest, and he would be met by a horse-drawn carriage at a chosen point at the foot of the property. One of my earliest memories is of being brought down to meet his railroad car and then riding back to the house in the carriage with him. He died when I was four, at the age of sixty-one, after an undisclosed illness of only a couple of days.

ATLANTIC COAST LINE
NEWS

WILMINGTON, N. C. AUGUST, 1944 VOL. XXV—No. 8

WITH PROFOUND SORROW
WE ANNOUNCE THE DEATH OF
MR. LYMAN DELANO
CHAIRMAN OF THE BOARD OF DIRECTORS
IN THE CITY OF NEW YORK
ON SUNDAY, THE TWENTY-THIRD OF JULY
NINETEEN HUNDRED AND FORTY-FOUR

Atlantic Coast Line News stationery announcing the death of Lyman Delano.

Lyman's death, unexpected as it was, didn't hold a candle to the suddenness of his father's. Warren Delano's demise was so sensational it landed on the front page of every newspaper in the nation, beginning with the *New York Times.* This was thanks in part to his standing as a coal baron and railroad tycoon, sportsman, and prominent member of society, but also to the fact that his nephew was the Democratic vice-presidential candidate. At the time of his favorite uncle's ghastly accident, FDR was off speechmaking in Maine and had to suspend his campaign to attend the funeral.

In our family, the accident—the freak accident—was decidedly not a story that was told over and over again. It was, rather, something unmentionable that had happened in the long-distant past—I mean, my mother was only a year old at the time her grandfather was killed. I remember irreverently thinking after first hearing the gory details, "What a way to go!" I could picture it, being no stranger to the scene. (Whenever I visited Grandma Delano at *Steen Valetje*, I would eagerly accompany the workers on the estate to pick up her mail at the tiny Barrytown station-cum-post-office.)

My great-grandfather's ardent hobby was his blooded horses, of which he owned some of the finest specimens in the world: hunters, saddle mounts, and harness and heavy draft horses (no prophet, he had loudly declared that the draft horse would never be supplanted by the automobile for short-distance hauls). His forte was the breeding of Norwegian Fjord horses. The first stallion plus six mares, "light-tan chunky ponies with cream-colored manes and a black stripe down their backbones," had been ferried to Barrytown from New York City in 1900, the night the century turned. From those, he succeeded in crossbreeding the ideal military horse, a "khaki-colored mount for a khaki-covered soldier."

On that fateful Friday morning of September 9, 1920, Warren hitched his wagon to an equestrian star—his favorite mount, the high-spirited Belle. She was a ravishing brown mare that he had entered in the harness class of the next day's Dutchess County Fair where he would be presiding as chairman of the show committee. Tethering her to his light buggy, he drove off to the station to fetch a trunk for one of his houseguests. He tied her up at the station's north end and, allowing for the fact that she was easily spooked by trains, calculated how many minutes he could safely spend inside. His timing was woefully awry. Faster than the speed of his own cognizance, the whistle of the New York Central's northbound "fast express" was sounding. He bounded out of the station, jumped into the buggy, and took the reins in a desperate attempt to quiet his already unruly horse.

Belle reared, then bolted, running amok around the station before plunging smack into the oncoming locomotive. Horse and rider were catapulted 150 feet down the tracks from the railroad crossing, at which point Belle, severed from the wagon, was propelled a full thousand feet further. She was badly mangled—literally torn to pieces.

My great-grandfather, in stark but somehow comforting contrast, was discovered intact, sitting upright by the buggy seat amid the splintered wreckage, not a scrap of whose wheels was ever to be found. A gash on his forehead was the only visible sign of the cataclysm. Death had been instantaneous, courtesy of a broken neck.

Warren Delano, cruelly struck down at the age of sixty-eight in the fullness of an active and eager life, was laid out on a blanket on the floor of the ticket office. Two of his daughters, my great-aunts Sarah Delano Redmond and Laura Franklin Delano, blissfully oblivious of the debacle, had meanwhile arrived at the Barrytown station to meet the train innocently carrying their mother home from a trip upstate. According to the local paper, "The two girls took Mrs. Delano between them to support her as they broke the news and approached the office. 'I've been expecting it for some time,' she said before entering the room" (a reference, one is left to suppose, to her husband's unbridled passion for breaking, riding, and driving horses). The Delanos' saddle and carriage draft horses that had been entered in competition at the horse fair were hastily withdrawn, and the two Delano daughters naturally dropped out as drivers in the mule race.

Warren was eulogized by his brother Frederic as a godlike, almost mythological figure. "With his wonderful physique and close-cropped Van Dyke beard, he was certainly good to look upon, and it appeared to us that there was nothing he could not do," Frederic intoned, pointing out how Warren had both revived their father's anthracite properties and bituminous mines and expanded and enhanced *Steen Valetje*.

At the conclusion of the service, the blossom- and flower-bedecked casket was carried to the hearse by a confederation of

Warren Delano, miniature by William Jacob Baer.
The Walters Art Museum

WARREN DELAN[illegible]
IS KILLED B[illegible]
LOCOMOTIVE

Noted Society Man and Sportsman Unable to Control Runaway Horse.

POUGHKEEPSIE, N. Y., Sept. 10.—Deep gloom has been cast over the Dutchess County Fair by the death of Warren Delano, uncle of Franklin D. Roosevelt, Democratic candidate for the Vice-Presidency. Mr. Delano, one of the most prominent members of the county's Summer colony, was in charge of the Horse Show, one of the fair's most notable features.

As a result of the bolting of his favorite horse, attached to a buggy in which Mr. Delano was riding, he was instantly killed by a locomotive at the New York Central Railroad crossing at Barrytown.

Mr. Delano had tied the horse at the north end of the Barrytown [illegible] way station, while he went inside. Hearing the approach of a train, he hurried out of the station and, [illegible]ting into the buggy, attempted to quiet the frightened animal.

HORSE BOLTED TO TRACK.

The horse bolted, running to [illegible] south side of the station and onto [illegible] track. The train hit the bug[illegible]

The New York Times.

NEW YORK, FRIDAY, SEPTEMBER 10, 1920.

WARREN DELANO KILLED BY TRAIN AT BARRYTOWN

His Favorite Horse, Frightened by Express, Dashed On Track, Carrying Him to Death.

BORNE 150 FEET BY ENGINE

Uncle of Franklin D. Roosevelt and Had Large Coal Interests in Pennsylvania.

OWNED STABLE OF HORSES

He Intended to Exhibit Animal He Was Driving at Dutchess County Fair Tomorrow.

Special to The New York Times.

POUGHKEEPSIE, N. Y., Sept. 9.—While driving his favorite horse, which he was to have entered in the harness [illegible]

Articles detailing the tragic death of Warren Delano.

the longest-serving employees on the estate—talk about feudal. As FDR drove mournfully away, there were boos mixed with the applause (come November, he and Democratic presidential candidate Governor James M. Cox of Ohio would be clobbered by Warren G. Harding, whose administration was destined to be remembered as the most scandalous in American history).

Warren was further eulogized, in the florid spirit of the era, as "one of the large-souled men of his time: kindly, genial, alert, anxious to diffuse happiness. There is no circle in which he was known in which his absence and tragic death will not be deeply mourned, while over those nearest and dearest to him a dark cloud must impend which many years cannot wholly lift." And indeed, he was shortly followed to the grave by his sixty-nine-year-old widow, my great-grandmother Jennie Walters Delano, for whom my mother would originally be named. On the occasion of *her* passing, the *New York Times* published a story with the subheading "Death May Clear Up Mystery of a Light Burning in Mansion 32 Years Since Daughter Married Against Walters's Will." Her widowed father, William Thompson Walters of Baltimore, multimillionaire railway director, steamship executive, merchant, and connoisseur (founder of the eponymous art galleries) had vehemently opposed the union—his only daughter, he held, was duty-bound to devote herself to him in his lonely old age.

Shortly after Jennie's insubordinate marriage, a ghostly "perpetual light" was detected burning in the vestibule of the Walters mansion, ostensibly to mark her absence. The story goes that when her father died in 1894, leaving her but fifty cents, her brother, Henry, chairman of the Wilmington, North Carolina-based Atlantic Coast Line Railroad and, according to the *Wall Street Journal*, the wealthiest man in the South, gave her half of *his* inheritance. My grandfather had been working on the railroad—all the livelong day, as the song goes—since 1916, and upon his uncle's death, in 1931, succeeded him as chairman, operating out of New York all through the Great Depression and well into World War II.

Standing steadfastly behind my grandfather as he ran his course in life was the woman he had married in 1908, my wonderful Grandma Delano. The former Leila Chapin Burnett brought to the Delano table, so to speak, golden Guernsey milk. Her grandfather Joseph Burnett imported the herds for richer quality and went on to found one of the biggest milk suppliers in Boston and, later, a booming vanilla-extract company called Burnett's Flavoring Extract. Along the way, he invented and patented the milk bottle, the old original one that looked like a bowling pin.

Joseph Burnett begat six sons, and when the oldest entered St. Paul's School, in New Hampshire, the headmaster encouraged Joseph to found (that is, fund) a comparable church school closer to home, which his five other sons could more conveniently attend. My grandfather Delano attended St. Mark's and, astonishingly, so did his wife: as the founder's granddaughter, my grandmother was the only female ever to do so, until the school went co-ed in the late 1970s.

Of the six children she bore, three were sons and three were daughters: Warren, Leila, Frederic, Margaret, Bobby, and Mummy (Jennie/Jane). Horses were the order of the day: Warren IV's was named Moldover; Leila's, Anthem; Bobbie's, Viking; Fred's, Elf; Margie's, Lucy Locket; and Jennie/Jane/Mummy's, Jack Horner. Bobby, the youngest son, committed suicide in June 1936 when he was twenty-three—there's a letter in the family archive from FDR to my grandfather expressing condolences that nobody doubted were profoundly felt. My mother and my grandmother, both of whom adored Bobby, commented many times on how much I looked like him.

Bobby was a student at St. Mark's at the same time as the poet Robert Lowell. A literary friend recently called to my attention the poem "Bobby Delano" in Lowell's *Collected Poems*. It begins bucolically with "sunlight gilding the golden polo coats / of boys with country seats on the Upper Hudson," but goes on to contain a number of troubling lines: "Bobby Delano, cousin of Franklin

My maternal grandparents, Lyman Delano and Leila Chapin Burnett Delano, 1943.

Delano Roosevelt— / deported soused off the Presidential yacht ... / his football, hockey, baseball letter at 15; / at 15, expelled. He dug my ass with a compass, / forced me to say 'My mother is a whore' ... / he shot himself in Rio, / odious, unknowable, inspired as Ajax."

The Notes section of the volume offers a brief exegesis of the poem by the editors that, to my non-academic mind, amounts to overkill. To wit: Bobby Delano shares characteristics not with "the Greater Ajax but with Ajax the Lesser, the Son of Oileus or Ileus, the Locrian chieftain: 'of hateful character and on occasion grossly rude' (as in *Iliad* XXIII.473ff)." I have since learned, reconcilingly, that Lowell's nickname at St. Mark's was "Cal," short for Caligula, the Roman emperor renowned for his sadism. Could it not be said, then, that it took one to know one?

At least one biographical fact Lowell got dead wrong: Bobby took leave of his life not in Rio but in a small port town in northern Argentina where he had gone to work as a ranch hand (there exists a letter from FDR wishing him a jaunty bon voyage). More than three quarters of a century later, the question remains: with seemingly everything in the world to live for, why did he do it? The story was that the girl he was head-over-heels—in any case, unbalancingly—in love with dumped him, but who knows?

Bobby was a close friend, as well as a second cousin of the president's four sons, and on one occasion, he and Franklin Jr. went rogue and plied a young woman with drink. Word reached the president, who gave both boys a good old-fashioned talking-to, during the course of which Bobby confided how much he wished his own father would show a similar concern.

My mother's brother Warren became a commercial lobster fisherman in Maine, living in a simple house in Kittery Point, driving a pickup, and altogether leading the most basic kind of life. My other uncle, Freddy, worked in some capacity or other for the Atlantic Coast Line Railroad in Georgia. The brothers were just nice low-key guys, not prominent in any way, certainly not socialites leading fancy lives.

Owing to her close relationship with my grandmother, Eleanor Roosevelt would come to *Steen Valetje* for lunch from time to time. One such visit she described in her July 6, 1949, syndicated newspaper column: "Driving home, we followed as many of the old and unfrequented roads as I could remember, going past Bard College and the old Chanler place. I could not help thinking that in many ways Mrs. Lyman Delano's old house at *Steen Valetje,* in spite of being built in the Victorian era, has more real charm and sense of being a house where people have lived and really understood and loved their possessions than some houses where you have a feeling that a perfectly impersonal decorator was called in to hang the

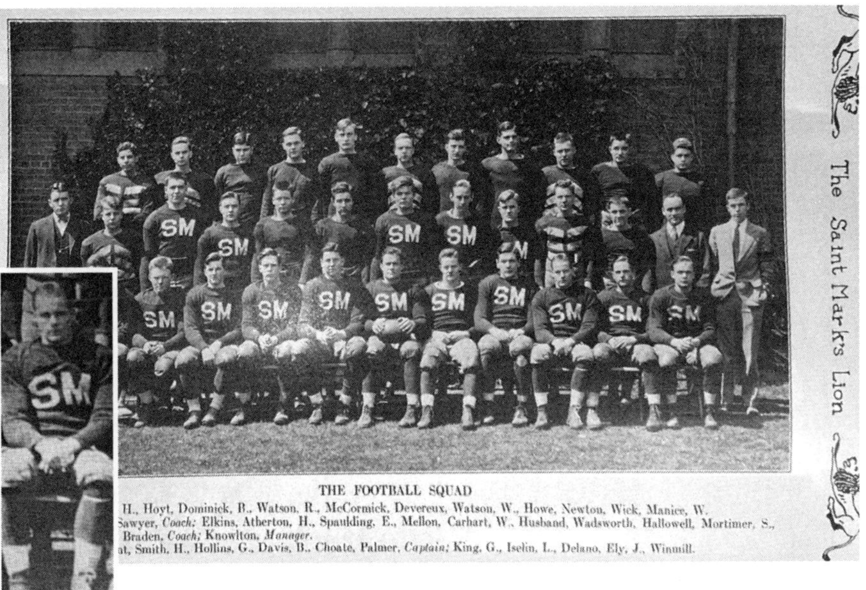

The St. Mark's football team. My mother's doomed brother, Robert Burnett "Bobby" Delano, is seated front row, third from right and inset.

Delano's Body Ready For Return to America

Resistencia, Argentina June 2 (AP)—The body of Robert B Delano, second cousin of President Roosevelt, was prepared for shipment to Buenos Aires today after he died from what police said was a self-inflicted pistol wound

Delano 21 shot himself in the mouth Sunday night the night police commissioner said at the town of Barranqueras in the Argentine Chaco He died at 11 p m

(A dispatch to the newspaper Critica in Buenos Aires said Delano killed himself because his fiancee had broken their engagement Another dispatch to the newspaper La Razon said the motive for the act was not determined)

Friends of Delano in Buenos Aires said he came to South America last year after leaving Harvard University He visited the wealthy and socially-prominent Debruyn family

Article describing Bobby Delano's suicide.

curtains and lay the rugs and choose and place the furniture. I am not very sure sometimes that the owners even choose the books and the piano. That kind of house never gives me a sense of being really representative of the personality of the people who live in it and without some feeling left by various generations a house remains a shell and never becomes a home."

Grandma Delano in turn would take us grandchildren to visit Eleanor at *Val-Kill*, the homy house of her own, now a National Historic Site, that FDR had grudgingly allowed her to build at *Springwood*. She would have parties for us with her grandchildren. In my experience, she was always friendly and attentive, asking me about school and whether I had enjoyed camp—questions I rarely got at home.

I look back at *Steen Valetje* as one of the all-out dispensations of my childhood. I spent about a month there every summer between the ages of eight and thirteen. My mother would ship me and my sister Laura off from Duluth to the Hudson Valley. Our cousins would already be there without their parents. The only adults on the place were my grandmother and her maids, of whom there were always about ten, plus a herd of outside people—that's how Grandma lived, right up until she died, in the mid-1960s. The cousins on hand were all girls, which I know sounds like fun, but when you're nine and ten and eleven you want to play with boys.

How now to adequately convey the Arcadian flavor of the place? I'll leave it to a Dutchess County weekly which ran an elegiac piece about the good old days: "Every July Fourth the lawns of *Steen Valetje* were the site of an 'ice cream and strawberry social' to which all the countryside were welcome. Most came on foot ..."

Every morning, I jumped into my grandmother's station wagon for the ride to the stables, which were quite a ways away—maybe two thirds of a mile. William, the stableman, would be there tending to the offspring of Warren Delano's special Norwegian horses. The one I was given to ride was Tony the Pony. Grandma Delano told me she had named him after me, and she let me ride him in

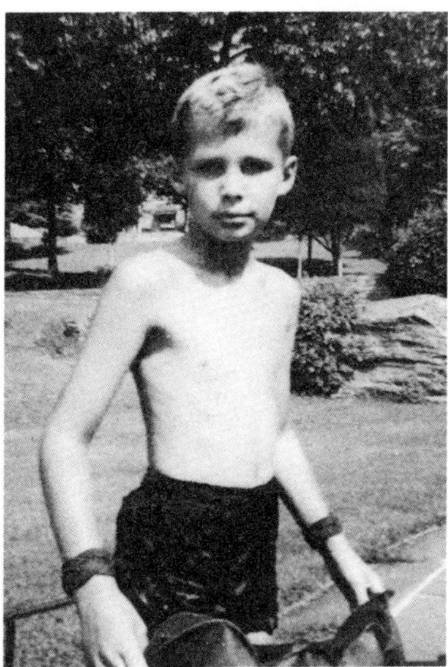

Age nine, at *Steen Valetje*.

Competing at the Dutchess County Fair on "Tony the Pony." I won a ribbon.

With my brother Peter and sister Laura, and three of our Delano cousins, straddling Grandma's Woody station wagon at the Dutchess County Fair, circa 1950.

a horse show. I rode for at least an hour almost every day, usually with an instructor, through field after field (by then, the property was down to 500 acres).

In the afternoon, we all went for carriage rides; there were about fifteen of these conveyances, some of them, if not on their last legs, at least beginning to show their age. Grandma would be driving (it was written of her after her death that "she treated horses as she treated people, with wit and understanding"), and sometimes she would hand the reins to me for a bit.

Afterward, I would hang around the cow barn. One day, I mustered the courage to ask the farmer to show me how to milk. I didn't have the touch—sensing I wasn't their regular guy, the cows withheld their milk. The fresh milk we grandchildren were given to drink had lumps in it—disgusting clots—and we would procrastinate in drinking it. The minute my grandmother left the breakfast room we would get up from the table in unison, open the window, and pour our milk into a big trough that thankfully happened to be below.

Grandma told us how Mummy, when she was a little girl, would go ice sailing on the frozen-over Hudson in a small boat without a hull but with blades. When we were taken to the FDR Library in Hyde Park, I got to see some of *his* boyhood ice-sailing boats in kind of a museum-like setting in the basement of the main house.

The south wing of *Steen Valetje*—the wing with the famous ballroom—was closed off but my cousins and I would sneak in there and lift the cloths off the furniture and the marble statues. The most surprising thing I remember uncovering—for its sheer aesthetic incompatibility—was a pool table.

Conceitedly calling ourselves The Steen Valetje Players, we presented a play every summer in the ballroom, which was opened expressly for the occasion. I was always the male lead—it had to be me, I was the only boy. One year, we put on *Cinderella*. Eleanor Roosevelt attended that performance. The costumes came from Grandma Delano's attic and included the dress she had worn to her coming-out party—a baby-blue silk print trimmed with lace. My cousin Wendy played Cinderella, and my sister Laura was the wicked stepmother. The last scene opened with Cinderella on the arm of her Prince Charming (none other than little me), gliding down the aisle to Mendelssohn's "Wedding March." Grandma had a writer friend of hers compose a make-believe review, and it was read aloud at the dinner table: "The youthful players captivated a full house ..." My performance rated a fake rave.

Around 1950, when I would have been ten, my grandmother took me to see another Delano family house, an hour or so upriver on the bluffs near Newburgh, and to visit with my great-great-uncle Fred Delano, FDR's uncle, who was still living there. The place was

Some of my cousins and I—the self-styled "Steen Valetje Players"—practicing for our annual dramatic offering in the ballroom.

called *Algonac* (an Algonquin Indian name meaning "hill meets river"), and it was all sand-colored stucco and had a three-story tower. It had apparently been built around the same time as *Steen Valetje*—in the middle of the nineteenth century—by the first of the innumerable Warren Delanos, a prosperous opium dealer. The story told to me was that his first glimpse of the Hudson had been as a boy of sixteen when he accompanied his father to Albany for the celebration of the opening of the Erie Canal and that he had sworn to himself that when he grew up, he would build a house with a sweeping view of the river. Grandma pointed out the exact spot

"Cinderella" Performed By Steen Valetje Players

Entirely original and charming was the Friday matinee performance of "Cinderella" as presented by the Steen Valetje players. In costumes from their grandmother's attic, which included one of her "coming out" dresses - a blue silk print trimmed with deep lace - these youthful players captivated a full house at this, their yearly dramatic offering.

As a "curtain raiser," the blonde Delano twins, Diana and Daphne, sang a quaint ballad titled "Three Fishermen" - the fishermen were by name, Isaac, Jacob and Abraham.

Tony Ridder gave the epilogue. Cinderella, the beautiful little queen of the chimney corner, was played by Wendy Paul She was an appealing heroine, first seen dusting her cruel stepmother's house and running at the constant beck and call of her two vain stepsisters. The stepmother was played by ~~Lora~~ Laura Ridder; the stepsisters by Linda Paul and Daphne Delano. The fairy godmother, beautifully costumed, was Diana Delano.

Highlight of the play was of course the extravaganza scene at the Prince's ball - where Cinderella quite unrecognized by her mean relations, danced happily with the other merrymakers. The handsome Prince was Tony Ridder. At the stroke of twelve Cinderella vanished, leaving no trace behind except of course, a shoe. The Prince's servant, in the next scene, seeking the owner of the shoe, was played by Diane Delano.

The final dramatic episode, and the one perhaps which most nearly accounts for the generation-to-generation appeal of this fairy tale, opens with Cinderella on the arm of her Prince Charming. As they moved down the aisle, accompanied by their Court, a chorus sang the suitable and well-loved Mendelssohn's "Wedding March."

After the final curtain, the entire cast gave a comic feature number, called "Strut Miss Lucy."

A friendly (as in written by a family friend) review of "Cinderella," one of our annual juvenile productions.

where FDR's mother and father had, as I remember her putting it, "plighted their troth."

In the mid-1950s, New York State, exercising its right of eminent domain which allowed the expropriation of private property for public use, seized a slice of *Steen Valetje* to build a two-lane toll bridge spanning the Hudson. In the late afternoon, it was Grandma's wont to sit out on the veranda facing the river and, if it was a cloudless day, the Catskills beyond. I would be happily sipping a Pepsi or whatever, but I knew Grandma must be inwardly seething at the sight of the humungous structure bisecting her view:

the Kingston-Rhinecliff Bridge, which at its height hosted 20,000 vehicles per day. Nor, conversely, would she have been pleased as punch by the thought that *we* were visible to all those "motorists."

I remember fondly the forays we made to see my grandfather's flamboyant sister, my great-aunt Laura Delano. Her sprawling estate, *Evergreen Lands,* was south of us toward Hyde Park. She had had John Russell Pope, the architect of the National Gallery of Art in Washington, design a fieldstone-and-timber carriage house for her in the English Tudor-revival style and site it high on a rolling hill with breath-snatching river vistas. It's listed on the National Register of Historic Places.

Everybody in the family called her Polly because of her predilection since childhood for a drink with a funny name—Apollinaris—and, at least to my unsophisticated palate, a funny taste. It was a German carbonated mineral water, labeled "The Queen of Table Waters," and, irony of ironies, from the mid-1930s until 1945, the year FDR died, it was bottled at a plant controlled by the German SS (today it's owned by the what-could-be-more-American Coca-Cola company).

The concoction that Aunt Polly served us was a hybrid, part Apollinaris water and part pureed raspberries, and it was the most delicious reddish-orange color. Actually, it was her butler who served it, but she would mix it herself, sitting in her library, on the table in front of her, while the mosquitoes made a meal of us (Aunt Polly was a devout nonbeliever in screens, on the grounds that they would spoil her view). It was said that when she served the Polly water to Winston Churchill—straight, no pureed raspberries for him—he spat it out on her fieldstone terrace and that they spent the rest of the evening glowering at each other. But when it came to FDR's four sons, it wasn't Polly water she naughtily served them but, rather, their first alcoholic beverage.

Aunt Polly was FDR's confidant and near-constant companion—while Eleanor was usually off doing her own thing, Polly and the president lounged around having cocktails and gossiping about

My fabulous great-aunt Laura "Polly" Delano, widow-peaked and bejewelled, cradling a couple of her long-haired dachshunds at her estate in Rhinebeck.

friends and relations. It was at Eleanor's vindictive insistence that Polly was excluded from the famous picnic at Hyde Park in honor of the visiting King George and Queen Elizabeth where they were fed that most All-American of rations—hotdogs.

Stumping with FDR on his cross-country trips during his first campaign for president, Polly was memorably photographed sitting in the motorcade with him and his Scottish terrier, Fala, while cradling one of her Irish setters in her lap. She was one of the four women with the president when, all unexpectedly, he died at the "Little White House" in Warm Springs, Georgia—not to mention *the* one to whom, as she was helping to convey him to his bedroom, he uttered his last words, "I have a terrific pain in the back of my head." That FDR's former mistress, Lucy Mercer, who once upon a time had been Eleanor's social secretary, was also in attendance was something that Eleanor, though reportedly managing to remain expressionless, was horrified to learn in the immediate aftermath of her husband's death. Aunt Polly always slyly maintained that, when asked point blank who else had been there on that fateful afternoon, she couldn't bring herself to lie to dear Cousin Eleanor.

Aunt Polly was a tad flashy—picture colored silk pajamas, velvet pantaloons, and show furs, not to mention all manner of earrings, necklaces, bracelets, bangles ... She dyed her hair purple and styled it every morning in a distinctive widow's peak and wore red nail polish at a time when that was roundly frowned upon (one of her more conventional sisters, eyeing Polly's incarnadine fingertips, inquired if she had been disemboweling rabbits). But for all her frippery, she had also handled her father's horse-drawn carriages at the Dutchess County Fair like a professional.

After imbibing Aunt Polly's Polly water, my sister Laura and I would be allowed to wallow in real water. *Evergreen Lands* had a swimming pool, which *Steen Valetje*, by design, did not. My memories of it remain ever green.

Aunt Polly lived to a ripe old age, dying at eighty-six in 1972 in her four-story townhouse on Sutton Place. I had visited her there as

Aunt Polly (center) with FDR on the presidential campaign train.
The Franklin D. Roosevelt Presidential Library

Aunt Polly on the arm of Governor Nelson Rockefeller at Eleanor Roosevelt's funeral, Hyde Park, New York, 1962.

well, with Grandma Delano and some of my cousins, and I recall it as being exceptionally dark. When the eminent Chinese American architect, I. M. Pei, purchased the house from Aunt Polly's estate, he naturally opened it all up. After he died—at the age of 102, by the way—it was marketed as a "light-filled masterpiece." I had to laugh.

CHAPTER FOUR

Dad Goes to War … I Get Wounded

SHORTLY AFTER HIS honeymoon, Dad started at the Ridder paper in Aberdeen, sent there by his father as, a generation later, I would be sent there by mine. Many a young Ridder started there—the operation was so small you could work in almost all the departments and learn all the angles in short order. Dad's nineteen-year-old bride was quick to enroll in a local stenography and typing class to be of help to my father (I wonder now if this could possibly account for Mummy's making my sister Laura and me take typing lessons at a business college in Duluth when we were in our teens).

Dad was working in the advertising and circulation departments but still pulling in only $15 a week, barely a living wage. South Dakota in the late 1930s was a bare-bones economy—the Dust Bowl had exacerbated the impact of the Great Depression and ground farming families into poverty. Dad told me how he and the circulation manager would barter subscriptions for produce and eggs and live chickens, which they would then exchange for cash to put in the paper's coffers. One day, emerging fresh from a local farm with the whole back seat of the company car loaded with eggs and caged hens, they collided with another vehicle—nobody got hurt, but the road was awash with whites and yolks, and cacophonous with clucking.

When my father was playing in the Northland Invitational in August 1939 and my mother suddenly went into labor with Laura, my grandfather said to him, "Why don't you just stay in Duluth and work for our paper there?" Dad accepted the offer and was assigned to the advertising department, where he rose in the ranks to manager and then ad director. Step by baby step, he was learning the newspaper business.

Dad enlisted in the Navy in 1942. He was assigned for training to the Naval Mine Warfare School in Yorktown, Virginia, where he wound up spending a year and a half on the administrative staff. My mother accompanied him, taking my sister and me with her, and stayed with Dad until he shipped out to the Pacific Theater of Operations, at which point she rented a small apartment on Manhattan's Upper East Side for the duration.

In Yorktown, Dad was befriended by the officer chosen to command an Essex-class aircraft carrier that was in the process of being built—the *USS Bunker Hill.* Given the position of gunnery officer, he put in two and a half years of steady sea duty, rising from ensign to lieutenant and getting to participate in the largest carrier-to-carrier engagement in recorded history—the Battle of the Philippine Sea, which involved twenty-four carriers and deployed more than 1,350 carrier-based aircraft.

Dad was later transferred to the office of Commander in Chief Pacific. His job was to escort enlisted naval correspondents to the various vessel-cruisers, carriers, and battleships in the Pacific war zone, the objective being morale-building (the newsmen were primed to file feel-good stories about the crewmen for the latter's hometown papers).

Dad never wanted to talk about his war—it had been nothing less than traumatic for him, as was the case with many veterans. The first and only time he opened up to us about his time in the Navy was—fittingly, one might say—on the high seas. In 1981, he and my mother, my wife Connie and I, and my youngest sister Jill were sailing on the *QE2* from New York to Southampton to play golf in

Dad in the Navy, early 1940s.

Scotland, at Turnberry and Muirfield. One night we were unwinding on deck over Singapore slings, a potent cocktail that legend has it was created just before World War I by a bartender at the Long Bar of the storied Raffles Hotel. The concoction consists of cherry brandy, gin, Cointreau, Benedictine, Grenadine, Grand Marnier, and fresh pineapple juice. I've knocked back a few since, but only on cruise ships. We were all having them, except for Connie, who didn't drink alcohol, when Dad piped up, "This is what the Brits were doing in February of 1942—sitting on their asses drinking Singapore slings on the front porch of Raffles when the Japanese were sailing into Singapore Harbor, getting ready to inflict the single worst disaster in British military history." Suddenly the floodgates had opened, and Dad was talking about the war.

It was a conversation that continued in fits and starts over the course of a couple of days. He regaled us with stories of the naval battles he had witnessed and how his ship had sustained two Kamikaze attacks and suffered severe damage and heavy personnel losses. She had had to limp back to her shipyard on the U.S. mainland—Bremerhaven in Washington State. I had heard from Mummy that Dad succeeded somehow in getting a secret signal or code to her approximating his time of arrival. She hopped on the train to Seattle but ended up having to cool her heels there for a couple of days. When he finally turned up, they were allowed only a day or two together, and as for the ship, she was never again to see active service and was scrapped in 1973.

While Dad was off at war, something bad befell me here, at home. Something horrible. For the summer of 1944, my mother, together with one of her Greenwood girlfriends, had rented a small place a couple of blocks from the beach in the Connecticut-shore community of Pine Orchard. In late August she was driving back to New York on the Merritt Parkway going sixty miles per hour or so. I was three, almost four, and safely installed in the back seat. Laura, thirteen months older, was sitting up front with Mummy. I was fiddling with the door and had gotten it slightly ajar when suddenly it opened all the way and I fell out. I remember so clearly bouncing onto the highway, and that there was a truck right behind us that had to swerve to avoid turning me into raspberry jam. Laura, who had seen me fly out the door, alerted Mummy who had no choice but to keep going until she could securely circle back for me.

I had managed to crawl or roll over to the side of the road. Cars had come to a screeching halt, and there were people crowding all around me. When Mummy finally pulled up, some of them helped get me into the back of her car. Full-speed ahead to Yale New Haven Hospital, where they gave me a glass of orange juice—to this day I remember how good it tasted. Then they put me in traction—a pulley on my leg. Mummy called her mother in a panic, and Grandma Delano got hold of the foremost orthopedic surgeon in New York, who she either knew or knew of—those were the good old days when the name Delano could open any door. He told her without hesitation that what they were doing with me at Yale New Haven was the wrong thing, that I should definitely not be in a pulley. The good doctor advised her to call an ambulance and send me on to him and he would operate on me himself. And that, ladies and gentlemen, is the one and only reason I can stand and walk upright today.

The bone between my pelvis and left knee was practically shattered—the femur, the longest and strongest bone in the human body—and other bones, including my hip, were broken, fractured, or cracked. I remember lying in the O.R.—they were putting an ether mask over my face, and I wasn't having it—I was trying to push the damn thing off. When they got me under, they removed the bone fragments, inserted a plate, and set the leg. Three months later, they had to perform another operation, to remove the plate.

I was in the hospital for all that time—a private facility somewhere on the Upper East Side that no longer exists. I had a cast on my left leg all the way up to my waist, and another on the right side that went from hip to knee. Talk about downtime: I couldn't move a muscle. I don't remember doing any walking. Mummy was terrified I would never walk again. *Well*, I have run four New York City marathons—1980, '83, '84, and '86—in addition to one in Montreal in '81, plus the *Mercury News* race that I ran every year I was in San Jose. I went the distance in all of them.

I'll never forget the exhilaration I felt at the start of my first New York marathon. I ran across the Verrazano Bridge at full strength. There were at least ten helicopters circling overhead and fire boats shooting water 100 feet or more into the air, and huge crowds cheering everyone on, and the Statue of Liberty visible in the distance in all her height and glory. I discovered belatedly that my rebuilt left leg could take me comfortably only as far as eight miles, because, beyond that, my knee was killing me—and ahead lay almost twenty miles of body punishment. One of the race officials yelled out at about the twenty-five-mile mark, "When you finish the marathon, you win the marathon." I crossed the finish line at three hours fifty-six minutes.

But getting back to unadulterated body punishment, the day finally came when I was discharged from that hospital. My room was crawling with stuffed animals and fidget toys, and Mummy told me to say goodbye to them, that I had to leave them for the children who came after me. I pleaded with her and, in the end, she let me take one toy—a stuffed bear. But I wanted them *all*—I had come to regard them as my friends.

Whenever I have a massage, if I forget to tell them and they rub me the wrong way—that is, on my scar—it hurts like hell. The first time my wife saw it up close and personal, she went, "What is *that*?" I mean, it's eighteen inches long. When I had the accident, it was only a few inches, because I was only three at the time, but it grew along with me. It runs down my left leg, from hip to knee, and when I'm wearing shorts, you can't miss it. Literally hundreds of people have asked me about it over the years. Including, and especially, my grandkids.

One Christmas, when the youngest was three or four, they were really after me to tell how I got it. I eventually gave in and let them have the whole story: how I had fallen out of the back of a speeding car and gotten broken into a lot of little pieces, how I was lying on the side of the road in terrible pain, and how their great-grandmother and their great-aunt Laura, who was the age some of them were then, had to turn around and come back for me. Oh, and how there had been this big truck behind us when I fell out of the car and that if it had squished me, they wouldn't be here to hear the story. Well, what can I tell you—they ate it up and made me tell it all over again.

When my mother was pushing ninety, I had a godawful time getting her to give up driving. She was refusing to put her seatbelt on, among other worrying things. I would say, "Mummy, please, buckle up—it's making the most awful noise." I finally had to take her car away from her—she was a menace on the road. Where Dad had always been a foot-dragger at the wheel, Mummy was a lead foot (something I inherited from her). She complained to my sisters, "Will you please tell your brother I want the keys to my car back!"

Mummy was eighty-three when Dad died in October 2002, in San Mateo, California, at the age of eighty-six, of a stroke. The *Pioneer Press* eulogized its former longtime publisher as a "man with the air of a patrician, the accent of a Bostonian, the build of a tall Vikings linebacker, the golf swing of a professional, and an ego disproportionate to his size and status—a man with an amiable manner and a calmly civilized approach to the problems of life and the businesses he ran." Mummy was totally bereft, and her bosom friend Betsy Beinecke flew to her side and slept in my parents' bed as a comfort to her. (When Betsy's husband, Carl Shirley, died some years before, my mother, who was matron of honor at their wedding, had flown to Betsy's side and slept in bed with *her*. Those Greenwood girls!)

With every passing year, Mummy was slipping a little more. She and Dad had been very much in love and all but inseparable throughout their marriage of sixty-three years. She would say to my sisters and me, "When I go to bed, I say goodnight to your father and I tell him that I hope I can be with him soon." I would say, "Mummy, don't say things like that, there's still so much for you to look forward to," and I said it as if it were true. She lived on into her ninety-fourth year, succumbing to a stroke in 2013.

When Dad went off to war, I was a year and a half old, and when he came back, I had just turned five. Immediately on his return he was promoted to assistant general manager of the Duluth paper, still nominally being run by his malingering uncle Victor. The first six months or so after we moved back to the Midwest, we lived in a rented house, and then my parents purchased 3901 Greysolon Road. As I would learn later in school, the street was named after the seventeenth-century French soldier and explorer who was the first European to visit the area: Daniel Greysolon, Sieur du Lhut. The name got anglicized as "DuLuth," and he became the city's namesake.

I could sit in our living room with its big picture windows and look all the way down to Lake Superior five blocks away without seeing a single house. The pristine setting was certainly not lost on Eleanor Roosevelt when she came to stay with us in June 1947, two years after FDR died in office. She wrote in her nationally syndicated column: "It is a cold climate, but it is very beautiful there and I have seldom seen a lovelier homesite than that of my cousin Mrs. Bernard Ridder, Jr. Her house is hidden among trees and looks out over the lake, yet it is only about a ten-minute drive from the business district."

During my childhood it was my mother who did the disciplining. Dad was disengaged from that sort of thing—he left it to Mummy

My mother with her cousin and friend Eleanor Roosevelt, Duluth, 1947.

The relatively modest gray-shingle house in Duluth that I mostly grew up in.

to raise us pretty much. At some point he started referring to her as the Grand Marshall, and we picked that up and ran with it. No question, she ran the show. I was never spanked—punishment rarely took the form of anything more severe than a scolding. When I did something unspeakably bad, I would be sent to my room without supper. The most painful punishment Mummy ever meted out was when I was nine and dove into my Christmas presents a few days before the holiday. Most of them were just the usual boring stuff—shirts and socks and pjs. But my main present was something I had hinted I wanted desperately and that I was counting on getting: a turbine-powered Indy 500 racecar. When Mummy discovered I had unwrapped it ahead of time, she took it away from me, promising I would never see it again. And she kept her word.

With Laura and Peter, Duluth, 1950.

I was enrolled at the co-ed Lab School at the University of Minnesota-Duluth (UMD), a small academy administered by the college's teachers program. I went there through the eighth grade. There was no foreign language taught, and no Latin, no Ancient Greek. And no algebra, which was a disappointment, because math had always been my forte. In the sixth grade my math aptitude was rated twelfth-grade level. All told, the education I received at the Lab School was probably no better than what I would have gotten in a public school.

Dad hosted office parties at the house—usually for twenty couples or so. They would drive up, and I would have to park their cars. I was only twelve, but I had taught myself to drive. The guests who had brand-new cars looked nervous handing them over to me. Some of them would say, "Are you sure you're old enough to drive?" I always said, "Don't worry, I'm a good driver." I mean, what could they do about it—they worked for Dad. I must say I got a real kick out of driving the length of our long driveway and parking out on Greysolon Road.

I had a newspaper route in Duluth around this time—my first regular job. I had to get up every day at five. I made sure to dress warm. There was always so much snow on the ground I couldn't ride my bike. I would head out on foot to a path through the woods that took me to Superior Street where I picked up the papers that had been left for me on the side of the road by the delivery truck. There would be at least fifty of them and I put them in my carrier bag and trudged all the way along Superior from 39th to 33rd streets—my route was about a mile and a half. I would carefully place the papers between the customers' storm doors and their front doors—I never tossed them.

I would then proceed two blocks east to Mr. Hoff. He was one of the Boy Scout leaders and some sort of a hotshot businessman. He had a couple of sons, who I knew from school, but they would be sound asleep. If his light was on, I'd knock, and he would invite me in. He would usually be drinking a cup of coffee, and he would offer to make me a hot chocolate, and we would talk about Minnesota football or, more likely, hockey.

Duluth was the hotbed of hockey in this country, primarily thanks to its being so cold. The best hockey players in the 1920s and '30s all came from Minnesota. Every year, the top collegiate hockey player receives the Hobey Baker Award, the equivalent of the Heisman Trophy in football. (Baker was a legendary Hall of Famer. He had played at my alma mater, St. Paul's, where modern hockey got its start in the U.S. in the late nineteenth century, on the Lower School Pond, and then at Princeton.) I played hockey in grade school in a public recreational league—a city youth league. I was on the same team and the same line as Tommy Williams who went on to play

Olympic hockey, and then major-league hockey, first for the Boston Bruins and then for the Oakland Seals.

From Mr. Hoff's I plodded north, up Greysolon Road six blocks to where most of the rest of my customers lived. I was supposed to collect money from them once a week after school, but I always had trouble getting paid in full because not everyone would be home. I took the bus downtown to the paper to pay my bill as best I could. If I didn't have all the money, they let it go till the following week. My take-home pay amounted to the difference between the subscription and wholesale prices and came to only a few dollars. Most of it I spent on lifesavers in assorted flavors—strawberry was my favorite—and on candy bars, Baby Ruths mainly.

I bought a broken-down Doodle Bug scooter from one of the Hoff brothers—think of it as my "Rosebud." I paid for it with what was left over from the money from my paper route that I hadn't spent on candy. I could never get that Doodle working right—I just wasn't mechanical. I asked the Hoff kid for help in fixing it, but he wasn't mechanical either. Dad was angry with me for buying it—he felt that I had let the Hoff boy take advantage of me somehow, and he was also concerned that the contraption was dangerous. Later, when I got to the University of Michigan, I bought myself a third-hand Vespa, but I made sure Dad never knew a thing about it.

My paper route came to a natural end in June when Laura and I were shipped East to *Steen Valetje* and Grandma Delano. From there, six weeks later, I was dispatched to Brooksville, Maine, and Robin Hood Camp, where you can bet your last dollar I was *not* taught to steal from the rich to give to the poor.

Paper boy was not by a long shot the only job I had growing up. During those Duluth summers, I raked what golf traditionalists call bunkers, a name for the dugout areas on a golf course, particularly around the green. This was at the Northland Country Club where I also worked in the pro shop cleaning golf clubs. And I was a caddie, too. I especially enjoyed caddying for Dad since he always played with other accomplished golfers.

At Robin Hood Camp, Brooksville, Maine.

Dad didn't talk to me much on the course, but sometimes he would give me five dollars, which was a pretty good deal for caddying. More often, though, it was more like two or three dollars—for four and a half hours. One time when I was eleven or twelve, I was caddying for a St. Paul friend of Dad's, Larry O'Shaugnessy, and he asked me how far it was from his ball to the pin on the green. I answered, "150 to 175 yards." That evening as I was walking by our living room, I overheard Dad and his friends laughing about "Tony"—clearly, they were dining out on something I had done. I asked Dad the next day what was so funny. He told me, "Tony, when a player asks you how far, you need to give them the exact yardage, not a range."

My colorful great-aunt Laura "Polly" Delano, FDR's favorite first cousin, with some more of her beloved dogs.
Franklin D. Roosevelt Presidential Library

There were chores I was responsible for around the house as well. Mummy adored her aunt Polly Delano. She idolized her to the point that, in Duluth, she started raising the same breeds—Irish setters and long-haired dachshunds. They were all either for show or for sale, and Mummy was very particular about who she sold them to. She had a kennel built with three thirty-yard runs, but a select few of the dogs ended up living in the house.

When Aunt Polly visited, she would always bring four or five of her own. She had a Mercedes convertible with a trailer attached, and a liveried driver by the name of Cundee to whom *she* was attached. Everybody suspected it was one of those Queen-Victoria-Mr. Brown situations. Flirtatious as Aunt Polly was, she never married. Once upon a time, she had been engaged to the first secretary of the Chinese embassy in Washington—a nobleman of some sort. It was the usual story—her father disapproved (but then, so did her fiancé's father).

There were always too many dogs around as far as I was concerned. I was the one doing the grunt work, picking up after them. In the spring, summer, and fall I hosed down the runs, and in the winter I had to use a snow shovel. Whenever one of the bitches got pregnant, Mummy delivered the puppies herself, and my sister Laura and I helped clean up the bloody mess. We helped Mummy with the dog shows as well. We would load up the station wagon with four or five for the drive to Chicago or Minneapolis. Sometimes we took the train and the dogs were confined in the kennels on board. More than a few went on to win championships—there were ribbons all over the house, blues and reds (no third-place yellows or fourth-place whites).

Dad was not in the least interested in our dogs. I don't remember him ever petting one. He didn't even know their names. Well, names were never his thing. I don't know that he ever would have been able to tell you the names of all his grandchildren. Except for my son. Par was Dad's favorite out of nine. He regularly read the newspapers and *Time* magazine and even as a kid could make intelligent conversation with adults about current events. Dad's mother, Nell Ridder, used to take me to restaurants in New York like the 21 Club and announce, "This is my grandson Tony from Duluth, Minnesota, and he is my favorite grandchild." So, I knew what that felt like—it used to embarrass the dickens out of me.

I never allowed myself to get attached to any of our dogs. We had a gorgeous Irish setter, Sue, who disappeared on us one day. We went looking for her, driving around and calling her name out the car window—calling and calling. She was never found. During my long, married life with Connie, we had dogs, generally yellow Labs, but there was also a golden retriever, and an Irish setter called Cinnamon. They lived mostly outside but slept in the kitchen. I never paid much attention to them—they were just dogs for the kids. But now, in my old age, my pugs have come to mean the world to me.

The lawn between the house in Duluth and the garage easily extended a hundred yards, and on fine summer days my mother would leave my baby brother, Peter, outside in his crib to bask in the sun. People in Duluth were big on deer hunting with bows and arrows, and the park bordering our six acres of woods had a practice archery course. One afternoon, Mummy found Peter playing with a sharpened arrow. Somebody must have taken a wild shot, and the weapon had landed in his crib.

Holding brother Peter close, Duluth, late 1940s.

CHAPTER FIVE

Packed Off to School

In early September 1954, my mother, my sister Laura, and I went to stay with Grandma Delano at *Steen Valetje* for a few Arcadian days. Dad, with his age-old aversion to the place, didn't show up until the eleventh hour—the night before the morning that he and my mother were set to drive me to Concord, New Hampshire, for my first year at St. Paul's. The only time Dad ever set foot on the school grounds was when they dropped me off that day.

Mummy was the parent who oversaw my education, and when it was time to pick a boarding school, she chose St. Paul's over St. Mark's, the so-called family school, on the proven grounds that it was academically superior. I was never even taken to visit the place, but at the age of thirteen you have to do what your mother tells you to—and it wasn't like I had had my heart set on St. Mark's.

In sports I started out playing football, then switched to soccer because you're running all the time and I thought that would get me in better shape for hockey, which was my big love after golf. Dad was proud of the fact that I was becoming a good junior golfer. At St. Paul's, I got to play five days a week and I was number one on the team my last two years. The summer after my junior year, Dad came out to watch me in the final rounds of the Duluth city junior championship and the North Lakes championship, both of which

I won. He never went out of his way to watch me play in any other tournament, not that I ever won another.

When I first arrived at St. Paul's, I was at a decided disadvantage because I had hardly ever cracked a book—unless you count *The Hardy Boys* series, and that didn't seem to count for much. I don't remember Mummy ever handing me a book to read and suggesting that when I finished it, we should sit down and discuss it. I was one of a very few students who had gone to what essentially amounted to a public school. I was also coming from a place that my classmates viewed as a backwater. However you looked at it, I was behind across the board, and I ended up in the bottom quarter of my class.

Because I have always been disposed to liking people, I didn't find making friends to be a challenge, so I wasn't at all lonely—zero periods of homesickness. But I was also happy when vacation came around and I got to go home and see my parents and siblings.

Duluth was a bit too far to go for the short Thanksgiving holiday. Mummy's brother Uncle Warren Delano, the commercial lobster fisherman, would pick me up at school and drive me to his house in Maine for the long weekend. One Thanksgiving I ate around ten lobsters. Uncle Warren said I had set the record, that he had never heard of anyone eating more than six at one time. I was always hungry at St. Paul's. We had something called a tuck shop, where we would go after sports, and I would buy a peanut-butter-and-jelly sandwich. There were no candy bars or bags of potato chips on the premises.

St. Paul's didn't have a sister school, and I was reduced to going out with the local girls who babysat for some of the masters. I realized I was flirting with something a lot more serious than girls—I was flirting with disaster, playing with fire, since I could have been expelled.

I tended to listen to whatever the popular music of the day was—traditional kinds of stuff, Frank Sinatra and Ella Fitzgerald. I was never a Beatles or an Elvis fan. Movies, I always enjoyed, but they were not a passion of mine. I remember being taken when I was twelve to see the first 3-D feature-length film in color—everyone got handed a pair of Polaroid glasses made of tinted cellophane and cardboard. *Bwana Devil*, it was called: an African-adventure B movie based on the true story of the Tsavo Man-Eaters of East Africa, the lions that regularly feasted on the natives who were building the Uganda Railways. I've never forgotten the movie's thrilling tagline: "A lion in your lap! A lover in your arms!"

Another film I remember seeing was *Magnificent Obsession*, the weeper where Rock Hudson plays a worthless playboy who accidentally blinds a pretty woman—played by the first wife of Ronald Reagan, Jane Wyman—then goes to medical school to learn how to miraculously restore her sight. It was ludicrous, but I teared up on cue.

Each day at St. Paul's started with compulsory Chapel. My most stimulating teacher was in fact a priest: the Rev. John Walker, who the school had recruited to head its sacred studies and history departments. He was down to earth for a priest—he used to drive some of us to the movies in town on Saturday nights in his Renault.

He was the only African American on the place and, if I'm not mistaken, the first ever. He later wrote a piece for the alumni magazine recounting that he had come to St. Paul's only "after considerable publicity and discussion" and that "perhaps my very coming can be said to be the first big change in a decade that was to see many innovations in the life of the school." He added—euphemistically, as I would discover—that his "first year was made unforgettable by the almost overwhelming positive response of the boys" and that "by the end of the year I was convinced that, whether or not it was self-conscious, there was a great deal of Christianity at least residually present."

I re-encountered the Rev. Walker in the early 1980s at, of all things, the annual convention of the American Newspaper Publishers Association at the Waldorf Astoria in New York. He was on a panel discussing how members of the clergy viewed journalism and I went up to him afterward and said, "I don't know if you remember me

Faculty of St. Paul's School in the late 1950s.

from St. Paul's, my name is Tony Ridder." What he said to me next was in shocking contradiction to the account of his experience that he had rendered so affectingly in the alumni magazine. He said, "Tony, I remember you so well, because there were only five or six students in the whole school who, I felt, considered me a human being. I could tell simply from the way they looked at me, but I could see in your eyes that you recognized and appreciated me for who I am."

I remain deeply embarrassed to confess that I had never realized how alone and uncomfortable he must have felt. The only Black people I had ever known worked in the locker room of the Northland Country Club shining shoes. John left St. Paul's after seven years to take up duties as a canon at the Washington National Cathedral. By the time I ran into him at the Waldorf, he was not only a trustee of St. Paul's (and with a son there) but the dean of the cathedral

The Rev. John T. Walker, my favorite teacher at St. Paul's School and, later, my good friend.

and the episcopal bishop of Washington, D.C.—an eminence with a capital "E." We made a point of keeping in touch. He was on the board of the Berkeley School of Theology, and when he came out to California for meetings, he would arrive a day early, or stay an extra day, so he could spend the night with Connie and me in Saratoga. She felt the same way about him that I did.

At St. Paul's I did well on my college boards—I always did well on aptitude tests—and I got into my first-choice college, the University of Michigan. I had picked it because, having grown up happy in Duluth, I wanted to go to school back in the Midwest. If I had gone to Harvard or Yale or, for that matter, Princeton where Dad went, it would have amounted to just four more years of boarding school.

Neither of my parents ever attended a Parents Day at St. Paul's, nor did they attend my graduation, but both of my grandmothers showed up. Mummy, who was my more caring parent, visited me once in my sophomore year. I would have liked for both her and Dad to make an appearance from time to time, but it wasn't any kind of issue. In all fairness, most of my classmates' folks lived nearer to the school—Boston, New York, Philadelphia, Greenwich … Most of my classmates had never been west of Philadelphia, or even the Hudson.

One day one of them, Guy Rutherfurd, came up to me and said, "I just found out you're a Delano—I had thought you were just some guy from Duluth, Minnesota. I don't think there's anybody else at St. Paul's who knows that you come from a very wealthy family." I said, "That's news to me—all I know is my grandmother has a very large house." I didn't know this then, but it turned out this guy's grandfather's wife—second wife—in other words, his step-grandmother—was Lucy Mercer who, I remembered, had once been FDR's mistress and was with him when he died.

I was curious, so a few years ago I inquired of the school if there had ever been a student from Duluth before me, and they wrote back confirming what I had suspected, that in the entire history of St. Paul's, which was 150 years old by then, I was the one and only.

The summer after I graduated, Dad got me a job working in the newsroom of the Duluth paper for about five weeks as a clerk doing stock tables and running errands. Then he and Mummy magnanimously invited Laura and me to join them on a five-week, grand-tour-like trip to Europe. We sailed on the *SS America*, where I was euphoric to discover there was no age limit for drinking beer. And it was German beer, too—*bester Geschmack*. I had never had the courage to cadge a beer at home, and in my four years at St. Paul's I might have had a total of only three or four—you had to figure out a way to buy it, usually by finding someone to buy it for you, and then sneak off somewhere safe to drink it. One day a friend and I went down to Boston and I experimented with hard liquor—I ordered a gin martini and promptly threw up. So, when I got to college, I stayed off the hard stuff and continued drinking only beer. Oh, if there was a party at my fraternity, I might have laid in some cheap champagne, and I *mean* cheap—two dollars a bottle. The next time

My yearbook photo, St. Paul's School, 1958.

I had a gin martini I would have been in my late twenties, and I managed to keep it down. Or maybe it was a Tom Collins. Anyway, I certainly drank my fill of beer on the ship going over.

One night on deck, my parents, some friends of theirs, and Laura and I were enthusiastically playing round-robin ping-pong. There were quite a few Catholic priests on board bound for the first stop, Cobh, a seaport town in County Cork, Ireland, which happened to have been the *Titanic*'s last port of call in 1912. One of the Good

Fathers was walking past, and I asked him respectfully if he would like to join our game. To this day I can't for the life of me imagine what set him off, because, the next thing I knew, he hauled off and slugged me, *pow right in the kisser.* He knocked me off my feet—decked me. Dad and his friends went chasing after him, but he managed to slip away.

Mummy and Laura helped me back to our cabin and called the ship's doctor, who checked me out, put me to bed, and told me to stay quiet. First thing the next day, Dad registered a complaint with the senior Catholic on board that this was exceptionally unbecoming behavior for a servant of God, to which, instead of being contrite, the cleric replied, "And what were *you* doing, may I ask, letting your son stay up till all hours, and from what I've been told, he was drinking beer." I mean, I *might* have had a bottle of beer in my hand, but so what?—it was allowed. Dad said, "There's no excuse for how your priest reacted to a perfectly innocent invitation to join a ping-pong game." Dad added that it was clear from the way he was walking—kind of weaving—that the fellow was tipsy. The incident was the talk of the ship.

There was a "ship's pool" where the first-class passengers could bet on how many miles the vessel would cover in a given day, with the pot going to whoever came closest. Dad handed me twenty dollars to put in the pool—quite a bit back then. And, blow me down, I won. It was a bonanza—six or seven hundred bucks. Dad said, "I gave you the dough for the pool, so I'm going to take half your winnings." Mummy appealed to him to let me keep the whole caboodle but, being Dad, he wouldn't budge.

My parents, to save on the fare, had me and my eighteen-year-old sister share a cabin. When Laura and I were with kids our own age late at night, I got a charge out of saying stuff like, "Time for bed, Sis—let's go to our room." Which would totally get her goat—every time, she died a thousand deaths. Which made me do it even more. She pleaded with our parents to make me stop embarrassing her. But even if Mummy and Dad had intervened—said something like,

"Come on, Tony, grow up!"—I couldn't have stopped. I *couldn't* grow up, I *had* to embarrass my sister. I'm not sure she's gotten over it to this day.

In Paris we stayed at the Hotel Vendome where Mummy told us she had always stayed when she was traveling with her parents. Laura and I had to share a room there, too, but there was wasn't anyone our age around to embarrass her in front of. I took the half of my winnings that Dad let me keep and put them in my wallet and went for a walk in the Tuileries Garden. A seedy-looking guy sidled up to me and whispered, "*Monsieur désire?*" and then, in broken English, "Wanna see some dirty pictures?" and he whipped out a greasy card deck. They were nothing special—just soft-focus photos of naked girls—but while he was displaying them, he managed somehow to pick my pocket. I didn't realize my money was gone, along with my good leather wallet, till I was quite a ways away, and I raced back to the spot, but of course he had disappeared. Dad found this incident pathetic—"If you were stupid enough to fall for that …" he said.

The next night he took us all to the Folies Bergère. There was an act featuring a magician, and when he asked for a volunteer to come up on stage, Dad said, "Why don't *you* go, Tony," and he raised my hand for me. So I got up there, and this Houdini wannabe ran through his repertoire. When he asked me what time it was, I gazed down at my wrist and discovered my watch was missing. Dad was never one to do a lot of laughing, but there he was, in the audience, yucking it up. Mummy, too, I was shocked to see.

Next, we went to Spain for two or three days, to San Sebastian where we stayed in some hunting club on top of a mountain. Dad and I played golf a couple of times, and we, all four of us, took in some bullfights. Mummy was quick to identify a glamorous-looking woman sitting a few rows in front of us as former Queen Soraya of Iran, whose husband, the Shah, had sent her packing when she couldn't bear children. Mummy had read somewhere that she was having a torrid affair with the bullfighter.

Scotland was next on the menu. We played all the great golf courses—Troon, Prestwick, Turnberry, Carnoustie, St. Andrews, Muirfield. You could say we played the field. I never had any trouble breaking eighty. Dad was proud of me.

Then we were off to London. We stayed at the Charing Cross Station Hotel, where Laura and I were made to share a room again. Dad was on the executive committee of the board of the U. S. Golf Association, which was hosting a U.S. Amateur at the Olympic Club in San Francisco, so he had to leave us to our own devices and fly over the pole nonstop to California. Lockheed had recently come out with the Constellation, aka the "Connie," a plane with kind of a comical three-winged tail. Howard Hughes had bought the first twenty-five of them for his airline, TWA. The Connie went on to break a transcontinental speed record, and President Eisenhower was using one as Air Force One. They didn't have sleeper seats back then, and I don't know how far back the seats went, but poor Dad—it was a twenty-three-hour flight.

Mummy, Laura, and I continued on to Brussels for the World's Fair. The hotels were full, and we ended up staying in some cheap motel, all three of us in the same room, and on top of that, we had to provide our own soap and towels. We then boarded a boat on the Rhine to go upriver to Wiesbaden, which we found looking a lot like what Gaza looks like today—rubble everywhere. Mummy rented a car and we drove to Munich and then over the Brenner Pass to Venice, where we stayed for a few days at the Luna Hotel—three in a room again—across an alleyway from the famous Harry's Bar. Then it was on to Rome, where we stayed three-to-a-room at the five-star Hassler.

From there we flew coach on the Connie to New York and just kept on going—back to the All-American Midwest. It felt good to be home.

CHAPTER SIX

Michigan and Marriage

I HAD BEEN so well prepared at prep school that when I entered college I was much more advanced than most of the other freshmen. The downside was that I felt free to not take my studies seriously. My parents visited one weekend in my freshman year, and Mummy came one other time—I had had the, ahem, half-baked idea to use a sunlamp and fallen asleep under it and was being treated for burns in the infirmary. I never used a sunlamp again.

I was dating a pretty freshman, a graduate of Abbott Academy named Sue Moore, who had grown up in Port Huron, Michigan, where her father was the head of a big salt company. One day she sprung on me that she was thinking of going to the spring dance at Williams as the date of an old hometown boyfriend. I gave her an ultimatum: "If you go, we're over." She went, and we were.

In the fall of my sophomore year, I was elected to Psi Epsilon and moved into their fraternity house on campus. I was fooling around a lot and irregular in class attendance, and my grades sank to below C level. My best friend was a bright guy from Scarsdale, New York, with a great sense of humor, Moss Galpeer. We spent a lot of time together in his off-campus apartment. When I asked if he had any interest in joining my fraternity, he answered an enthusiastic yes. Moss was Jewish, and it was a fraternity that traditionally didn't take Jews—I mean, there were fraternities *for* Jews at Michigan. By the time he came up for election, I was no longer active in Psi Upsilon, and he didn't get in. But I had the sneaking suspicion that it *was* on account of his being Jewish. In any case, he was disappointed, and I was disappointed for him, but it didn't impact our friendship.

I had a girlfriend back in St. Paul—Tracy Bement. We had started going out the summer after my freshman year when I had a job at the *Pioneer Press*, working in the pressroom and the control room. When I came home for Christmas vacation of my sophomore year, we took up where we had left off. My next-to-last day in town before I had to return to Ann Arbor, we decided on the spur of the moment to go skiing at Mount Telemark, a resort in the Wisconsin Lake District.

We quit the slopes around 3:30 and headed for the lakeside cabin her parents owned, about five miles away, outside the town of Cable. We wound up having to break in. After building a fire, we had a couple of beers and promptly fell asleep. We woke up at midnight, remembering in a panic that both sets of parents had been expecting us to be home by dinner, and we hit the road.

About halfway to St. Paul, we were pulled over by the Wisconsin Highway Patrol. It turned out that Tracy's father, fearing we might have been involved in an accident, had contacted Dad, who had had the police put out an APB. Mr. Bement had then picked Dad up, and they were pretty far along in the three-hour drive to Cable when the police radioed them where to come get us. They sped to the site. Dad jumped into our car and grabbed the wheel, while Tracy jumped out and into *her* dad's car.

And what were the first words out of Dad's mouth? "Congratulations, Tony, you now have a serious legal problem on your hands—you violated the Mann Act." I said, "What's that?' Dad said, without missing a beat, "Knowingly transporting a female of any age across a state line for immoral purposes. I hope they throw the book at you."

A day or two later, I looked up the Mann Act in the college library and got really scared. Nothing came of it in the end, in any sense. I never saw Tracy again—I didn't want to risk inciting Mr. Bement to pursue the matter.

My sister Laura was also now at Michigan, as a junior, having graduated from Bradford Junior College near Boston, and she had introduced me to an extremely attractive girl who lived across the hall in her dorm. Connie Meach and I had been going out since the fall. I rationalized that it was okay to have two girlfriends at the same time so long as they weren't living in the same city. I had given my fraternity pin to Tracy and couldn't face asking for it back, so I got another one from the frat to give to Connie. Back then, to give a girl your fraternity pin meant you were getting serious about her—there was real significance to the gesture.

The tit for tat was that I introduced Laura to the person *she* wound up marrying—one of my frat brothers, Ned Evans. I offered him a case of beer if he would take her out, and he wouldn't do it unless I gave him two. They've been married now for sixty-five years and counting.

Connie and I hit it off right away. As far as I could see, she had it all: in high school she had been Homecoming Queen, a National Merit Scholar, and an ace athlete—Central U.S. Ski Champion, as well as good at tennis and golf. She was a shoo-in for the most selective sorority on campus, the one with the highest-achieving members, Kappa Alpha Theta (to get considerably ahead of the story, all three of our daughters would wind up pledging it).

I had no money to take Connie out to restaurants, and the college dining rooms were gender-segregated; women weren't allowed in my fraternity house; and Connie's dorm was a mile away. But we were determined to make it work.

Meanwhile, what I was neglecting to make work was my schoolwork. At the end of sophomore year 1960, I flunked out. I came home to my parents in St. Paul that summer with my tail between my legs. I was in the doghouse, for sure—in deep shit. Dad was pressuring me to enlist in the army: "It'll teach you discipline, which you seem to be sorely lacking."

I quickly got my act together and applied to Macalester in St. Paul for the fall semester. Academically, it was the highest-rated college in the Twin Cities—a goodly number of distinguished people had gone there (Joan and Walter Mondale, Kofi Annan, Ari Emanuel ...). Dad was an acquaintance of the college president but wouldn't lift a finger for me. I got accepted on my own, which he gave me credit for.

Dad warmed up toward me by degrees, and in mid-June he invited me to go with him and Mummy to Denver, where he would be attending U.S. Golf Association board meetings and taking in the U.S. Open. I got to witness Arnold Palmer win—the most dramatic comeback in U.S. Open history. Mummy and I then flew on to Wyoming to spend three days with Laura and Connie at the lodge at Jackson Hole where they were both working as housemaids.

It was while we were in Jackson Hole that I proposed to Connie, not on bended knee, as that would have literally upset things—we were in a rowboat in the middle of Jenny Lake in Grand Teton National Park. She said yes and, realizing that this would probably be her last summer to spend with her parents, she decided to go home to Traverse City, Michigan, but she wasn't one to just sit around the house—she went out and got herself a job as a waitress.

I, meanwhile, was getting ready to set out for Canada to start the summer job that Dad had lined up for me at a newsprint company in Fort William, Ontario, called Great Lakes Paper. I was in Canada for about ten weeks. For the first half I was in the engineering department, basically taking inventory of the wood on site. I would climb to the top of ... not quite a mountain, not even really a hill, just an enormous pile of cut-up logs. I would move from point to point on the pile and, using a pole-like device, call out readings from various angles—there would be someone on the ground taking notes. I was staying at the local YMCA, which had more the feeling of a homeless shelter. There was a communal bathroom on each floor, thankfully with a shower. I felt uncomfortable there and began locking my door at night.

The other half of that summer I spent deep in the woods doing land surveying. I was assigned a section of forest to walk through. Did I say "walk"? We had to *fight* our way through the underbrush, it was that dense—almost junglelike. More than once, I accidentally stepped on a beehive and got badly stung. I don't remember seeing an actual bear, but there were plenty of them around, or so we'd been warned. The guy I was partnered with would be calling out the diameter of the trees and what species they were—"Hemlock eight inches ... White Spruce four ..."—and I noted it all down on a pad.

The cut logs got dumped in a lake, and I spent my last few weeks in Canada going out on a two-man rowboat with a big pole that had a sharp hook on the end to dislodge the ones that had gotten caught on the side. Once we had pushed them off, they flowed seamlessly down to the sawmill. At that point I was basically functioning as a lumberjack.

I was now living in one of the logging camps, but not with the loggers—they had their own digs—rather, with the guys who were doing the inventory. There were between thirty and forty of them. Most were in their twenties and thirties—immigrants from Scandinavia. I couldn't believe the amount of food they could put away. None of them ever said a single word between mouthfuls—the only sounds were their forks and knives scraping the plates. The minute they were through they got up and, well, lumbered back to their beds. I had always prided myself on being the world's fastest eater—at home, at prep school, in my college fraternity, at any number of country clubs, nobody had ever surpassed me in speed-eating. But I was gobsmacked by how fast *they* ate—I definitely met my matches in the Canadian woods.

My parents had rented a car for me for the summer, and every other weekend, I made the fourteen-hour trip to Traverse City to see Connie. This entailed driving all the way down to Duluth and crisscrossing Wisconsin to up around Lake Michigan across the

Mackinac Bridge. I would get there about seven Saturday morning. And before I knew it, I would be driving back the next night, which meant losing two nights' sleep—leaving Traverse City around dinnertime and reporting straight to work, either in Fort William or further up, in the woods, at 8:00 a.m. sharp—needless to say, bleary-eyed.

In the fall I matriculated at Macalester, and Connie went back to the University of Michigan. A few weeks later, she found out she was pregnant, and we sat down and set a date for our wedding—November 6. This was most definitely not a case of pregnancy forcing the issue; I had already bought her an engagement ring. Admittedly it was a mere speck of a diamond—it set me back me $200, all that was left of the money I had made in Canada.

In late October, Connie dropped out of Michigan and went back to Traverse City to stay with her parents for the two weeks before the wedding. Dad was very unhappy with me for *having* to get married, although that was not the way I saw it, since I had my heart set on marrying Connie anyway. And never mind that Dad had married Mummy under the exact same circumstances.

He was insisting that Connie have an abortion. He told me, "You don't have a choice—you don't have a nickel to your name. How do you figure on supporting a wife *and* child? I'll arrange to get the thing done, and I'll even pay for it."

I was in no position to pick a fight with Dad, but I stood up to him, nonetheless. "Connie is going to have our baby come what may. And nothing and no one is going to stop us from getting married."

On my way to Traverse City for the ceremony, I stopped in Detroit to pick up the car that Mummy and Dad were giving us for a wedding present. It was the least expensive Ford on the market, a two-door Falcon that came with not a single extra: no window power, no FM, and an engine not much more powerful than a lawnmower. The coincidence that Grandpa Ridder had given my parents a car after *they* had had to get married didn't escape me.

We had only immediate family at the wedding. My parents gave

Connie's parents short shrift. I don't think Dad and Mummy ever saw or even talked to them again. Connie was from a traditional middle-class Midwest family with solid values. Her father was the owner of a dry-cleaning establishment, where her mother also worked. The two sets of parents, clearly, had nothing in common. When Laura got married a year later, it was a very different story—Ned was from the fancy Detroit suburb Grosse Pointe, and his father was CEO of a Fortune 500 company.

Dad was very distant to Connie at the beginning. Mummy was warmer, but if Connie had ever tried calling her "Jane," she would have been brought up short. At the end of the day, by which I hardly mean the wedding day—it took a little longer than that—my parents liked and valued Connie more than all the other in-laws combined. They thought the world of her and more—they thought she walked on water. Out of all the lawyers they had on call, it was Connie they entrusted with the task of doing their trusts.

Our honeymoon consisted of the 388-mile drive from Traverse City to St. Paul and spending the night along the way in a cheap motel called the Edgewater. We set up house in a bare-bones apartment near the Macalester campus that my mother was paying the rent on behind my father's back. She would also slip us a little something from time to time, but I had been made to understand that once I graduated from college, I would be entirely on my own. I remain grateful that my parents didn't spoil me—they were doing me a favor. Knowing that I wouldn't be able to rely on them financially motivated me to study even harder—to try and surpass myself.

I got a job in a Brooks-Brothers-type men's clothing store downtown, Hubert White's. Women came in to shop for their husbands, and some of them, friends of my parents, recognized me. And Connie was working as a salesgirl at Powers Department Store in a part of town called Highland Park.

I was only at Macalester for that one semester of junior year. On the strength of the respectable grades I received, I was readmitted to Michigan for the spring semester, beginning in February. Connie

Connie Meach and I were happily married on November 6, 1960, in Traverse City, Michigan, with my parents (left) and hers (right) in attendance.

and I moved into a little stand-alone house in a low-income area on the outskirts of Ann Arbor. Eventually we got accepted into student housing, which consisted of a two-room apartment on Michigan's north campus, and we lived there till I graduated.

We allowed ourselves the rare diversion. When I was single, I used to go to the track in Detroit and Toledo with Moss Galpeer, but after I got married, I went only once. That race was in Toledo, and Moss insisted he had the inside track, that a horse by the name of Mister Scoot was a sure bet. Connie and I were living literally hand to mouth, subsisting on chili and spaghetti, yet I went and wagered twenty dollars. As the entrants were being called to the gate, I confessed my recklessness to Connie. She took it badly: "How could you do this to us? We can't afford to lose that money."

As I was weakly protesting that the horse was a shoo-in, the mounts zoomed by the stands, with Mister Scoot only in fourth place. Connie burst into tears. But lo and behold, he went on to finish first. Connie continued with her crying, and she stayed mad at me for weeks on end. More than just mad—*irate*. Didn't matter that we had taken forty dollars home. You can bet I never bet on a horse again while I was in school.

Connie went into labor on the afternoon of July 18, 1961. I rushed her to the University of Michigan Hospital. As the resident loaded her onto the gurney elevator, he introduced himself, "My name's Dave Middleton—I'm going to be delivering your baby." I exclaimed, "Surely not the Dave Middleton who's going to be the starting wide receiver for the Vikings?"

The answer was a resounding—and astounding—yes. This was the Minnesota Vikings' inaugural season as an NFL professional football team, and Ridder Publications owned the largest stake—Dad, in fact, was the chairman of the Vikings board. It turned out that back in 1955 when Dave was the number-one draft pick of the Detroit Lions, pro-football players were allowed to go to school in the off-season and he had enrolled in medical school; after six seasons, he announced he would be available for only a couple of more, and the Vikings had acquired the rights to him in a special expansion draft.

Our Katie was one of Dave's first deliveries. She looked just like baby pictures of Connie and, like her mother, grew up to be not only beautiful but accomplished—an interior designer with an international reputation. A few weeks after bringing Katie into the world, Dave took a leave of absence from the hospital to play his final season in the NFL. That fall, Mummy and Dad came to Detroit to visit Laura and Ned, and we all attended a Detroit Lions/Minnesota Vikings game. Midway through, there was an announcement over the public address system: "The chairman of the board of the Vikings is in the stands today—Bernie Ridder. Dave Middleton, who just caught that pass, recently delivered his

With Katie in front of the University of Michigan student housing building, where her mother and I lived when Katie was a baby.

first grandchild." Dave went on to enjoy a long run as an esteemed obstetrician-gynecologist in Ann Arbor.

I was certainly no Lion, but the summer Katie was born I experienced my own rite of passage in Detroit. Dad had gotten me a job as a reporter intern at the *Detroit News*, which was not a Ridder paper. I worked the night shift, 5:00 p.m. to 1:00 a.m. My first assignment was to interview the parents of a child who had rushed out into the street in front of their house and been run over and killed. They refused to talk to me—they were outraged that I was even attempting to ask them questions. That day, I recognized that a reporter's job wasn't easy, that there were issues of moral ambiguity.

I was majoring in economics but during senior year I gave serious thought to applying to Michigan Law School. When I broached the subject with Dad, he said, "Fine, but how do you propose to pay for it? I guess you could try for a scholarship. Or maybe even get a job."

I blurted out, "What about a job in the company?"

Dad said nothing—radio silence. But a few months later, he called me: "If you still want to work for the company, I can arrange an entry-level job on the *Aberdeen American News*, which is where I got *my* start, as you know, but if you don't perform, if you try and slide through on your name, I'll have you pulled right out." That there was to be no free ride in the company was just about the most useful thing Dad ever said to me, because it scared the living daylights out of me.

And so, it was decided: I would be heading to South Dakota come summer. The irony is that, although I never got to law school, Connie did. When a couple of decades later she was considering applying, I told her that that way I would be getting to go myself, vicariously.

CHAPTER SEVEN

"Springtime for Hitler"

I SAID EARLIER that I didn't remember my mother ever recommending a book to me. But one day during my senior year at Michigan, when I was on the phone with her, she said, sounding a tad uncomfortable, "There's a book just out that has some extremely negative things to say about your grandfather Ridder and his brothers." I ran right out and got it.

My Life in Court turned out to consist of detailed accounts of six civil cases in its author's long career at the bar. A big yawn, right? Except that the author happened to be Louis Nizer, the most famous trial lawyer in the world (also, according to *The Guinness Book of World Records*, the highest priced—his client list would come to include Salvador Dali, Mae West, Johnny Carson, and Julius Erving). The book would go on to spend a phenomenal seventy-two weeks at the top of the *New York Times* nonfiction bestsellers list.

The chapter devoted to the Ridders had the hair-raising title "Honor: Issue of Nazism in America." I was blown away reading it—or at least knocked sideways—having had no clue, not even an inkling, that in my own immediate family there was a link to one of the greatest infamies in world history.

Nizer went to great lengths (literally—his chapter on the Ridders ran to eighty pages) to frame the occasion for the court case. In the early 1940s, a renowned German émigré professor/scholar published an open letter in pamphlet form in which, among other things, he bitterly accused my great-uncle Victor Ridder of having been a Pan-German activist and Nazi propagandist—altogether a demagogic supporter of supremacist ideology. Victor, who enjoyed a reputation as a social-minded citizen, chose not to take this calumny lying down. He retaliated by publishing an incendiary pamphlet of his own, accusing the professor of spreading "knowingly malicious falsehoods against persons whose integrity and devotion to the ideals of this country have been unquestioned." Adding fuel to the fire, Victor petitioned the New York County District Attorney to indict the professor for criminal libel. When that failed, he pressured the president of Columbia University to deny him a position, and the Brookings Institution to terminate its sponsorship of him. He also sought punitive damages.

The professor turned around and sued Victor for libel. Enter Louis Nizer. The ensuing litigation metastasized into what that seasoned trial lawyer unhesitatingly summed up as "one of the most remarkable libel suits in legal history."

Now, Victor was a formidable figure in far more than the field of journalism, in which, by the way, he had succeeded no less than the august publisher and owner of the *New York Times*, Adolph Ochs, on the Associated Press board. In 1935 no less than FDR had appointed Victor, steadfast Republican though he was, the New York administrator of the massive New Deal federal program, the Works Progress Administration (WPA). And no less prominent a Jew than New York governor Herbert Lehman had appointed Victor, who was already a member of the national executive council of the Boy Scouts of America and a board member of countless Catholic and German American societies, president of the New York State Board of Charities.

Victor was also a close friend and ally of legendary New York mayor Fiorello LaGuardia, who in 1938 had invited him to address an anti-Nazi rally at Carnegie Hall, where he shared the stage with no less than archbishop Fulton J. Sheen and uber rabbi and Zionist leader Stephen S. Wise. The next year, Victor was presented with the "outstanding protector" award by the New York lodge of the B'nai B'rith.

For all this, his pet charity essentially remained the New York Society for Crippled Children. Himself stricken with polio as a child, and further afflicted in adulthood with tuberculosis of the hip bones, Victor throughout the trial would have to be carried to the witness stand in his wheelchair: a spine-chilling visual that served only to heighten the courtroom drama.

In his account of the case against the Ridders, Nizer came out of the gate swinging. To wit: "The moment Hitler came into power [January 30, 1933, when he was appointed Reich Chancellor], the Ridder brothers began to visit him. Victor Ridder saw Hitler and his Nazi associates for a month during April 1933. He returned to visit Hitler again two months later, and repeatedly thereafter in 1935 and 1936. While Victor Ridder was on his way back to the United States from his first trip, his brother and *Staats-Zeitung* co-publisher Bernard Ridder visited Hitler, and another brother and co-publisher, Joseph, also visited Hitler in interim periods. Victor Ridder attempted to explain these visits as journalistic enterprise by an American publisher of a German-speaking newspaper ..."

Nizer saw it as a case of conflicted loyalties: the brothers' to their Motherland versus their allegiance to the United States of America where they were born. If the three Ridders were warmly received in the most exclusive circles of the Third Reich, it would have been with the not unreasonable expectation that they would chauvinistically promote the German cause in the *Staats-Zeitung*, the largest and most influential German-language daily in the U.S.

From Nizer and other sources, I further learned that on May 20, 1933, the Nazi Minister of Aviation, Hermann Goering, dispatched a plane to Bremen, which my grandfather was visiting, to transport him to Berlin to conduct a "personal interview" with Hitler, which extended to an unheard-of hour and three quarters.

The *Staats* ran a blow-by-blow front-page story on their meeting. When my grandfather declared, "I am ninety percent Nazi," the Führer exclaimed, "That is not possible," insisting he account for the missing ten percent. My grandfather replied that he "agreed with the National Socialist ideas one hundred percent, with the single exception of the racial question ... Like many of my American fellow citizens, I cannot agree with the German conception in respect of the Jewish question."

Hitler, who blamed the Jews for the national trauma caused by Germany's ignominious defeat in World War I and who continued to believe that they were hell-bent on turning the world against Germany, nevertheless sought to allay my grandfather's concerns. He classified the so-called Jewish question as a "picayune issue"—one that he was determined to not let "hamper" him. He asserted that "to be rid of them, Germany would gladly pay the freight of its Jewish inhabitants to the U.S. and make each and every one of them a present of a bank account in addition, if President Roosevelt and America would only harbor them ... That is the truth, and may I ask you, if the American press may print the truth, then let it disseminate the German truth."

The Führer left my grandfather with the impression that modification of his anti-Semitic policy was in the offing: that the quota of Jews permitted to practice at the bar would be extended from one percent and the ban on the enrollment of Jewish children in schools mitigated.

My grandfather was appeased—one could go as far as to say pacified. Two weeks after this interview, still in Germany, he exulted to the *Berliner Illustrierte Nachtausgabe* that, being a poet at heart, he had been moved to write an ode to the "exhilarating spirit" of Hitlerism. Moreover, he vowed to "declare and reiterate" when he returned to America that "the present Hitler government is the greatest thing that has ever come to Germany." He took care to add: "I have found substantiation here for my belief that certain groups of Jewish fanatics had exaggerated, sensationalized, and falsified reports [in other words, that the Nazi acts of cruelty toward German Jews, already bordering on barbarism, were in fact no more than what Hitler was dismissing as 'atrocity stories'] in order to stage their propaganda more effectively." As far as my benighted grandfather could see, "No Jew need be uneasy about events in Germany. Anyone who has walked through the German streets with his eyes open, as I have, and spoken with the leading German political functionaries knows that it is utter nonsense to cite the existence of the Nazi Storm Troops and the Steel Helmet men as evidence of a militaristic spirit in the country. These troops are solely for protection against Communists, that and nothing more." He urged Jews not to overreact.

My grandfather concluded: "The German people do not think of war, Hitler does not want war—he is a man of peace." It was chilling, to put it mildly, to read that my grandfather in 1933 believed any of these things, let alone stated them for the record.

His brother had also gotten a free ride, literally. Hitler had had Victor flown to Munich, where he granted him a short interview. On the strength of the twenty-five minutes he was allotted, Victor rhapsodized to the *New York Times* that "Adolf Hitler is one of the most sincere, honest, and open men I have ever spoken to ... He is going to keep Germany safe from war."

Victor proceeded to do two interviews with Hitler's Reich Minister of Propaganda, Joseph Goebbels. In an article he later wrote for the *Staats*, he commended Goebbels for his "extraordinarily wise propaganda" and described him as "world-renowned ... a person of unusually quick power of perception who knows what to do in any situation ... a speaker second only to Hitler ... exceedingly kind and forthcoming. I found a certain bond with him as a newspaperman ... I would be more than happy to welcome him in America."

Upon returning from one of his trips to Germany in the mid-1930s, Victor launched a weekly Sunday supplement in the *Staats*,

"The New Germany: One Reich, One Will," to promote the aims and aspirations of the regime, and appointed as its feature editor a card-carrying Nazi. (It would be revealed during Victor's trial that his private secretary at the newspaper, the man with whom he shared his very office—one Karl Gunther Orgell, out of whose surname the word *ogre* could gratifyingly be carved—was also a rabid Nazi.) The first article in the new section was titled "The Resurrection of the German people under Hitler."

In the summer of 1933, the Nazis brazenly embarked on a campaign to infiltrate German American societies and expel their Jewish members. The chief Nazi henchman in America, Heinz Spanknöbel (a name often deliberately misspelled "Spanknoobel," "Spanknoodle," and "Stoopnagel" in newspaper accounts), duly installed himself in the Yorkville section of Manhattan as the leader of the so-called Friends of New Germany.

One day, Spanknöbel stormed into the offices of the *Staats* demanding that my grandfather and his brother Victor, in the latter's words, "submit to his censorship—he attempted to dictate directions to us as to what could be included and what must be excluded from our publication." The Ridders defied his determination to intimidate them (in point of fact, terrorize them, as their visitor was known to have at least four hundred blackjack-wielding Storm Troopers in full Nazi regalia ever at the ready). Victor and my grandfather published an account of this despicable incident in the *Staats*. Spanknöbel in turn accused them of "treason to their German blood."

By the mid-1930s, the reservations the brothers had initially expressed regarding "certain alleged excesses in regard to the persecution of the Jews" had morphed into "emphatic condemnation of the wholly unwarranted and senseless persecution of the Jews of Germany." The *Staats* ran several anti-Nazi editorials. But at the same time, starting in 1933 and continuing into 1940, it published the programs of the German shortwave broadcasts, not to mention the official dispatches devised in Goebbels' Ministry of Propaganda. And in 1941 and '42 the newspaper solicited contributions from its

THE NEW YORK TIMES, TUESDAY, MAY 2, 1933.

HITLER'S SINCERITY PRAISED BY RIDDER

Publisher, Returning From Tour of Germany, Says He Saw No Disorders There.

Victor Ridder, secretary of the Staats-Herold Corporation, returned on the North German Lloyd liner Bremen yesterday from an unofficial good-will misson to Germany where he went April 8 with Colonel Herman Metz.

"Adolf Hitler is one of the most sincere, honest and open men I have ever spoken to," said Mr. Ridder. "We went to Germany to acquaint German authorities with the true state of public opinion in the United States."

"We presented this opinion," he continued, "to the real leaders of German influence and were agreeably surprised at the reception we received. The Germans we conferred with were extremely patient. Colonel Metz and I are definitely of the opinion that we have some good results from our ..."

Among those they conferred with, according to Mr. Ridder, were Dr. Hjalmar Schacht, president of the Reichsbank; Wilhelm F. Frick, Minister of the Interior; Dr. Ernst Hanfstaengl, head of the foreign press in Germany, and Vice Chancellor von Papen. He added that he had flown with Colonel Metz from Berlin to Munich to see Chancellor Hitler and had a twenty-five minutes' interview with him.

Speaking of present conditions in Germany, Mr. Ridder said he had spent ten days visiting Berlin, Dresden, Munich and other cities and did not see any signs of trouble.

"No Jews were molested in the streets or stores or in their houses, so far as I could learn, and the situation is now quite tranquil," he said.

Lord Duveen of Millbank, recently created a peer by King George, returned on the Bremen from a brief visit to London, where he found general conditions, financially and commercially, to be improving. He said he is returning in June to take his seat in the House of Lords.

Frederick M. Sackett, the retiring United States Ambassador to Germany, arrived on the liner with Mrs. Sackett, after spending five weeks in France. He declined to comment on conditions in Germany.

Also on board the Bremen was Jacob Gould Schurman, former United States Ambassador to Germany, who went abroad last January to travel through the Near East.

Trinidad Has "Crime Wave."

Special Cable to THE NEW YORK TIMES.

PORT OF SPAIN, Trinidad, May 1.—The second motor bandit hold-up in the history of Trinidad occurred early yesterday morning when three gunmen bound and robbed Raymond Joseph, proprietor of a wayside gasoline station. Luckily the cash drawer contained only $4.

WHEW! WHAT
THE TIRE WA

RIDDER SEES CHECK ON NAZI INJUSTICE

Publisher Bases Prediction on Visit to Berlin and an Interview With Hitler.

CALLS HIM 'MAN OF PEACE'

Says Chancellor Told Him He Would Not Have One Man Killed for 100,000 Square Feet of Land.

Bernard F. Ridder, publisher of The New York Staats-Zeitung, who has just returned from a visit to Germany, said yesterday that modification of the Hitler government's anti-semitic policy may be expected soon.

Recent developments had led him to hope that the injustices to the Jews would be mitigated, he said. His opinion was based upon observations in Berlin. In the interior of Germany the Jews' plight was worse, he thought.

Mr. Ridder characterized Hitler as "a fanatic" with absolute powers who has so impressed the Germans that he would get 80 to 90

New York Times articles on my grandfather's and great-uncle's visits with Hitler, 1933.

readers for the relief of German war prisoners in the U.S.

It must be said in the Ridders' collective defense that as soon as America entered the war—on December 8, 1941, in the wake of Japan's "unprovoked and dastardly attack" (FDR's stirring words) on Pearl Harbor—the newspaper went from isolationist to interventionist, as it had done when America entered World War I. And that, more or less, was where things stood with the Ridders vis-a-vis the Nazis—until the advent of Victor's trial and tribulations in 1945.

My great-uncle did not acquit himself well: he lied nonstop on the stand. By the end, he was forced to admit to certain dark doings, including to having belonged, until the very year before, to a subsidiary of the Nazi organization, the German American Bund. On June 29, 1945, Nizer began his closing argument in New York Superior Court. It was a stifling day, the windows had been flung open, and suddenly, martial music and passionate cheering started up from the street. At that moment, in City Hall, which was hard by the courthouse, the man of the hour, of *any* hour—Dwight D. Eisenhower, five-star general of the Army and Supreme Commander of the Allied Expeditionary Force in Europe—was being received by the mayor, and the most tumultuous ticker-tape parade in the city's history was getting off the ground, with four million people lining the streets.

The jury took but an hour to return a verdict of guilty, finding for the professor in the full amount requested—$100,000 ($1.74 million in today's currency). Victor's counsel counterargued that it was "the excitement of the day, welcoming General Eisenhower from his triumph in Germany," that had swayed the jurors, and the judge reluctantly agreed. "A substantial award to the plaintiff was amply justified by the evidence," he acknowledged, while allowing that it was "difficult to avoid the conclusion that the jury in fixing the amount of damages may have been either consciously or unconsciously influenced by a species of patriotic spirit to which the issues peculiar to this action would make a ready appeal." When all was said and done, the penalty was vastly reduced, but the professor/plaintiff had proved his point and then some.

I remember combing through my grandfather's self-published collection of his poetry at one point, hoping and dreading—both at once—to find the ode that he said he had written to the Führer who would go down in flames.

What I did come across was his elegy on the death of his brother Joseph, Victor's twin, in 1966 (Victor had died a couple of years earlier). It was titled "Flowers, Not Flames," and contained the following lines: "What do you meet after / The gate has finally closed. / I think flowers and not flames, / A kind of floral forgetfulness ... Only my brothers, / For me, are missed in the throng. / Who shall be there to greet them: / Flowers, not flames, shall meet them."

Wishful thinking perhaps. But if my grandfather is destined to lie for all eternity in the bed he made, may it not be in hellfire but, rather, in those beds of tulips so lovingly laid out in brilliant prisms in his Minnesota garden.

Mummy never again alluded to this deplorable Nazi business. She and my father were positively not like that. Growing up, I never heard either of them, not to mention my grandfather, utter a single disparaging remark about Jewish people. True, there weren't too many in St. Paul and Duluth. But one summer in my late teens, I dated a nice local girl whose last name was Epstein, and my parents didn't say a thing one way or the other about that.

CHAPTER EIGHT

On the Way to San Jose

Now we can cut to the chase.

Connie and I had made plans to spend Christmas of 1961 with her parents in Traverse City. I was a senior at Michigan, and she had dropped out to get married and have our baby. We set out from Ann Arbor in the late afternoon, with five-month-old Katie in a make-shift crib in the back seat. If you were to drive from Ann Arbor to Traverse City today, it would be mostly on a freeway, but in 1961 the last half of that 250-mile drive was on back roads.

It was nine or ten at night and pitch-black when a pickup truck came up behind us like a bat out of hell. In the rear-view mirror, I saw what looked like roughnecks in there, and before we knew what hit us, they were bumping into us, accidentally on purpose. Now we were in a horror movie.

I knew I could never get up enough steam on the Ford Falcon to lose them. And now they were back to bumping us, trying, it was clear, to run us off the road—and, perish the thought, maybe even kill us in cold blood. Around the fourth time they rammed into us, I noticed a police car coming from the opposite direction and began furiously flashing my lights, at which the pickup veered off down some other dark deserted byway. Murder averted.

Then and there I resolved at all costs never to experience that feeling of utter helplessness again, of being trapped, and ever since, almost every car I've owned has had a powerful engine. I've had Mercedeses, Jaguars, and Porsches, and these days I zoom around in a BMW.

I didn't go to my graduation at Michigan. I was in pretty good shape with my parents now—they were feeling a lot better about me—and Mummy had gone to the ardent trouble of arranging for Connie and me to enjoy a belated honeymoon in Jamaica. Her old Greenwood friend Polly McDonnel Coffey, who also happened to be my godmother, had a "cottage" in the exclusive Round Hill resort. On the almost certain-to-be sweltering day when my classmates would be sporting mortarboards and gowns, I would be in a bathing suit, immersed in water the temperature of warm tea. So, that June of '62 Connie and I drove to Traverse City—in broad daylight this time—to leave Katie with her parents. We then flew to New York to stay with Grandma Delano at *Steen Valetje* for a few days before heading for the Caribbean.

Jamaica turned out to be the idyll of our heart's desire. Polly was a Weyerhaeuser heiress originally from St. Paul, and her so-called cottage was nothing if not deluxe. She was a ton of fun besides, a woman of spirited determination who piloted her own King Air. But then it was back to Traverse City and reality. Connie's father had a friend with a used-car lot who gave us a good deal on trading our Ford Falcon for a Chevy wagon with an ample enough engine (her dad generously made up the difference). We drove to Aberdeen with all our belongings, including, I daresay, Katie, now just about a year old.

My job paid next to nothing—$105 a week—and I had no other money coming in. I was one of only two general-assignment reporters. All the county offices plus the chamber of commerce and the sheriff's department constituted my beat. One of my first stories, on a guy who'd been passing bad checks all over town, backfired on me big time. I had found his address in the phonebook and included it in the article, but it turned out to belong to another fellow with that same name, who then raised holy hell, justifiably.

After this blunder there was added pressure to prove myself. I decided to go after the county auditor-cum-treasurer with a vengeance. Not that it wasn't a fair story—the woman was inefficient at best and deserved to be called out, and the story I wrote resulted in her improving her performance. After about six months on the beat, I was transferred to the production department, with a stint in the press room and another in the composing room where the materials for the ads were prepared. In those days, newspapers still used the hot metal linotypes that were not all that different from what my great-grandfather had used at the beginning of the twentieth century.

My grandfather had given me some of his ties to wear on the new job, and one of the first things I did in Aberdeen was throw every last one of them away. I was a young man striving to get ahead and not wanting to call any attention to his wardrobe. I mean, those ties were really loud. They suited my grandfather—only *he* could pull them off. I had certainly never caught Dad in any of his old man's neckwear.

Connie and I were happy in Aberdeen. We lived in a very small house a mile from downtown. We joined the country club—it cost practically nothing—and we enjoyed a nice quiet social life. In the millennial year 2000, I was invited to give the keynote address commemorating the 125th anniversary of the Aberdeen Chamber of Commerce. During the nine years I was president of KR's newspaper division, I would find myself back in Aberdeen from time to time. I had a soft spot for the place; it represented a significant steppingstone in my life—my first job out of college and all that. It had kept its small-town quiddity despite being the third biggest city in South Dakota (after Sioux Falls and Rapid City). That statistic was hard to miss when you were on the road there: a South Dakota license plate starting with the number three signified that the car was registered to somebody from Aberdeen (number one denoted Sioux Falls, and two stood for Rapid City).

Round about the time I went to Aberdeen in 1962, the bill came due, so to speak. Or rather, so *not* to speak. Let me elaborate. Uncle Joe drove a Rolls Royce (the sole Rolls in San Jose) or, more accurately, got driven around in it because he was an alcoholic; and my cousin BJ drove a Bentley. Those luxury cars were purchased for them and continued to be owned by Ridder Publications. The Ridders overall led extravagant lives, and the company underwrote them.

The "due bill" was a concept originated by my grandfather in St. Paul to stimulate advertising in the *Pioneer Press*. The company would encourage stores that were hurting to advertise on credit, which would have the benefit of prompting their competitors to increase *their* advertising to keep up. The practice morphed over time into advertising being traded for merchandise. In the multifarious cities where Ridder owned newspapers, the family regularly bartered ad space for goods and services, including travel and lodging, artwork, clothing (especially furs), and housing. It had never occurred to me that they—we—were living the lifestyle of freebies.

Uncle Hank was cut from the same cloth as Uncle Joe. He furnished his office lavishly and lived in a sumptuously decorated and fully staffed house on the tenth hole of the Long Beach Country Club. The fancy house in St. Paul once occupied by another brother, my Uncle Dan, was also company-owned, as was my great-uncle Victor's yacht, the *Maid Marian*, which plied Lake Superior until the day he died (and was sold the next day).

Dad, in contrast, was not one for trappings. He personally owned our house, and he and Mummy had no household help other than the couple who had come with the place in Duluth and moved with them to St. Paul. We kids had a wonderful nanny—Carrol Kasey, who I called "Kay." She hailed from a small town twenty miles north of Duluth called Two Harbors, and she remained with us until my younger sisters Robin and Jill, both of whom called her "Kay Kay," left home in the mid-1960s. They would be quick to say she virtually raised them.

For Christmas one year in the early '50s, Dad's present to Mummy was a Ford Woody station wagon. It was waiting outside the house in Duluth, all bright and shiny. I said to Mummy, "You don't seem all that excited. I can't imagine a better present than what Dad just gave you." She replied, "I don't want to talk about it." A long time later she fessed up to the fact that it was a due-bill car—Dad had traded advertising in the paper for it.

In the years before I went off to boarding school in 1954, one weekend every fall, I would travel from Duluth to St. Paul to take in a University of Minnesota football game and I would stay with Grandpa Ridder. He would take me on a shopping spree, shepherding me from store to store, encouraging me to pick out "whatever you want." I would be satisfied with, say, a football helmet or a pair of ice skates, but he wouldn't let up, he would go, "Is that all you want? Pick out some more stuff," and I would go, "No, no, you're too generous." At the Saturday lunch he hosted at the Town and Country Club, even before getting up to recite some of his cornball verse, he would relay to his cronies, "I took my grandson shopping yesterday—go ahead, Tony, tell them what I got you."

Turned out it was all due-bill booty—every last item.

The Ridders' comeuppance was a long time coming. The bill was way overdue. It wasn't until 1962 that the IRS cracked down. The company was fined, individual family members were compelled to settle significant sums in back taxes, and the practice was unequivocally put to a stop.

In May 1963 my time at the *Aberdeen American News* was up—I was assigned to the *Pasadena Star-News*. I drove Connie and Katie to California in the Chevy wagon. I worked first as a classified and then as a retail ad salesman, followed by stints in accounting and production. During the nineteen months I was there, I trained in every department except circulation, learning step by step how a paper was put together.

Our daughter Linda was born in Pasadena on July 24. Those were the days before amnio, so there was no way of determining whether

My eleven-year-old daughter, Linda, and I had just ridden our bikes 350 miles from Santa Cruz to the Los Angeles airport.

it was going to be a boy or a girl. The obstetrician, Dr. Muir, was convinced it was a boy that Connie was carrying—he said he could tell by the heartbeat.

He assured Connie, even as the baby was emerging, "You have a fine son." A few seconds later, Linda made her appearance.

He came out to the waiting room to console me. "It's all the same to me," I told him. "How are they doing?"

From day one, Linda was a winner in every sense. In any sport she had her hand in, whether swimming or tennis or girls' baseball, she was the star—captain of the varsity tennis team at the University of Washington, Ladies' Golf Champion at both Cypress Point and the Seattle Golf Club, and so on. Just a wonderful athlete. A *phenomenal* athlete—the best in the family by far. And she married an athlete—a six-foot-seven professional basketball player named Wally Walker (he played successively for the Portland Trail Blazers, the Houston Rockets, and the Seattle Supersonics, where he later served a twelve-year term as general manager and president). Post-basketball he got an MBA at Stanford, and by the time he and Linda got together he was with Goldman Sachs. Linda works with underprivileged children at a public school in Seattle—kids struggling to keep up. She has a big heart.

During my brief time in Pasadena, I also had to function as the paper's acting comptroller, because the fellow in charge of the accounting department had developed a bad back and was intermittently out of commission. I soon discovered that the general manager, Gustaf Nordin, who had been the editor in Duluth when Dad was the publisher there, was bilking the newspaper by having it purchase various supplies—carrier bags and so on—from an expensive boutique gift shop he owned with his wife, who ran it (a younger woman, not the one he'd been married to in Duluth). "Three Crown Imports, Ltd.," it was grandiosely called. This was a clear conflict of interest—to use plainer language, Gus was little better than a swindler.

To go to the publisher, my cousin BJ, would have been kind of delicate because he and Gus were mates who went out drinking together every noon. BJ might well have known about this and not given a damn. I wouldn't have put it past him to tell me to mind my own business—in effect, to drop dead. So, I went instead to the business manager, who told me he didn't want any part of it, to just leave it alone, that it would lead to nothing but trouble. But when Dad visited the paper, I let it all out. He promised to take care of it, and not long afterward Gus got fired. I had had him dead to rights.

Working for BJ was no stroll in the park—or should I say no lap around the racetrack. He was stuffy and stiff. He invited me to the

California newspaper convention in San Diego and drove us there in that big show-off Bentley of his, stopping en route at his ranch, named *Murrieta Stud* after the town it was in. Another time, he invited me to Santa Anita where he had a horse running, which I felt I had to bet on (it promptly lost).

Two or three Sundays a month, Uncle Dan's wife, Aunt Betty, would invite Connie and me for lunch at their estate near Long Beach, on Portuguese Bend in Rolling Hills, on the Palos Verdes Peninsula. They lived above the smog layer, while Connie and I lived within it (you could actually see this brown miasma over the L.A. basin creeping all the way up to our house). Aunt Betty's marriage to Uncle Dan was irretrievably broken by then. There was zero affection between them that I, at any rate, could make out. I don't know why they kept going—maybe "for the children." Uncle Dan had evidently not changed his stripes one iota. A close friend of Aunt Betty's eventually divulged to Connie and me that he was putting on this charade just for us. He wasn't even living at home—all those Sundays when we visited, the minute we left with our two young daughters he would hotfoot it back to an apartment he maintained for his "other interests."

I accidentally caught him in the act. Driving to a Los Angeles Dodgers game, I got held up in traffic coming into the stadium, and there, right next to us, was Dan at the wheel of a snappy Mercedes convertible with his arm around some attractive young woman. Well, he could afford to be footloose and fancy-free because, God knows, he wasn't doing much at the paper from a business standpoint. Anyway, a few years later, he met an East Coast woman by the name of Frani Ackerman and settled down with her to an enduring domestic happiness. When the Oakland Raiders played the Vikings in the Rose Bowl in Pasadena in 1977, Connie and our four kids stayed with them in Long Beach, and we all enjoyed ourselves. Dan was just somebody everybody liked—I run into people all the time who were crazy about him.

In December 1964 I was transferred from Pasadena to the *San*

Jose Mercury News. When Ridder Publications purchased the paper in 1952, San Jose was just a sleepy, sprawling, largely agricultural region at the base of San Francisco Bay surrounded by orchards and popularly depicted as the "valley of the heart's delight." By the early '60s, it was growing like, God forbid, wildfire. Today, with a population of around a million, it's the third largest city in the state (after L.A. and San Diego) and the tenth largest in the U.S.

My first exposure to California had been in 1957 when Dad invited me to tag along on a business trip, and that whetted my appetite to live there someday. He took us to dinner at Chasen's in L.A., where he recommended I order the house chili and Mummy pointed out a couple of movie stars. The next day, he checked us into the Pebble Beach Lodge, and within the hour we were teeing off at Cypress Point. I spotted Bing Crosby and Bob Hope on the golf course, thereby giving Mummy a run for her celebrity spotting.

When we got to San Jose, Dad parked outside the *Mercury News*, and I wandered around on my own while he went inside to confer with Uncle Joe. I just had this euphoric feeling that California was the ticket, *the* place to be. Today, of course, the state is experiencing a population drain: people are leaving in droves—for Texas, Utah, Idaho, Florida—half a million or so every year. But back then, it was considered the land of milk and honey, and when I returned to St. Paul's for my senior year, I couldn't stop raving about it to my classmates. I told them that my dream was to live and work there. And now I was.

When I first came to town, I made a point of joining the Rotary Club. I was never a particularly good Rotarian, not that that was something I ever aspired to. I saw membership strictly as a way to learn what was going on in the community. I also saw to it that I got admitted to the Sainte Claire Club, the city's old-guard men's luncheon club, which occupied the whole of a Mission Revival building that had withstood the legendary 1906 San Francisco earthquake that killed more than a hundred people in San Jose alone. There I got to know the owners of the businesses downtown and the former mayors and other politicians who had led the city back in the 1940s and '50s.

It was at the Sainte Claire Club that I would hear talk, or at least catch snatches of conversation in muted voices, about "poor Brooke Hart": "I think *she* was in the crowd that broke into the jail and took the law into their own hands," or "I'm pretty sure *he* was involved in the lynching," or "He's denied it all these years, but he was there all right." I always wondered if the *Mercury News*' longtime attorney, Duncan O'Neill, who would have been around seventy-five at the time I first knew him, had been among the horde, but I knew better than to bring that up—nobody was ever going to own up to having been there.

The two men who were lynched had kidnapped and viciously murdered the twenty-two-year-old golden-boy-movie-star-handsome scion of the owner of the L. Hart & Son department store, which at one time was the largest between San Francisco and Los Angeles. In the early 1960s, just before I came on the scene, Macy's had tried to open a store in downtown San Jose, but the property owners didn't want them there. They ended up in the shopping center called Valley Fair, out on Stevens Creek near the border of Santa Clara. Hart & Son had been invited to be the development's original anchor and passed up the opportunity, not foreseeing that, by the end of the decade, malls would become *the* place to shop.

L Hart & Son was a dependable *Mercury News* advertiser, which is how I got to know Alex Hart, the murder victim's younger brother. He was a good friend of Uncle Joe's, being gay—or at least everybody said he was. Like Joe, he was always dressed to the nines. He would come on the annual men-only trip to Las Vegas—two nights and three days—which Uncle Joe organized for our largest advertisers and some of our civic leaders. The *Mercury News* would host a cocktail party, then whisk everyone off to one of those flashy dinner shows. It would get out at 10:30 or 11:00, leaving plenty of time for those inclined to gamble the night away. The next day, we would all play golf—everybody, that is, except for Uncle Joe, who did not

EXTRA

THE POST ENQUIRER — EXTRA

OAKLAND, CALIFORNIA, MONDAY, NOVEMBER 27, 1933 — THREE CENTS

SAN JOSE VIGILANTES LYNCH 2 HART KILLERS

MOB STORMS JAIL, HANGS KIDNAPERS ON TREES IN PARK

By Ralph Jordan

SAN JOSE, Nov. 27 (INS). — Vigilantes today had ridden again in California!

In a fierce throwback to the tumultuous days of '49, they stormed the county jail here, seized two confessed kidnapers and murderers, stripped the clothes from their bodies, strung them to elm trees in the public square and then attempted to make a pyre out of the body of one of their victims!

They hanged Jack Holmes and Thomas A. Thurmond, who admitted the abduction and killing of Brooke L. Hart, 22, Santa Clara university graduate and son of a wealthy San Jose family Nov. 9.

They fought a terrific pitched battle with the combined forces of Sheriff William J. Emig, Chief of Police J. N. Black and the state highway patrol.

They battered down the doors of the jail, dragged the two accused men from the jail across the street into St. James park, the public square of San Jose, and strung them to two elm trees as 10,000 men and women looked on.

Thurmond Pleads for Life;

Sheriff Battles in Vain

VIGILANTE JUSTICE FOR BROOKE HART SLAYERS

Mother Begs Mob to Spare Thurmond Life

Posse Too Late to Prevent Lynching

SHERIFF HURT IN JAIL FIGHT

MOB RUSH INSPIRED BY TOTS

BATTLE TOLD BY DEPUTY

GOV. ROLPH HAILS LYNCHING AS 'LESSON'

KILLERS NEAR VICTIM'S BODY

Today's Post-Enquirer

Apartment House Owners

Oakland Post-Enquirer headline, 1933.

play. So: a couple of days of golf and a dinner show or two on the newspaper—not a bad deal. Everybody loved it—everybody, that is, except for me. Some of our guests took advantage of being away from home and in a fleshpot like Las Vegas to hire hookers. I felt increasingly uncomfortable with *that*, and after I became general manager of the paper, I rang down the curtain on the Vegas trip. I would take the advertisers to Pebble Beach instead, where they made a perfectly happy adjustment to just playing golf.

To return, unhappily, to Brooke Hart. In November 1933, he was abducted as he exited the family emporium he was being groomed to take over. The kidnappers finished him off a couple of days later—bound his hands with wire, attached a couple of twenty-two-pound concrete blocks to his feet, and tossed him from a bridge into San Francisco Bay. They were rounded up in short order, but the county jail wasn't sufficiently garrisoned. An out-of-control mob of riled-up San Jose citizens were able to storm it and drag the prisoners from their cells to St. James Park across the street. They hanged them from the branch of a rock elm, which instantly entered the annals of infamy as the "gallows tree." The approximately 10,000 eye-for-an-eye onlookers—men, women, and children—broke into song and dance.

The governor of California joined the chorus and sang the praises of the baying vigilantes, depicting the lynching as "a fine lesson." But when it was broadcast as a "live event" by a Los Angeles radio station, it ignited a world-wide firestorm. Nazi propaganda minister Joseph Goebbels seized the chance to spin the lynching as prima-facie evidence of America's inhumanity.

The Hart tragedy passed into popular culture. It inspired a short story by the future Nobel laureate John Steinbeck, titled "The Vigilante." Later, some Faulkner wannabe turned it into a pulp novel, and later still, somebody made a feature-length pulp movie titled *Try and Get Me*—one of four films based on the case. And almost half a century further on, the *Mercury News*' lead political reporter and columnist, Harry Farrell, wrote a riveting account of the case titled *Swift Justice: Murder and Vengeance in a California Town*. Leave it to Harry to have been the only one to ever gain access to the kidnappers' kids. He was a San Jose native who knew the city by heart—its unofficial historian, if you will. More than that, he was an institution in the state of California—he had a great working relationship with every major political figure, from Pat Brown to Ronald Reagan. His book won the prestigious Edgar Award in the "best true fact crime" category in 1992. My friend Tom McEnery, the most effective mayor in the history of San Jose and a history buff himself, purchased the play rights to Harry's book, then sat down and wrote the play himself. It was produced in 2016 by a local theater company, and I drove over from Pebble Beach to attend a performance with him. The audience lapped it up.

Six months after we moved to San Jose, on May 18, 1965, Connie all of a sudden felt she was about to have Susie. The hospital was a half hour's drive from where we lived. The freeway consisted of two much-trafficked lanes in each direction, plus an unpaved dirt lane for emergencies. Automotively, I had graduated by then to a Ford station wagon with a large V8 engine, and I gunned it to eighty, with the dirt flying. Connie delivered Susie uneventfully shortly after we arrived.

Susie grew up to be not only athletic like her sisters but also the best student of my four children. She was the star of the Saratoga High varsity track team and set the freshman record for the high jump, a spectacular five feet, four inches. She wound up going to the same law school as Connie, the University of Santa Clara—not that she's ever practiced. But today she works for Nordstrom in a capacity where her legal education comes in handy. Her husband, Lance Lopes, is executive vice president and general counsel for Seattle's NHL team the Kraken—the same positions he previously held with Seattle's Seahawks.

Connie and I found a new house we both liked, in a tonier section of Saratoga. The only problem was the price—$52,000. I didn't have anywhere near that much money on hand and had to borrow from the newspaper. We lived there from 1965 until '68 when we found we would need slightly larger quarters, since Connie was pregnant again.

We had decided to make one last try for a boy. Either she was going to deliver this time, in both senses of the word, or we were just going to have to make do with four daughters. We were naturally buoyed when that April we finally had a son.

The new house was anything but—it was a century-old farmhouse on three and a third acres, for which $85,000 changed hands (I was earning more by now). An antiquated swimming pool, rundown barn, stable, and goat enclosure came with the property. We had a

Northwest Publications, Inc.
NEWSPAPER PUBLISHERS NWP RADIO AND TELEVISION
55 EAST FOURTH STREET · ST. PAUL, MINNESOTA 55101

October 31, 1968

Dear Tony:

The four colored pictures that you forwarded to us are marvelously good, and I shall never forget the glorious scene of myself holding a fifth generation Ridder on his lap.

It was a magnificent sight to behold in the church of San Jose, the miracle being performed of a Ridder turned into a Christian at the baptism on a Sunday morn. Now that he is a Christian, I wonder how many of the Ridders can call themselves in the same class. Whoever took the pictures you sent on, did his photographic work remarkably well, and they shall be a constant reminder of the family we belong to.

On my desk in St. Paul, I have a picture of my father and my mother and their family taken in 1880 and, alongside of it, will be this lovely full-color picture done 88 years later. It is an indication of the beginning of this family and the widespread of years over which it has developed.

As the only surviving member of the second generation, I take an enormous personal interest in the development and success of the members of the fourth generation in which you already play so prominent a part. Many thanks for the fine reminder of a lovely day of the great "B's" beginning with baptism, followed by banqueting and booze and ending with a final "B", your grandfather, Ben.

Love,

Granddad

Mr. P. Anthony Ridder
750 Ridder Park Drive
San Jose, California

(Left) Letter from my grandfather regarding our son's baptism.

(Below) Four generations of Ridder men.

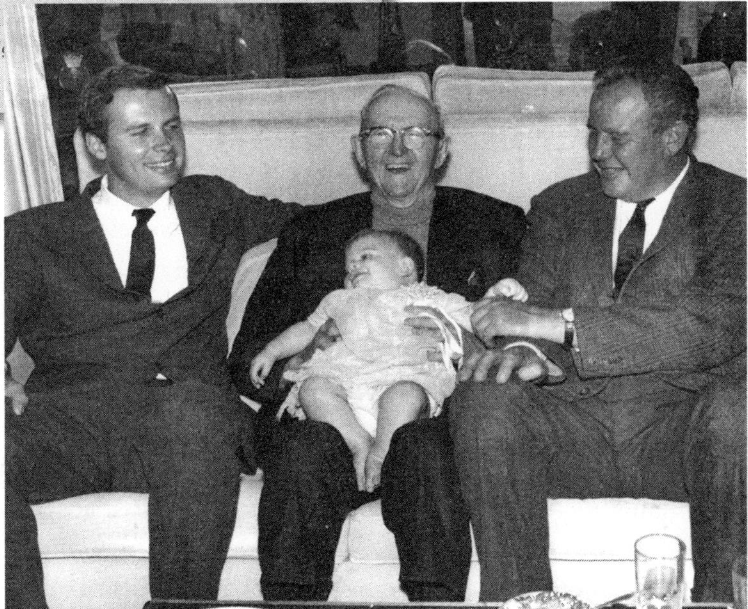

Our house in Saratoga where we lived from 1968 through 1986.

horse at one point, for Susie, but we never got a goat. The house was only 2,600 square feet: the three girls slept upstairs, two of them together, and all four kids shared a bathroom (eventually we built a room downstairs for Katie). The only drawback was that the house faced a busy street, so we built a fence around the property. Connie set about creating a bountiful flower and vegetable garden (with the help of a young man who she whimsically described as "blow-and-go," on the grounds that he blew in for a couple of hours a week, then blew right out). She assumed we would be living in this house for the rest of our natural lives and envisioned all three girls being married in her garden.

I had started out at the *Mercury News* in the circulation department and, after a few months, I was named district manager. One of my early assignments included hiring (and, when necessary, firing) around thirty-five or so carrier boys, all of them between the ages of twelve and seventeen. Since we were an afternoon paper at the time, I didn't have to leave the premises to attend to that part of the job till 3:30, having by then been in the office for seven hours answering complaint calls and doing clerical work. The delivery trucks would have dropped the newspapers off throughout my territory, at the corners near which each carrier lived. I cleared the "drops," which meant making sure the carriers had picked up their bundles. If they hadn't, I had to try to round them up. I had a list of their addresses (not that it was always up to date), so I could track them down. Their mothers would open the door and usually say the boys weren't home, whether they were or not, in which case I would be obligated to deliver their papers myself—all fifty or sixty or even seventy of them. Shades of my old paper route in Duluth.

Somebody in the accounting department tipped me off to a scam. The newspaper paid solicitors to secure new subscriptions, but the checks were all being made out to people with fictitious names and getting cashed at the same place—a bar, of all things—and then honored by our bank because they were *Mercury News* checks. I methodically tracked all the phony orders, then went to our general manager with the evidence. He promptly canned the circulation director and the assistant director—for, in effect, making the checks out to themselves.

I took a week off from my circulation duties, and Connie and I rented a tiny house in Lake Tahoe four blocks from the beach. My Michigan classmate and close friend, Moss Galpeer, joined us there, using a week of his vacation from the Manhattan firm he had joined after graduating from Columbia Law. We had made him the godfather of Katie, who was born while we were all at Michigan together (since a godfather is traditionally supposed to teach about religion I guess it was odd that I would pick a Jew). In Tahoe, he was not the same Moss we had known and loved. He confided, without going into any detail, that he was seeing a psychiatrist—at that time, a fairly drastic thing to be doing, or at least it seemed so to me. Connie and I had hired a live-in babysitter, an attractive local girl of sixteen, and Moss, who was twenty-six, was all over her. I kept telling him to lay off, to keep his hands to himself, and he just wouldn't. The girl didn't seem to mind, but that was hardly the point. They were getting too cozy for comfort—*ours*. Connie was as disappointed and disgusted with Moss as I was. I ended up having to ask him to leave—I had to practically pry him out of the house. I lost track of him after that, and it was only long after the fact that I learned he had killed himself at the age of thirty-five.

In 1967 I was made business manager of the *Mercury News*. I was twenty-six and, if not yet briskly climbing the proverbial ladder, at least working my way up, little dreaming that one day I would achieve the highest rung. I had been promoted on the strength of my herculean efforts in planning and overseeing the move of all the non-production facilities located in the newspaper building, 211 West Santa Clara Street, to our new headquarters, a single-story structure with double the press-production space, at 750 Ridder Park Drive (it was Uncle Joe who named it that). The facility was in an undeveloped area that's now a cluster of city streets tenanted by high-tech companies. I executed the move over the course of a single weekend, with what my colleagues described as the precision of a military operation. All the grunt work I had done in advance kicked in: organizing the new phone systems, deciding what furniture to purchase and where to put it, and, finally, what to do with all the old stuff.

CHAPTER NINE

End of an Era: Sold Down the River

"WHAT TO DO with all the old stuff." You can say that again, and I just did.

In 1964 Grandma Delano suffered a stroke, in the middle of June, just as she was about to make the move to *Steen Valetje* for her forty-third consecutive summer as its chatelaine, tutelary spirit, and guiding light. She lived two years more, for the most part bedridden and not capable of much conversation. The obituaries celebrated her lifelong devotion to the national and international Girl Scout movement, but one of them aimed higher, borrowing the winged words crafted by F. Scott Fitzgerald to epitomize the protagonist of one of his classic short stories: "He believed in character; he wanted to jump back a whole generation and trust in character again as the eternally valuable element. Everything else wore out." Character was incontestably the element my grandmother embodied: it shone in her and emanated from her and will always glow in my memories.

Mummy and her two sisters and two brothers assembled to select what each of them might want from the house's store of treasures before the whole lot was put up for auction. As in all things, Mummy was careful not to overdo it; she held back and wound up taking practically nothing for herself. She selected from her father's study a pair of andirons in the form of dachshunds, which she had once bred, linked by a brass chain, and from the elegant breakfast room a mid-nineteenth-century Italian village street scene, which she later gave me. I have it hanging in my home office in California. That and a pair of antique copper cranes are my only mementos from *Steen Valetje.* The latter grace our garden in Pebble Beach, as they had previously embellished our gardens in Saratoga and Woodside. They're identical to ones that Connie and I encountered when we visited the emperor's palace in the Forbidden City of Beijing (in Chinese mythology, cranes, which mate for life, are symbols of longevity).

Our garden in Pebble Beach, with the copper cranes from *Steen Valetje.*

The sale was held at the house over the course of four long action- and auction-packed days and netted a then impressive quarter of a million dollars. The county paper described it as a "gala rummage sale ... crammed with miscellaneous marvels ... a forest of furniture, stacks of fine linen, and barrels of precious plates and dinnerware from Imperial China dating from Franklin and Laura Astor Delano who built the place a hundred years before. From fine guns to broken bassinets, everything went under the hammer except the wine cellar, which was divided under a private treaty between the heirs. At one point the painted panels were sold off the top and sides of a gilded chest." One is left to wonder which high bidder carried home—and whether she was ever able to carry off (perhaps at some Gilded Age costume party or ball)—the feathered headdress worn by Laura Delano at her presentation at the Court of St. James's.

With Grandma's death, the estate passed out of the Delano family, as none of her children had the bottomless resources necessary to maintain it. William Stix Wasserman, a prominent investment banker with a country house in nearby Tarrytown, was able to raise the several million dollars it took to purchase it. At least nominally, he was not a stranger to us—his daughter Marie Stix Wasserman happened to be married to our cousin, Victor Ridder's son Walter, who was the very capable longtime head of our Washington, D.C., bureau.

I had a second coincidental connection to Bill Wasserman. He owned a Christmas-tree farm, *Skyline Ranch*, in the Santa Cruz mountains that was only fifteen miles from where Connie and I lived in Saratoga. Whenever Marie visited her mother there, she would have us over for lunch, after which she invariably invited us to join her for a swim. She practically had to shame us into setting foot in that dank body of water, a literal hole in the ground that they were classing up by calling it a lake.

Wasserman had vowed to keep *Steen Valetje* intact, to leave both the land and the house in one piece, but no sooner had the deed been drawn up than he began dramatically altering the mansion for the worse, all in the name of "sprucing it up." He had the entire south wing that housed the ballroom torn down, along with the port-cochère, one of the most beautiful of the old touches, not to mention the grand staircase that was nothing short of spectacular. He also demolished the brick towers, the brick terraces, the wooden verandas, and all the decorative iron work. Most sacrilegious of all, at least in the eyes of my mother, was the sandblasting of the original earth tone of the façade in favor of a brick-pink with white trim—Wasserman's misconceived attempt to turn a classic Tuscan-style edifice into a bastardized English neo-Georgian affair.

Early in his stewardship an article appeared in the local paper headlined "New Master, New Man, New Name," which was the first inkling any of us had that he might be contemplating the unthinkable—I mean, it had been *Steen Valetje* since the day it was built. He nevertheless went ahead and rechristened it *Mandara*—after, we were told, an African kingdom of that name that had existed in the fifteenth century in the volcanic mountain range of present-day Cameroon. Make what you will of that (stretching the connection exponentially, one could posit that *Steen Valetje* in its original glory exuded the feeling of a feudal realm).

Among the first things Wasserman installed was his mistress, a much younger woman by the name of Sylvia Stratton. Mind you, she was not some floozy—she was attractive, educated, well-spoken. It turned out he had bought the place for *her.* She loved horses, and the one true improvement was in the stables. He made over to her the white farmhouse by the barns, along with a fifty-acre parcel, and that was where she lived for the most part. It made sense to us that she wouldn't want to be rattling around all by her lonesome in the main house, which remained enormous—around 17,000 square feet—even with assorted towers and wings lopped off. But whenever Wasserman was in residence, she moved up to the big house and snuggled in with him.

I would come to New York, usually with Connie, at least once a year from wherever I was based, San Jose and then Miami, for an

The iconic port-cochère at *Steen Valetje,* torn down after the sale.

ANPA board meeting, and on one of those occasions my mother happened to be in town with Dad, and my brother Peter and his wife were also on hand. Mummy said, "Let's see if we can go up to *Steen Valetje* and see what's going on." She got on the phone and arranged the visit through Sylvia.

This was the first time any of us had been to *Steen Valetje* since Wasserman had made his unfortunate architectural alterations. He had left it to his mistress to oversee the interior redecoration, and she was more than happy to show us around. My ultra-diplomatic mother managed to keep smiling throughout the house tour, though it broke her heart that so many important parts of the house had been dismantled.

When Wasserman died, in 1979, his children put *Steen Valetje* up for sale. After languishing on the market at $12.5 million for several years, it sold at a lesser price to a Long Island catalogue magnate who proved to be a responsible custodian. He kept up the landscaping and saw to the needed repairs. Above all, he recognized and respected the sanctity of the property and resisted the temptation to subdivide it, which had always been our greatest fear.

Steen Valetje's next owner, who ponied up $8.9 million for it in 1993, was a billionaire money manager described by *Barron's* as a "gray-haired guru with a style that harkens back to the days when Wall Street was full of gunslingers and go-go." For all the hype, the news story announcing the sale was quietly headlined "Noted Dog Breeder Buying *Mandara*." He and his wife were nothing less than America's top breeders of standard poodles, one of which had won the highest accolade in the dog world—Best in Show at Westminster. The new owner immediately renamed the estate *Atalanta* after the private investment management company he had founded, and the couple went on to name two of their new-home-grown poodles "Breakfast at Tiffany's Atalanta" and "Atalanta Prometheus Unbound." No comment.

In 2020 they listed *Atalanta*-aka-*Mandara* né *Steen Valetje* for $22 million. Suzy Wetlaufer Welch, the widow of GE chairman Jack Welch, snapped it up for $16.5. To her credit, she reinstated the estate's original name, then set about painstakingly restoring the original architecture—with the help, it goes without saying, of a veritable army of preservation experts and artisans. But just two years into the ambitious project, she startled everyone involved when she announced that she was moving, full time, to Manhattan—to a double townhouse on the Upper East Side. A that point, *Steen Valetje* reentered the real estate market at a whopping $25 million. It ended up selling to the co-CEO of KKR for $18.5 million, which nevertheless set a record for Dutchess County. The new owner and his multifaceted design team are reportedly embarked on "significant upgrades" to the house and a plan to "reclaim the landscape."

Letterhead for my seventy-fifth birthday "reunion" tour of *Steen Valetje*.

Franklin and Laura Astor Delano can presumably stop spinning in their graves.

Before I take final leave of *Steen Valetje*, permit me a couple of more grumbles. For my seventy-fifth birthday, in 2015, I rented a bus to transport my four siblings and my four children, plus all their spouses, to the old stomping ground in Rhinebeck. I had gone to considerable trouble—multiple phone calls and emails—to arrange the visit, which was to be followed by lunch in nearby Millbrook at the whimsical and much-admired house that Katie and her prize-winning architect husband, Peter Pennoyer, had recently built for themselves. But upon our arrival at the front door of *Steen Valetje*, we were callously informed that the house was "not available to be visited." In other words, we were being refused admittance, denied entry, left out in the cold—however you want to put it. As if we were just any old strangers to the place. We were allowed only a fast drive through the property.

There had been an earlier assault on our dignified dynastic sensibilities. As part of a Hudson-centric Delano reunion, we made a pilgrimage to the FDR Library in Hyde Park, after which we repaired to *Steen Valetje* for a visit that had been scheduled for a time when the owners were not in residence. (I hesitate to specify

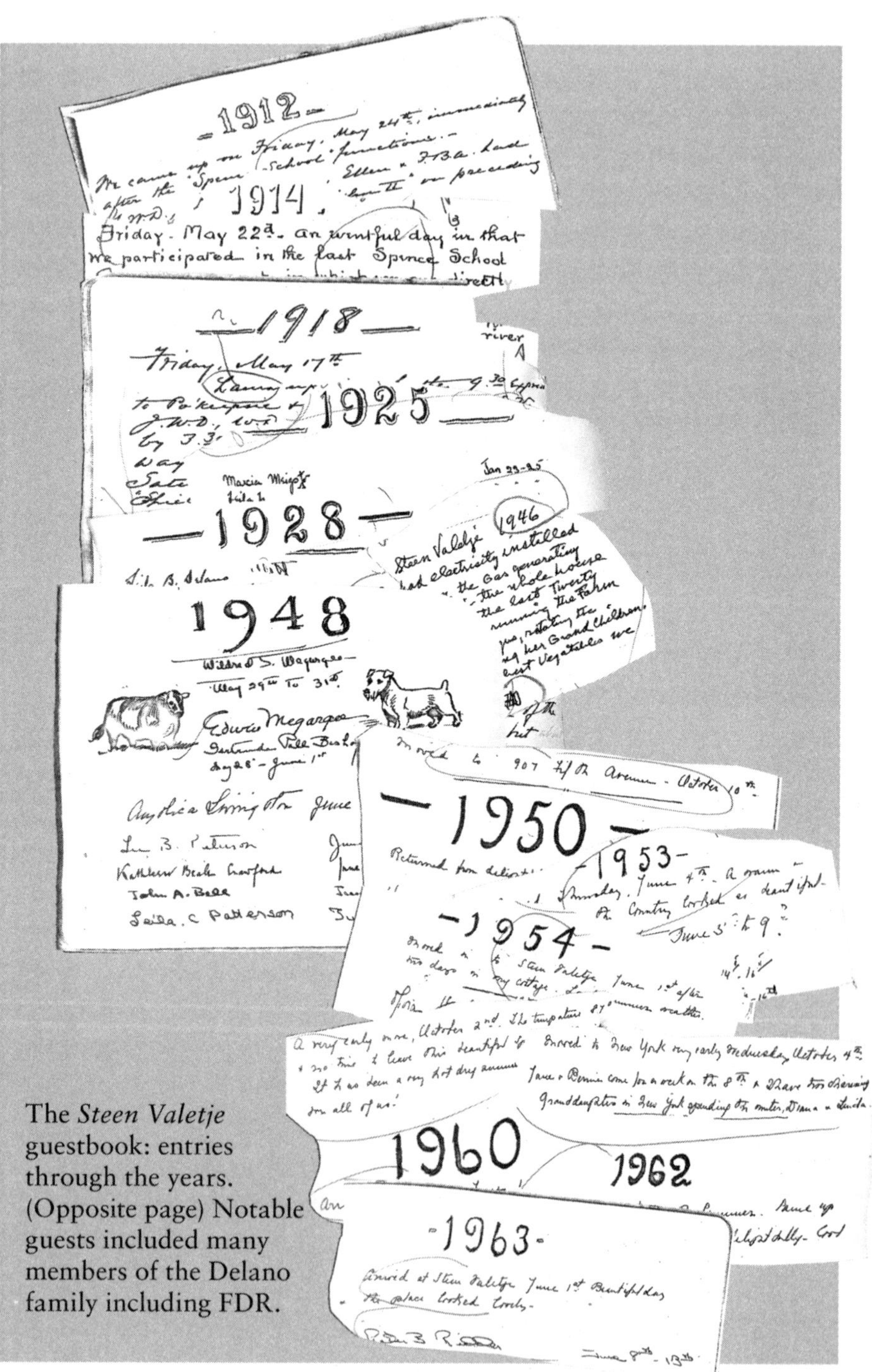

The *Steen Valetje* guestbook: entries through the years. (Opposite page) Notable guests included many members of the Delano family including FDR.

Laura D. Ridder

Tony Ridder — July 1st - Aug 31st

"

Sara Delano Roosevelt — 1934 — ... 2nd, 1940

Warren Delano.

Jane Delano

Margaret Delano

"A swell Party"! Feb. 21st - 24th

Ellen & Laura arrive from "Wilhelmina" on Tuesday Valetje at 6.20 p.m.

" 15th - 18th "

G. Peabody G. Franklin D.

Annie Delano Hitch — August 21 - 23

Franklin D Roosevelt — August 21 -

James Roosevelt — My 35th consecutive July 4th in the Lyman Delano home

Champion McD Davis — July 1 - 4

Lyman died July 23rd

Jean W. Edgell — July 25 - 26

Thalia Delano — July 26th - 44

July 25th - 27th

Eleanor Butler Alexander — July 25th - 27th

Wm Watson

Franklin D. R.

W. Porter Buck — July 13 - 14

Dorothy W. Buck — July 11 - 18 '35

Franklin D Roosevelt — July 20 - 21 '35

H Walters — Aug 14 - 15

Tony Ridder — June 20th - 22nd

Connie Ridder — June 20th - 22nd

which ones they were, for reasons that will all too soon become apparent.) After wafting through the grand reception rooms, we headed upstairs. The first thing I noticed as I crossed the threshold of my grandparents' sacrosanct master bedroom and the past took hold of me was a giant TV propped on a stand at the end of the bed. I didn't remember there ever having *been* a TV at SV. Then we noticed the disks. Homed in on, they turned out to be dirty videos—porn. Talk about a disconnect.

CHAPTER TEN

Going Public … Merging … Submerged

Dad had relinquished the position of publisher in St. Paul in 1969 when he became president of Ridder Publications. He was a good friend of Paul Miller, CEO of Gannett, the largest newspaper chain in the country, and lost no time initiating discussions about a merger.

In addition to myself, there were three up-and-coming young Ridders working at the company: Mike Ridder in St. Paul; his brother, Barney, in Long Beach; and my second cousin, Mark Mattison, in Gary. We were invited en masse to a Ridder board meeting at the St. Regis Hotel, in New York, to be drawn out on what we thought of the idea. I, for one, was against it—I didn't understand why my father and some of his cousins suddenly felt the need to sell, rather than just continuing to run the company themselves. The other young Ridders agreed with me. The older generation—Dan, Eric, and Joe Ridder—was also dead set against a sale but thankful to be able to use us as a foil—they hid behind us in a way. "Maybe we should listen to *them*," they proposed. "If *they* don't think we should sell, then maybe we shouldn't." Dad ultimately gave in. "With the family this divided, it's clear we shouldn't pursue a sale to Gannett," he conceded, adding, "We'll go public instead."

Every so often after that, whenever Dad was frustrated with what his brothers and cousins were doing, or not doing, he would remind me, "If you younger Ridders hadn't opposed the sale to Gannett, we wouldn't be in this situation. *They* would be running things, and I can assure you that not for a minute would they tolerate the kinds of performances, and lack thereof, that I have to put up with. Now that we're a public company, we can't afford to go on operating as if we were still private. I grant you we were able to do an awful lot of things as a private outfit that we can't get away with now that we're under continuous pressure to increase earnings and keep the price of our stock up. Our institutional shareholders are counting on the company to be run in an entirely professional manner." He never succeeded in getting his brothers and cousins to go along with him on that.

Dad had been made president and CEO of the public company, with his cousin BJ, the other oldest member of the seven Ridders in Dad's generation, as chairman, and the board consisting, in addition to them, of Robert, Walter, Eric, Dan, and Joe Ridder, as well as three newly elected outsiders. If Dad now had the ultimate title, what he did not have was the authority that normally goes with it. All of his male family members, many of whom owned far more shares than he, considered themselves, at the very least, his equals and behaved accordingly. Dad was in no position to crack the whip—on the contrary, his brothers and cousins could together tell *him* where to get off. As a consequence, Ridder Publications was still functioning less as a unified company than as a welter of fiefdoms.

Dad went on fretting about the glut of Ridders in the company and how most of them didn't take their obligations seriously enough. Grandpa Ben, on the other hand, when interviewed by the trade magazine *Editor & Publisher* on the occasion of his eighty-sixth birthday which happened to occur the year the company went public, boasted that the Ridders were a "dynastic family." He had only to point to the second, third, and fourth generations in the business: Dad sat astride the Ridder Publications board; Uncle Joe was the publisher in San Jose, Uncle Dan in Long Beach, and BJ in Pasadena; Eric was running the *New York Journal of Commerce*; Walter was in charge of the D.C. bureau; Mike was business manager in St. Paul, Barney in Long Beach, and I in San Jose; and Robert managed our TV and radio interests.

It was understandable that every young male Ridder would want a piece of the action. Being a newspaper publisher was a rewarding job in every sense. You were powerful—you wielded considerable autonomy—in many cases you were the leading citizen in your community, more important than the mayor, the police chief, or the school superintendent. As publisher of the *Mercury News*, I had the privilege of spending time with a host of sitting U.S. presidents: Gerald Ford, Jimmy Carter, George H. W. Bush, Bill Clinton, and George W. Bush. Oh, and Ronald Reagan, though at the time, he was just the governor of California. With the Reagans, I attended a reception for Queen Elizabeth on the *Royal Britannia* when it was anchored in San Francisco Harbor. I remember saying, "Your Majesty, I've always admired you." (I also remember empathizing with the British commoner who, after meeting the queen, commented, "You say the first thing that comes into your head, and you carry the memory of your foolishness with you to the grave.")

At the 2005 White House Correspondents' Dinner, I was seated between George W. Bush and his wife Laura. The newly re-elected president had the podium on his other side, leaving me as the only person within shouting distance that he could talk to, and it was a long dinner. For me, it was more like a two-hour one-man press conference, and the president and I covered a lot of ground. He was refreshingly open about everything I asked him. Except when I posed a pointed question concerning the privatization of social security, a kick he was on at the time. He looked stumped and said, as he scribbled a note to himself, "I'm surprised I don't know the answer to that—I need to find it out." He told me he was frustrated to be getting so much pushback on immigration from within his own party and that he was determined to resolve the issue once and for

With President George W. Bush at the White House Correspondents' dinner, 2005.
Photos, this page and opposite, by John Harrington, John Harrington Productions

all. Then he lightened up and mentioned how much he was looking forward to bicycling the next day at Quantico Marine Base, and he asked if bike riding was something *I* liked to do, then neglected to invite me along. Other than that, he couldn't have been friendlier—he was that kind of guy.

Connie, meanwhile, was seated between Jane Fonda and the Chairman of the Joint Chiefs of Staff, General Pace. She reported to me afterward—and Connie was never careless with words—that she had heard him say to Fonda, "I always admired what you did during the Vietnam War." Connie couldn't believe her ears, and even Jane Fonda could have been forgiven for thinking that her own ears had deceived her.

With Jane Fonda at the White House Correspondents' dinner.

Another precipitating factor for our having gone public was the Ridder women in my father's generation grousing that the Ridder men were earning big fat salaries running the newspapers in addition to receiving dividends, whereas *they* had only their dividends to live off. It was perfectly true that this wasn't fair—they had never been given equal opportunities.

Dad finally, if somewhat reluctantly, decided to dump the whole Ridder problem in somebody else's lap and thereby became the catalyst for the biggest merger up till then in American newspaper-publishing history. The combining of Knight and Ridder grew out of conversations that he held in 1974 with Knight's then chairman and CEO, Lee Hills, a longtime friend. Dad reasoned, "Let the Knights, who went public the same year we did, figure out what to do with the Ridders—let *them* run the show." Knight, he knew, had loftier expectations of their top people: they expected them all to actually work.

The first I heard of any of this was when my mother called one afternoon in 1974 to say, "Your father would kill me if he knew I was telling you this, but Ridder is about to merge with Knight Newspapers." Well, that made sense. Knight was a much better bet than Gannett had been. Its values were far superior to those of Gannett, where the publishers weren't allowed much autonomy—they were expected to adhere to the script they were given. The company was tightly controlled by its colorful CEO, Al Neuharth, whose ethics were, to put it politely, open to question. Under him, Gannett had grown ever more regimented. He lived and operated like a king: there was Al on the throne, and beneath him was everybody else—it was very much a top-down organization. At Knight Ridder meetings, on the other hand, editors and publishers would be encouraged to push back, to be strong and outspoken. (I don't remember our ever losing a key executive to Gannett.)

There were two conditions of sale imposed by Knight. One was that we divest ourselves of all our radio and television holdings (we owned half the controlling interest in WCCO television in

Minneapolis, which had an enormous audience, plus all the TV and radio in Duluth), lest we run into trouble with the FCC.

The other, more personally painful condition of sale was that, since Knight didn't believe newspapers should own professional sports teams, we would have to unload our interest in the Minnesota Vikings, one of only two teams I ever avidly followed, my alma mater, the University of Michigan, being the other. Ridder Publications held the largest single ownership position, and Dad had served as chairman of the Vikings board right from the team's founding in 1960.

We sold our shares to the other owners in 1977 and said goodbye to all that. To all that history. In the mid-1920s, there was an NFL team called the Duluth Eskimos that was solely owned by an amiable Swede by the name of Ole Haugsrud. When it folded after a couple of years, part of Ole's deal with the NFL granted him the option to buy up to fifteen percent of any franchise the league awarded Minnesota. It wasn't until 1960 that the NFL got around to doing anything about that, and when they did, Minneapolis insisted on having the majority interest, with the team based there, while St. Paul lobbied for the division to be fifty-fifty. The league ruled in favor of having three investors from Minneapolis at twenty percent each: Bill Boyer, a major Ford dealer; Max Winter, part owner of the Minneapolis Lakers, which later became the Los Angeles Lakers; and H. P. Skoglund, an insurance bigwig. And that's when ol' Ole weighed back in, exercising his option at ten percent. For sentiment's sake he was allowed to both name the team and choose its colors—purple and white, those of his Superior, Wisconsin, high school football team.

This left only thirty percent of the stock available to St. Paul. That's when Dad jumped in and had Ridder Publications snap it up. The Vikings minted money from the start, going on to play four times in the Super Bowl—without ever winning, I might add (sadly). The franchise value of the team today would be around $4 billion.

But getting back to Ole (fyi, a Scandinavian name derived from Old Norse, meaning "ancestor's descendant"). Midwest friends would tease me by sending me those once absurdly popular "Ole and Sven" Scandinavian-American jokes. There was even one that poked good-natured fun at the Vikings: "Ole and Sven, drunker than skunks, die in a snowmobiling accident and go to hell. The devil observes that they are really enjoying themselves there. He says to them, 'Doesn't the heat and smoke bother you?' Ole replies, 'Well, ya know, ve're from nordern Minnesooota, da land of snow an ice, an ve're yust happy fer a chance ta varm up a little bit, ya know." So the devil decides that these two aren't miserable enough and turns up the heat even more. When he checks in on them, he finds them in light jackets and hats, happily grilling walleye and drinking beer. The devil is astonished and exclaims, 'Everyone down here is in misery, and you two seem to be enjoying yourselves?' Sven replies, "Vell, ya know, ve don't git too much varm veather up dere at da Falls, so ve've just got ta haff a fish fry ven da veather's dis nice.' The devil is absolutely furious. He can hardly see straight. Finally he comes up with the answer. Because the two guys love the heat because they've been cold all their lives, he decides to turn all the heat off in hell. The next morning, the temperature is sixty below zero, icicles are hanging everywhere, and people are shivering so bad they're unable to even gnash their teeth. The devil smiles and heads over to Ole and Sven. He finds them back in their parkas and wearing their bomber hats and mittens. They're jumping up and down, cheering, yelling, and screaming like madmen. The devil is dumbfounded: 'I don't understand, when I turn up the heat you're happy. Now it's freezing-cold and you're still happy. What is wrong with you two?' They look at the devil in surprise and say, 'Vell, don't ya know, if hell iss froze over, dat must mean da Vikings von da Super Bowl.'" *That* old Ole joke still brings a smile.

The team played an important part in Dad's life, and he got a big kick out of playing golf with the coaches and the general manager. I had a small part myself—no more than a walk-on, really—in the Vikings playbook. When the team's Hall of Fame quarterback Fran Tarkenton left to join the Giants in 1966, Dad flew to Lake Tahoe to recruit the elite Latino quarterback, Joe Kapp, and took me with him to help negotiate the deal. Joe had been playing for the Calgary Stampeders and the British Columbia Lions—he was a huge star in Canada. The Oakland Raiders and the San Diego Chargers were after him but he had just signed with the Houston Oilers. Dad and I, with the encouragement of Joe's lawyer/agent, were able to persuade him to break his contract and sign with the Vikings. He was the team's ticket to victory in the 1969 NFL Championship Game, and the next year, when the Vikings made it to the Super Bowl for the first time, he was the star quarterback.

It took a good eight months to work out the details of the merger with Knight. Both Uncle Joe and Eric Ridder had made it known that they would vote their shares against it. No matter: the Ridder board approved the merger in July 1974, agreeing to accept five of the fifteen seats on a combined Knight Ridder board. Those seats were filled by the D.C. power lawyer Clark Clifford, who had joined the Ridder Publications board in '69 when we went public; Ridder CFO Ben Schneider, a lawyer who had joined the company when the family got in trouble over the due-bill imbroglio; and Dad, BJ, and Walter, representing the three major branches of the family (each of them to serve only as long as he continued to hold a significant amount of stock).

Although all involved, on both sides, were at pains to portray the deal as a merger, it was anything but: Knight, with two thirds of the stock, would be calling all the shots. The Ridders, for their part, were contributing their majority interest in nineteen dailies in ten states, while Knight was bringing to the table their sixteen dailies in seven states, exchanging 0.06 of their common shares for one share of Ridder stock.

The merged behemoth, with a staff numbering around 15,000, would be publishing in twenty-six cities across the country, with a combined weekday circulation of almost four million, the largest of any newspaper group at the time. In addition to quantity, there would now be greater quality. Knight's exacting standards would

Dad, the president and CEO of Ridder Publications, and Lee Hills, the chairman and CEO of Knight Newspapers, shaking hands upon the completion of the merger of the two companies in 1974. Looking on, Ridder chairman B.J. Ridder, left, and Knight president Alvah Chapman.
Photo by Tony Spina. Walter P. Reuther Library, Wayne State University

have to be met and maintained, which would mean fair and balanced reportage. This approach would be validated, and then some, by the forty-seven Pulitzer Prizes that Knight Ridder newspapers would go on to garner between 1980 and 2004—a grand total in both senses.

Lee Hills continued to serve as chairman and CEO, with Alvah Chapman as president and Dad as vice chairman. Five years later, in March 1979, when the board was disinclined to give the title of chairman to Alvah, Dad was elevated to the position. In his case, it was a title without portfolio, his sole duty being to preside over the four annual board meetings. The merger marked the end of his day-to-day responsibilities. Dad ceded the chairmanship to Alvah in 1982, and nine years later, when he turned seventy-five, he relinquished his seat on the board. Goodbye to all that.

My parents sold their big place in St. Paul in the mid-'80s and purchased a townhome. Dad would spend part of the morning at his office at the newspaper, talking with the publisher and/or the editor—he enjoyed keeping a hand in—and doing personal business. His secretary, Sue Fillion, who he now shared with the publisher, handled his and Mummy's affairs (Dad paid her privately). She had been my grandfather's secretary as well and would go on to be my brother Peter's and finally my son Par's. Talk about continuity. Talk about loyalty.

Every other Christmas, Connie and I would visit my parents in Florida, where they had owned a small apartment in Ocean Ridge since the mid-'60s. (When they were considering where to buy, it was so like my mother to veto places like Palm Beach. She was determined to be not only not in the social swim but as far away from it as possible.) Whenever I was able to get Dad alone, I would try to pry information about the company out of him. His default response was, "You know I can't talk about that." But later when our roles were reversed and I became the president, he would try to get information out of *me*.

There was never any question as to which culture would predominate in the new organization: Ridder, which was the more business-oriented, or Knight, which put a higher premium on top-quality journalism. Before the acquisition, every Ridder newspaper had operated on its own; there wasn't much in the way of company-wide standards. Knight immediately imposed a number of this-is-the-way-we-do-things strictures—they centralized a lot of functions, such as newsprint purchasing and insurance. Suddenly there were rules. All this required a certain amount of adjustment, but I don't remember its being particularly burdensome. As long as it saved the company money, I was for it.

The Knight newspapers as a rule had not had publishers; it was general managers who oversaw business operations, and editors who oversaw content, reporting only to the head of the news division at the corporate headquarters in Miami. When Alvah became CEO in 1976, he championed the publisher system of management, and by the mid-1980s all Knight Ridder papers, with the exception of the *Philadelphia Inquirer,* were operating under it. The Ridder papers, on the other hand, had always had on-site publishers, with ultimate authority over editorial and business matters. Knight made a commendable effort to make the merger work by refraining from replacing every Ridder executive with a Knight one. When, for instance, Gannett bought a newspaper, they would typically replace the entire top management team. The Knight organization understood that to be successful in a deal of this nature, magnitude, and complexity, it would need to secure the cooperation and loyalty of the people it had bought.

When Dad became CEO of Ridder in 1969, the company had let him have a small jet, which he had had painted the purple and white colors of the Vikings. Knight didn't have a plane of its own and, at a 1975 board meeting that I happened to be present at, Jack Knight said to Dad, "Why is it *you* have a plane in St. Paul when *we* don't even have one in Miami where our corporate headquarters are?" I had never heard anybody talk to Dad like that but, Knight having bought Ridder, what could he do? In harshly short order, Dad's plane—complete with co-pilots—was consigned to Miami. Knight soon replaced it with a Lockheed JetStar. Ten years later, around the time I moved to Miami to head the newspaper division, the company was flying high enough to purchase a second JetStar.

CHAPTER ELEVEN

Working in San Jose ... Making San Jose Work

IN JANUARY 1975, six months after Knight took over, I was promoted from business manager to general manager of the *Mercury News,* succeeding Tony Peterson who had been in the job since 1963 (at the time of the merger the year before, he had made it perfectly clear he had no intention of sticking around and working for "those people"). I now had the directors of advertising, circulation, production, and human resources, as well as the comptroller, reporting directly to me. I handily took the reins, having already led the effort to jettison our ancient linotype machines in favor of computer-generated technology.

The newsroom remained the only area where I was not the final authority. Although there were certainly talented people on staff, the *Mercury News* was, in terms of its journalism, a mediocre paper—it was much more of a business success. I was convinced that if we put out a better-quality product, our circulation would grow concurrently, but there was little I could do about it. Corporate in Miami was a hundred percent behind our improving the tenor of the paper, but Uncle Joe was loath to follow up on anything they wanted done.

Promotion was always his strong suit. His first big splash had been his 1952 brainstorm "Dollars from the Sky." He ran an announcement in the newspaper that at eleven o'clock on such-and-such a morning, a helicopter would fly over downtown San Jose dropping thousands of gilded ping pong balls. He got his money's worth in advertising and publicity—upward of a hundred thousand people showed up, and Uncle Joe, from his perch on a nearby rooftop, reveled in watching the crowds go crazy.

He also continued the annual treasure hunt gambit that he had originated in St. Paul, where it had been a huge community event. It was Uncle Joe's baby, but the day would come, sometime in the early 1970s, when even he had to agree that the negatives were outweighing the positives. Treasure seekers were digging up shrubbery and committing all sorts of property damage. Whenever it got to the point where the destruction was getting out of hand, we would make the clues increasingly specific so the treasure could be discovered sooner rather than later. Bluebeard's treasure it was not—all it consisted of at that stage was a *Mercury News* medallion. But—*presto magico*—when you turned it into the newspaper you received five thousand dollars. The burying part had worked better in St. Paul where the treasure could be effortlessly submerged in a mountain of snow as opposed to San Jose where it had to be strenuously hidden in hard ground.

I was one of a handful of people privy to the exact location of the hiding place, usually in some park and not necessarily even in San Jose—it might be Santa Clara or some other neighboring community. A friend of mine, John ("Jay") de Benedetti III, a shopping-mall and office-center developer and an enthusiastic golfer, had a son, John IV, who had tragically lost his vision at age ten through some kind of virus. Every July the president of the 49ers, Lou Spadia, another friend, would invite me to watch the team's practice session at the San Jose State football facilities, and one year I took Jay's son along. Being blind, he naturally couldn't see a thing, but he could hear the whistles and all the rest of the hoopla, and he got to have lunch with the team.

As we were driving back to Saratoga that afternoon, young John began pumping me about the treasure hunt, which was happening that week—the paper was running daily clues. As a lark, I drove by the spot, Lafayette Park in Santa Clara, where I knew the treasure was hidden, and I told John, "We are now within sight of where it is." Later that day I got an excited call from his father saying that John had been able to describe the burial place.

He must have figured it out by ... frankly, I could never figure out *how* he had figured it out, and out of delicacy I never asked. All I knew is that it would be bad optics if it turned out to be the son of one of my good friends who found the treasure. I had the *Mercury News* promotion department release a fusillade of clues to get it found ASAP. Fortunately, it was someone other than young John who won the day. But in another, more heartlifting sense, that kid was a winner. He wound up getting into Stanford, and his mother went with him and sat in on all his classes and read the texts to him. Today he works for a nonprofit that raises money for the blind.

The year of my promotion to general manager was a banner year for Connie as well. In 1975, fifteen years after she'd dropped out of Michigan to marry me, she decided to go back to school and earn her diploma. She enrolled at West Valley College, a public institution in Saratoga, where she proceeded to get straight As. Owing to those, she gained admission to Stanford, which she attended for three years part time, majoring in political science. She would fix breakfast for the family, go off to her classes, and come home and fix dinner.

When she was close to graduation, she asked me what I thought she should do next, and I encouraged her to go to law school. Stanford didn't have a part-time program, so she enrolled at Santa Clara Law School. Meanwhile she had to meet the obligations of the wife of a newspaper publisher, and she had taken on some civic responsibilities of her own as well. Four years later, she passed the California Bar, notoriously one of the toughest in the country, the first time around. Connie had several friends who had also dropped out of college to get married and who later in life tried to do what she did, but none of them was able to pull it off—she was the only one who had both the smarts and the determination. She was always

With Connie and our four children, Saratoga, mid-1970s.

one hundred percent committed to whatever she took on—Connie had the greatest follow-through of anyone I've ever known.

That June, just a year after the merger, I received an invitation from Jack Knight himself to play in the annual golf tournament—lightheartedly named the Knight Cup—that he hosted at the Pepper Pike Country Club outside Cleveland. I was left to wonder why, as the mere newly appointed general manager of one of his two-dozen newspapers, I was being so favored. Uncle Joe was testy about it, "Why *you*? I'm the publisher, or haven't you heard." I tried explaining that, for one thing, I played golf, and he didn't.

It would transpire that what corporate wanted *me* there for was to spend time with—in their parlance, "get to know"—the editorial-page editor of the company's *Philadelphia Inquirer*, Creed Black, who was the preferred candidate of both Lee Hills and Alvah Chapman to replace *Mercury News* editor Paul Conroy, who was on the verge of retiring. Aware of the delicate nature of my relationship with my uncle, corporate was using the golf tournament as an excuse to bring me to Ohio. But even when they stressed how important it was that the next editor of the *Mercury News* be acceptable to *me*, I failed to grasp that that could conceivably mean I could be the next publisher.

The Knight Cup was traditionally preceded by a morning board meeting in Akron, which was the home of the first Knight newspaper, the *Akron Beacon Journal*, and the city where Jack Knight maintained a home. The night before the meeting, I dined with Lee, Alvah, Dad, and Creed Black, and at eight o'clock the next morning I met with Creed alone for a couple of hours. He struck me as a very professional executive but just not what San Jose needed, which was a hands-on editor.

At about 10:30 I received word that my presence was required at the meeting. The minute I walked into the boardroom—I hadn't even gotten to sit down—Lee asked me to give a short presentation on the *Mercury News* and the Greater San Jose market. I had to speak extemporaneously. It was my trial by fire and, by all accounts, it went well—you *could* say that I really caught on.

After the meeting, Lee took me aside, wanting to know what I thought of Creed. When I stated that, in my opinion, he was not the answer, Lee asked who I *would* recommend, and I floated the name of Larry Jinks, the executive editor of the *Miami Herald*. Not long before, at a member-and-guest golf tournament at the Burning Tree Country Club in Bethesda, Maryland, I had been partnered with the longtime CEO of the Associated Press, Wes Gallagher, one of the most respected figures in journalism, and I had asked him outright who in his opinion was the best editor at any of the Knight Ridder newspapers. Without the slightest hesitation, he had answered, "Larry Jinks—he's an editor's editor." When I suggested to Lee that I would be happy to talk to Larry, he cut me off with "What makes you think he would have any interest in talking to *you*? The *Miami Herald* is a much bigger deal than *San Jose*."

Smarting a bit from that rebuff, I drove the two hours from Akron to Cleveland to play in the Knight Cup. Having been invited purely as a ruse, I was both amused and amazed when I went on to win. I returned on the next plane to San Jose and business as usual. I didn't encounter Jack Knight again until April of the following year when I attended the annual ANPA convention at the Waldorf Astoria in New York. It was always kind of a state occasion—typically you would have the president of the United States as your featured speaker. Knight Ridder had purchased three tables to accommodate its publishers and top editors, and I found myself seated next to Mr. Knight, which I recognized was no accident.

He asked me right off how I felt about my governor, Jerry Brown. I told him sincerely that I thought Jerry was doing an excellent job and I liked that he was fiscally conservative for a Democrat. Jack Knight said, "I'm disappointed to hear you feel that way, Tony. I hope you're not really serious. I think he's a loser. I just don't think he's got much on the ball." I was a bit shaken that my ultimate boss seemed to be losing confidence in me because I wasn't prepared to write Jerry Brown off as a flake—as "Governor Moonbeam," which was one of the pejorative nicknames people had come up with for him. The exchange made me more than a little apprehensive about my future in the company.

At the time, Jerry was a rising star, but doomed to dim out in the end. One of the things that did him in was, funnily enough, a mosquito. Or maybe a fruit fly—anyway, some kind of insect that had invaded the valley and infested fruits and vegetables, threatening the state's $40-billion-a-year agricultural industry. This tiny fly was responsible for not only an ecological nightmare but a political minefield. The people around the governor were recommending a widespread aerial spraying campaign, but Santa Clara County residents were rattled at the thought of all that pesticidal toxicity in the air. When the governor called me for advice, I told him I thought he should go ahead and spray, but he wasn't prepared to act. We had several follow-up conversations, looking at the problem from every angle. Finally he did spray.

I read just the other day that it was the turmoil in the wake of that decision that marked the beginning of the end of his political career—he went on to lose his race for senator to the Republican mayor of San Diego, Pete Wilson and, later when he ran for president, he never even got to first base. That insect was a real albatross. Oh, now it's coming back to me. What it was a fruit fly, a Mediterranean fruit fly—a Medfly, for short.

Speaking of Jack Knight, he was basically a middle-of-the-road Republican, and yet he had come out fairly early on against U.S. involvement in Vietnam. And publicly, too—in his weekly column, "Editor's Notebook," which ran in the Knight newspapers. I used to read him in the *Detroit Free Press* when I was a student at Michigan, and he was damn good—he won a Pulitzer in 1968 for editorial writing. His stance on Vietnam must have had something to do with his having lost his eldest son in World War II. First Lieutenant John S. Knight, Jr., was a Bronze Star recipient who was killed in action in 1945, in a German ambush—in Westphalia, of all places, which is where the Ridders originated. His wife was pregnant at the time, and the announcement of his death was withheld from her, and from publication, until she had safely delivered their baby.

John S. Knight III's story remained a sad one. He grew up to attend Harvard and Oxford and was embarked on a promising career as a reporter on some of his grandfather's newspapers, rising to assistant managing editor of the *Philadelphia Daily News*, but fate had other plans for him. He got stabbed to death in 1976, at the age of thirty, in his Rittenhouse Square apartment—a sensational, gay-motivated murder. Jack Knight's hopes and dreams all rode on this namesake grandson and died with him—he ended up leaving all his Knight Ridder stock to the now $2.5 billion Knight Foundation.

A long time elapsed without my hearing anything from Lee Hills about Larry Jinks. I went to Dad for professional advice—something I rarely did. I explained that I had stuck my neck out and shot my mouth off, that Lee had asked me what I thought of his and Alvah's choice for San Jose and that he was manifestly unhappy at my lack of enthusiasm. Dad said that if I felt that strongly about the matter I should stick to my guns. He turned out to be right on the money.

In late August 1975 I was in Durango, Colorado, attending an ANPA training session for publishers and general managers, run by professors at the Harvard Business School, when I got a call from Lee saying, "You wanted to talk to Larry Jinks, he's now willing to talk to you." Without delay I invited Larry and his wife to San Jose—he needed the opportunity to size *me* up as well. He would also need to placate Uncle Joe, who he would officially be reporting to, if he decided to take the job.

My job now was to clue in Uncle Joe, who had been left completely out of the loop. He went instantly on the defensive, announcing to the newsroom, "Tony thinks *he's* running the show around here, but I've got news for him—any future editor reports to *me,* period."

Connie and I accompanied the Jinkses to dinner at Uncle Joe's, a five-acre estate with a California-style ranch house atop a hill overlooking the valley and the southern end of the bay. (It was only three or four miles from where we lived, but we would normally be invited only when some family member came to town.) All the addresses on Uncle Joe's street, Saratoga Hill Road, had five numbers. His was 14751 but, at some point, he had gone and had a sign made—in non-compliance with the regulations—giving his street number as 555. I recognized those numbers—growing up he had lived at 555 Park Avenue in New York with his mother, my grandmother Nell Ridder.

Uncle Joe had moved to San Jose in 1952 not even knowing where it was, thinking it was in southern California—he had had to consult an atlas. With him was his new bride, Virginia Dunne, the tall, goodlooking daughter of his mother's closest friend. They separated

555 Park Avenue, familiarly known as "Triple Nickel," where Uncle Joe grew up with his divorced mother, my grandmother Nell Ridder.

around ten years later—Uncle Joe must finally have accepted that he preferred men. He acquired a close woman friend, a school administrator named Suki Hulburd, who he would trot out in public. She served admirably as his hostess-cum-beard at *Mercury News* and other functions, but she was nowhere in evidence the night Uncle Joe entertained the Jinkses.

The dinner, cooked by Uncle Joe's chef, Marcelle, and served by her husband, Ramon, the butler, didn't go down well—Uncle Joe was downright rude to Larry. More to the point, Larry and I hit it off; on the way home, he told me that he felt we had the same goals and would make a fine team. I told him that I was confident we could work around Uncle Joe. So, he agreed to take the job, starting the following May.

There was now, nominally, a Jinks waiting in the wings.

CHAPTER TWELVE

Making San Jose Count

IN LATE DECEMBER 1976, Alvah decided it was past time to sit down and have a talk with Uncle Joe. He flew out to San Jose accompanied by Byron Harless, senior VP of personnel and a KR board member (when a colleague once asked him how it felt to be the second most important person in the company, he replied, "Who's number one?"). Uncle Joe didn't think he had a thing to worry about. The *Mercury News* was a nationwide leader in ad lineage, and on his watch, circulation had increased from 73,000 to almost 200,000. He had been good for the paper in other ways as well. Early on, he had allied himself with San Jose's longtime city manager, "Dutch" Hamann, who was the most powerful man in Santa Clara County.

Dutch was out to develop San Jose at all costs and thought nothing of riding roughshod over zoning and environmental concerns. The results of that line of thinking spoke for themselves: subdivisions, shopping malls, car dealerships, and other commercial enterprises that crowded out fields and fruit orchards but translated into *Mercury News* ad spreads and classifieds—as Uncle Joe pithily put it, "Prune trees don't buy newspapers." Together, Dutch and Uncle Joe, working in a kind of unofficial partnership, transformed San Jose into the major city in the county. The one and only time they found themselves at cross purposes was when Uncle Joe successfully opposed the building of a slaughterhouse upwind of where the newspaper's new plant was to be located. (A couple of months after Alvah's and Byron's visit to the newspaper, Dutch and his wife—along with 581 other poor souls, including a horde of their fellow San Joseans homebound after a holiday in Spain—perished when their Pan Am Boeing 747 collided with a KLM Boeing 747 on the runway at the Tenerife airport in the Canary Islands: to this day, the deadliest accident in aviation history.)

Uncle Joe was scheduled to meet with Alvah and Byron at 9:30 on the appointed day, and I was to join the three of them for lunch in a private dining room at the Sainte Claire Club. In the event, Alvah and Byron spent most of the morning cooling their heels: Uncle Joe was a no-show. What could possibly be said in his defense? That he was rarely to be seen on the premises before three in the afternoon and that the first thing he was known to do upon arrival was repair to the bar that he had had installed in his office and fix himself a vodka and water? It wasn't until around eleven that Uncle Joe's secretary managed to get through to him on the phone. To little enough avail: he simply told her to tell us he would meet us at the club for lunch.

Suffice it to say, it was a fraught meal. Afterward we all went back to the newspaper, and Alvah and Byron followed Uncle Joe into his office and shut the door behind them. I learned later that they had read him the riot act: his management style was no longer acceptable, and from now on they would be expecting of him what they expected of all their other publishers, that he work regular hours five days a week. To which Uncle Joe responded, in effect, "I'm not going to do that. I've never done it—I can't do it, and I won't. I don't understand why you're even asking me to. That's what Tony's here for—*he* does all that stuff. You have nothing to be unhappy about. The paper's doing great."

Alvah and Byron left town in high dudgeon. Back in Miami they conferred with Lee Hills and both Knight brothers, all of whom agreed that the situation was neither tolerable nor tenable. Uncle

Joe for his part was steaming mad but still convinced they would back down.

A couple of weeks later, I received a call from Alvah, with Byron audibly at his elbow, informing me that I was being promoted to publisher and that Uncle Joe was being retired with the title of president and the directive to "consult with Tony Ridder." It fell unnervingly to me to spell things out to him: that from then on, there was going to have to be justification in terms of general news value for any story he proposed, and that there was going to be an arm's-length approach to dealing with politicians—the days when the city manager could just walk into the publisher's office and leave, having gotten whatever editorial he needed out of us, were over. Uncle Joe expostulated, "What do you mean! That's a terrible way to run a newspaper." And he was very cool to me after that.

He had been asking for it for years, it goes without saying. But still, his demotion had come as a jolt—to remove an elder Ridder was practically unheard of. My own sudden elevation was a high—and a surprise: the *Mercury News* was KR's second-biggest profit generator, behind the *Miami Herald,* and I had been concerned that, when the time for change finally did come, the company might feel I wasn't ready and bring in somebody from the outside as publisher.

I discovered belatedly—four decades later, in fact—that Alvah had first called Dad to tell him he was giving me Uncle Joe's job and that Dad had said, "I don't think you should do that, I'm not sure it's such a good idea—it'll put Tony in an impossible position vis-à-vis his uncles and cousins." I thought, retroactively, "Well, thanks a lot, Dad!" But in all fairness, he wasn't saying he didn't think I was up to the job, only that he was worried it would create a tough family environment.

The afternoon I was informed of my promotion, I called a staff meeting to announce the news. There was a photographer there to take a picture of the two of us, the outgoing and incoming

SAN JOSE CALIF., WEDNESDAY, JANUARY 26, 1977

SEPH B. RIDDER, P. ANTHONY RIDDER . . . Mercury News chiefs

—Staff phot

ph B. Ridder new president

Anthony Ridder new publisher the San Jose Mercury News

B. Ridder, publisher of se Mercury News since become president of the News and P. Anthony

He is a 1962 graduate of the University of Michigan and worked for the Aberdeen (S.D.) American News and the Pasadena

Governors of Goodwill Industries Board of Directors of the Boy Scouts of Santa Clara County; the President's Council of San Jose

San Jose Mercury News article announcing my promotion to publisher.

publishers, and as the guy was packing up his camera equipment, Uncle Joe turned on me. He said, "You son of a bitch, you stole my job!" There was a long, stressful silence, after which he conceded, "If anybody has to replace me, you're probably the best choice."

Alvah suggested I move into Uncle Joe's office right away—just as soon as he could be pried out of it. I protested, "Can't you just let him keep it? It's so important to him. There will be no confusion as to who's in charge, I assure you—if that's what you're concerned about." Alvah relented, and Uncle Joe stayed put. His bar, however, was swiftly dismantled, which he maintained was the single most humiliating thing that had ever happened to him. He came into the office less and less often after that, and one day in 1979 he upped and told Alvah he didn't want to be president anymore, that he was frustrated when friends asked him for favors he couldn't deliver on.

Uncle Joe lived another ten years, mostly in Honolulu (he was spending so much time there that he voluntarily gave up the apartment in San Francisco that the company had been paying for all those years). He died there in January 1989 at the age of sixty-eight, of complications from emphysema. On more than one occasion he had told me he was planning to leave me that trophy car of his—the 1963 Rolls-Royce Silver Cloud. But in the end, he bequeathed it to one of his men friends, a sheriff's deputy in the San Jose area named Crawford who he had also designated as executor of the California portion of his estate. As we know, it was originally a company car, but Uncle Joe got to keep it when they later bought him a Mercedes limo. I honestly had no expectations of inheriting a cent from him, given all the friction between us over his biased political endorsements and nonstop puff coverage of his cronies. And yet I inherited equally with all his other nieces and nephews, and I took the lead as the unofficial representative of the Ridder family to work things out with his estate. As far as the car went, Uncle Joe had never bothered to ask me if I even wanted it, and I wouldn't have wanted to insult him by telling him I wouldn't be caught dead driving around in a Rolls.

I had had Uncle Joe's office toned down before moving into it. A decorator friend of his from San Francisco, Sam Crocker, had done it up for him in the mid-1960s, with chairs upholstered in embroidered yellow silk and an enormous brass chandelier. Sam was an affable, good-looking, swish kind of guy, like Uncle Joe a fastidious dresser, and seemingly well-educated, well born, and well-heeled. He designed Uncle Joe's anteroom bar in knotty pine, which was quite a departure from the rest of the *Mercury News* offices. I don't mean that it wasn't in good taste—the problem was it was *too* good taste, if you know what I mean. The overall effect was more like something either of my grandmothers might have had than like the office of a newspaper publisher.

Sam decorated Uncle Joe's place in Saratoga, too, and later he did the house in Hawaii, which Uncle Joe had purchased from the estate of the industrialist Henry Kaiser. It was directly next door to one of the most spectacular women of the twentieth century, the magazine editor/playwright/politician/diplomat/beauty/trophy-wife Clare Booth Luce, who Uncle Joe regularly had as a dinner guest. He and Uncle Dan had been born on the same day, May 3, two years apart, and Connie and I flew over with my parents for their joint birthday party in 1972. The house was on Kahala Avenue, which Uncle Joe never got tired of describing as the Fifth Avenue of Honolulu. When Ridder went public in 1969, he had cashed in—or rather, cashed out—selling enough stock to buy that showplace. It sold for $40 million after his death. The buyers tore it down, leveling it off to just a flat piece of ground, then put up three townhomes in its place. Clare's house was subjected to the same fate. The poet Shelley nailed it: "The lone and level sands stretch far away."

To reflect for a moment on that over-the-top chandelier that Sam installed in Uncle Joe's office: in late April 1984 I was on the phone with Dad when the thing began swinging so wildly it was a miracle it didn't come flying right out of the ceiling. I said, "Dad, I gotta go. I think we're having an earthquake. I need to make sure everything's okay." We had four presses, each of which had a strong reinforced

Par, Connie, Susie, Linda, and I with Uncle Joe at his house in Honolulu, early 1980s.

foundation, but if any one of them developed a crack or got out of alignment, moved even an inch, it would impact our ability to print the paper. That was my worst fear—fortunately unfounded. It was a 6.2 Calaveras Fault earthquake, down in Hollister—the so-called Morgan Hill Earthquake. Although the newspaper was only twenty-four miles from the epicenter, we sustained no significant damage. I'd bet you anything Uncle Joe would have been more anxious about the state of his chandelier than our presses.

Speaking of which, shortly after being named publisher, I had to attend a KR board meeting to request permission to purchase additional presses. At dinner the night before at Lee Hills' place,

I was once again seated next to Jack Knight. As the largest shareholder—larger even than his brother, Jim, who he dominated in other respects as well—he naturally had the biggest say in the company. He right away began criticizing Alvah to me, which put me in a very awkward position, since Alvah was my boss. "He doesn't fully appreciate the journalism side of our business—the content of the newspapers and the creative people in the company," Knight went on. "He's one-dimensional, primarily concerned with the business side. He doesn't know how to deal with the gray areas, he's no good with ambiguities. And another thing, he doesn't look at things from the reader's point of view—the type in the papers is too small." (That last was reassuring to hear, in that it was the sort of thing *I* thought about—for example, in response to complaints that the print was rubbing off on readers' hands, I had switched to no-rub or low-rub inks.)

All during Jack Knight's rant, Alvah was sitting at an adjacent table and might well have heard what was being said. For all that, I need to add that Jack Knight understood that he needed Alvah. Lee Hills, who had come up on the news side the way Jack himself had, didn't understand the business side to the extent Alvah did. What Lee did fully grasp were the inner workings of a newspaper: the pressroom, the newsroom, the advertising and circulation and finance departments. That was one of my greatest strengths as well. I knew the *San Jose Mercury News* inside out, down to how the equipment worked. I used to go to the annual trade shows and talk to the manufacturers, so when my people would be touting some big new machine to me, I could tell them authoritatively why we didn't really need it. Anyway, for me, that dinner ended on a high note: Jack Knight told me, "I hear good things about what you're doing out in San Jose."

As publisher, I eliminated the two positions I had previously held, those of business manager and general manager. I felt that I was fully capable of functioning as all three—wearing all those hats. At the same time, I did away with freebies, which had gotten out of hand under Uncle Joe. Reporters were routinely on the receiving end of complimentary tickets to sports and entertainment events, not to mention free hotel rooms, meals, and trips, and even expensive Christmas presents. I had had heated altercations with Uncle Joe over the paper's sports reporting. My position was we shouldn't allow professional teams like the Giants and the 49ers and the Raiders to comp our people—we should pay our own way and not accept gifts. Uncle Joe had objected that it would be a waste of money to pay for ourselves—"They need us to cover them." I had countered that it made us beholden to them.

Ironically, the time was not long in coming when I was offered a highly desirable freebie myself. Early in 1979 I got a call from my old St. Paul's roommate, Steve Hansen, asking if I could spare the time to talk to his best friend, Paul Martha. Paul had gone from being an All-American football player at the University of Pittsburgh to playing professionally for the Steelers and was now executive vice president and general counsel of the 49ers. The team was owned by the shopping-mall magnate Edward DeBartolo Sr., who, Paul explained, had come to feel that his son, Ed Jr., who was running it for him, was in over his head—after two seasons of going through three coaches, the team was continuing to lose. I said right off the bat, "This is an easy one—hire Bill Walsh, the phenomenally successful head coach at Stanford." A few months later, Walsh was named the 49ers' head coach, and he went on to lead them to four of their five Super Bowl wins—the most, within a ten-year span, of any team in the history of the game.

Shortly after Walsh was hired, Paul let me know that DeBartolo was so appreciative of my advice that he wanted to give me a box at Candlestick Park for the 49er games. And it wasn't just any old box—it was on the twenty-five-yard line right next to the one he had gifted to the mayor of San Francisco, Dianne Feinstein. I explained that I wasn't free to accept, owing to my being in the newspaper business where such a gift would be considered an emolument, but that I would like to arrange for the *Mercury News to* buy the box.

I was told that boxes like that didn't grow on trees and were not for sale, but then, within a few weeks, they reversed themselves.

When Feinstein was facing a recall as mayor in 1983, the *San Francisco Chronicle* ran a story that she had failed to report as a gift the box she had accepted from DeBartolo. She quickly issued a statement denying that she had ever attended any games herself and claiming that she had made the box available to selected city employees. That was an out-and-out lie; she was there regularly. I witnessed her firsthand—saw her with my own two eyes—sitting pretty in the box next door to mine: just a glass wall separating us.

Speaking of Feinstein, I had always liked her politics because she was a moderate Democrat. But then, in the mid-1980s, the mayor of San Jose, my stalwart ally in civic causes, Tom McEnery, and I met several times with Bob Lurie, the son of the owner of the Mark Hopkins Hotel in San Francisco, a major real estate developer in his own right and the sole owner of the San Francisco Giants. He wanted to move the team to San Jose from Candlestick Park, the stadium built especially for them in Hunters Point, on the water, by the airport, after the previous owner had moved them from New York to the Bay Area in 1958. It was by all assessments an inadequate stadium, cold and windy and whatnot, and it was later renamed Monster Park, though only because a company called Monster Cable won the naming rights.

The next thing we knew, Tom and I received a letter from Dianne Feinstein putting us on notice that, as there was an unexpired lease between the City of San Francisco and the San Francisco Giants, we were attempting to interfere with a valid legal contract and about to commit a tortious act. We consulted attorneys for both the *Mercury News* and the City of San Jose, who agreed that we would be personally liable if Feinstein decided to sue us, which was what she was threatening to do. So, as much as we wanted to bring the Giants to San Jose, we couldn't afford to take the risk.

More than a decade later, to keep the Giants in the Bay Area, Safeway chairman Peter Magowan put together a team of investors to buy it from Bob. They had a suitable stadium built down on the water, near the Bay Bridge. That poor flustered sports ground would undergo a punishing number of name changes, from Pac Bell Park to SBC Park to AT&T Park to Oracle Park to … God knows what next. Talk about an identity crisis.

CHAPTER THIRTEEN

Making It to the Top

TOGETHER WITH LARRY Jinks, who took on the role of executive editor of the *San Jose Mercury News* in the spring of 1976, I began making extensive changes. The newspaper had a history of hiring virtually anybody who walked through the door, so there was, shall we say, room for improvement. We redoubled our efforts to recruit reporters and editors with an excellent track record, and word got out that we were committed to publishing a first-rate newspaper. The communications schools took note of the resulting transformation—journalists from all over the country suddenly wanted to come to work for us, the way musicians want to play for a great symphony orchestra. Also working in our favor was the fact that Silicon Valley was now considered an exciting place to live.

At the beginning of my run as publisher, the paper had only two business reporters, three editorial-page staffers, and a total of only 162 in the newsroom; by the time I left, we had thirty reporters in the business section and ten editorial-page writers and editors, and we had doubled the size of the newsroom staff. We were ranked among the top five papers in the country in full-run ad lineage, and circulation kept growing. In 1980, we had come up with a winning tagline for radio, television, and billboards: "The Bay Area's Best." Nobody now could reasonably challenge that assertion. The

Mercury News appeared regularly on industry lists of the ten best dailies in the country.

In 1986, we won our first Pulitzer Prize—the first that any northern California daily had won in a couple of generations—for a three-part series on the political and financial corruption of the Marcos regime titled "Hidden Billions: The Draining of the Philippines." We would be awarded a second Pulitzer in 1990 for general news reporting following the monster Loma Prieta earthquake in the Santa Cruz Mountains triggered by the San Andreas Fault. The upheaval occurred at the outset of Game 3 of the World Series when the San Francisco Giants were playing the Oakland Athletics in Candlestick Park—suddenly the whole stadium was rocking. It was the biggest quake in northern California since the earth-shattering San Francisco earthquake of 1906: the San Francisco-Oakland Bay Bridge collapsed, not to mention a major freeway and much else besides.

I had gone out of my way to be active in the Greater San Jose community. Most of our reporters were outside hires, with no history in Santa Clara County. As a member of various boards, clubs, and organizations, I had, over time, accumulated invaluable contacts and was in a position to alert the newsroom to stories they needed to get on top of. If some of those turned out to be unfavorable to elected officials and community leaders, even our advertisers, so be it: no kid-glove treatment.

Uncle Joe would cover the opening of any store by any advertiser, down to a tire store or drugstore, and readers were falling asleep. I eliminated practically all coverage of ribbon-cutting ceremonies. Every day of the week, there used to be a three-by-eight-column ad on the front page of the sports section, and I imposed a policy of no ads on section fronts.

Next, I tackled the graphics. I rethought the newspaper's trademark color—all our trucks, vending racks, and promotional paraphernalia were orange. Orange was "hot"—a fun color—but I opted for something cooler and more refined: blue-green and silver. And

Breakfasting with Bishop Desmond Tutu, Sacramento. He had just been awarded the 1984 Nobel Peace Prize for his role in the opposition to apartheid in South Africa.

when we made a $300 million capital investment in equipment for our two Philadelphia newspapers, I specified a blue hue for the sophisticated new presses.

One day in 1998, I found myself wondering, Why do we have to have that hyphen between the "Knight" and the "Ridder." It had been there ever since the two companies got together. I asked myself what would happen if we just dropped it—would it ever be missed, or did it in fact serve some useful purpose? I consulted with our general counsel on whether there could possibly be any kind of issue with our legal documents. The answer was no, so out it went. And while I was at it, I dropped the "Inc."

Another day, again out of the blue, it hit me that nowhere on the masthead of any of our newspapers did it indicate that they were part of Knight Ridder. I directed that each of them include the words "A Knight Ridder Newspaper." I was out to raise our profile with the public in every way. Whenever we won a Pulitzer or any other important prize, which we had begun doing with some regularity, I made sure we ran ads to that effect in magazines like *Fortune*, *Business Week*, and *Forbes*.

On fronts other than fonts, I was also up to my eyeballs. In 1984 the governor of California, George Deukmejian, who was of Armenian descent, drastically cut the proposed state budget. Around that time, we ran a big story about some Armenian terrorist. This inspired our editorial-page cartoonist to depict the governor with a sword in his hand and to caption her creation: "Armenian terrorist slashing and burning." I would normally be shown editorials before they ran, but not cartoons. I knew this Deukmejian—during my nine years as publisher in San Jose I was periodically invited, along with Silicon Valley bigwigs and the top people at IBM and Lockheed, to get together on a social basis with the sitting governor. Deukmejian was a thin-skinned guy to begin with, and he demanded an apology and a retraction. The problem was you can't really retract a cartoon.

This was a case where I fully accepted that we had crossed a line we shouldn't have. I was in favor of our publishing something along the lines of "Cartoons are largely political; they exist to poke fun at politicians, among others, but no way did the *Mercury News* mean to imply that the governor of California is a terrorist."

As a rule, if the paper published something that, in hindsight, I determined was unfair, I never had any hesitation in saying so. There was, however, a natural reluctance on the part of the newsroom to admit they were ever wrong. My position was, and is, there's nothing wrong with saying you're wrong when you *are* wrong. If you're not, great—hang in there.

Now, don't get *me* wrong—being a publisher had its fun side, too. In the early '80s, one of our editors came to me with the idea for a story that would need to be done in depth—literally, since it involved plumbing the depths of Lake Tahoe, which, at 1,600 feet, was the second deepest lake in the United States and, at least according to the editor, had never been gotten to the bottom of. I asked the next question, "What do you hope to find down there?" He said there were rumors floating around of fantastic things like gigantic mackinaw fish, and drowning-victim cadavers that were perfectly preserved thanks to the cold. He already had the perfect person to lead the expedition—a well-known marine biologist at the University of California at Davis. It sounded too intriguing to pass up, and I went ahead and leased a submarine from an oil company in Houston.

I came to feel that I owed it to my sense of adventure to go down with the biologist and the reporter. So down I went, and when we surfaced, there were a couple of boats with journalists and television crews waiting to interview us. No, we had not run into any cadavers, or even any outstanding fish. I mentioned in passing that we had gotten stuck on a ledge for a couple of nervous-making minutes. The AP reporter ran with that, for lack of anything better, and the story went out to the wire services headlined "Newspaper Publisher Stuck at Bottom of Lake Tahoe." My sister Laura read it in the *Detroit Free Press* and called our mother, and Mummy called me out on it: "Just what were you doing at the bottom of Lake Tahoe? Promise you won't ever do that again, Tony."

My vaunted sense of adventure was soon to be further tested. In the mid-1980s, Byron Harless and Bill Ott, KR's senior VP of operations, called to take the temperature of my interest in becoming publisher of the *Detroit Free Press*, which at the time was being run jointly by its general manager and its editor. I discussed the offer with Connie, our children, and Dad, and the unanimous feeling was it was a bad idea all around. It would have been an interesting challenge because, although the paper boasted the tenth highest circulation in the country, it was losing the ad battle to its competitor, the *Detroit News*, which had recently been purchased by Gannett.

A couple of years later, Alvah Chapman and Gannett chairman Al Neuharth combined the business operations of both papers in what's known as a Joint Operating Agreement. (In 1970, Congress had passed the Newspaper Preservation Act which allowed competing papers in local markets to sign such agreements if one of them was failing, which by 1985 ours was.) The structure took a couple of years to be approved by the Department of Justice, but it did the trick, boosting the profits of both papers after an almost thirty percent reduction in the workforce.

I may not have been sufficiently tempted by the Detroit offer, but when I was approached a bit later by the chairman of one of the biggest recruiting firms, Hedrick & Struggles, on behalf of the head honcho of Times Mirror, Bob Erburu, I pricked up my ears. When the headhunter asked me how I saw my future, I told him truthfully that I was perfectly happy where I was. He recast his question: what did I envision as my next step—did I, for instance, harbor an ambition to become a KR corporate officer? I explained that I had long ago ruled that out, as my family and I had zero interest in relocating to Miami. Within a matter of days, Bob Erburu himself called to ask if he could come to San Jose to talk to me.

I picked him up at the airport and took him back to our house in Saratoga where Connie fixed us a salad for lunch. He didn't beat around the bush—he asked me directly what it would take to get me to say yes to an offer from Times Mirror. When I dithered, he extended an invitation for Connie and me to be his guests in Los Angeles on a coming weekend.

Over morning coffee on his terrace, he proposed the position of Times Mirror senior VP, with the publishers of nine of their newspapers reporting to me, including the *Hartford Courant*, the *Baltimore Sun*, the *Denver Post,* and *Newsday.* The sole exception would be their flagship paper, the *Los Angeles Times*, whose publisher, Tom Johnson, would continue to report only to Erburu. He explained that Johnson was temperamental and would never sit still—would in fact never stand—for having it any other way. For me, that was the deal breaker. I would have liked to have *his* job. Back then, in 1985, the *Los Angeles Times* was arguably the second-best newspaper in the country, after the *New York Times*, and one of the most read, with over a million circulation.

Coincidentally or not, within the month I had a call from Alvah summoning me to Miami to discuss my "future at KR." Upon arrival at our hotel, Connie and I found an invitation to join him and his wife, Betty, on their boat the next day—the party was to include Byron Harless and KR president Jim Batten and their wives. My alma mater Michigan happened to be playing Iowa that day. As both teams were undefeated, it would be the decisive game of the season, and I wanted to watch it on the big TV in our hotel room. I was able to persuade Alvah to wait for the game to be over before pushing out of the harbor in Key Biscayne. I realized I was taking a risk but felt it was one I could afford to take, given that I wasn't looking to change jobs.

Deep-sea fishing with Alvah would always prove to be a command performance. The boat, christened the *Chris Dale* after the Chapmans's two daughters, was a fifty-foot fishing vessel, complete with captain and two-man crew. Once a year Alvah would host an extended fishing trip for four or five senior men in the company (wives not invited). He gave you so much notice—in, say, September he would say, "Put down March 2nd to the 5th for a little fishing expedition"—it was difficult to find a reasonable excuse not to go. He loaded you up with fish to take home—grouper and mahi-mahi and the like. I would just shove it in the freezer. All told, I probably never ate more than a quarter of my share of the catch—the rest I ended up tossing. I had bigger fish to fry.

The name "Alvah" was a dead giveaway. It was a tribal name of some kind, meaning a "biblical place," and he more than lived up to it. He would have somebody stand up and say grace before each and every business meal. I always felt uncomfortable with that, but the editor of the *Miami Herald*, who was Jewish, as were other officers of the company, was downright offended. My first meal on that first outing on the *Chris Dale* consisted of just a sandwich. I was famished and dug right in. Alvah said, "Wait just a minute, Tony, we haven't said grace yet." I had already gobbled it up.

I've been told all my life that I eat like somebody's going to take it away from me. So many people over the years have said, "Slow down, Tony." I hold the record for eating a hamburger faster than anybody in the history of La Rinconada Country Club in Los Gatos (a story that got wildly exaggerated, by the way—someone came up to me to say he'd heard I had eaten it all in one bite). At some point, Dave Lawrence, the publisher and chairman of the *Miami Herald* (and, before that, the publisher of the *Detroit Free Press*), challenged me to a speed-eating contest. What *he* proceeded to eat was humble pie—he conceded the title to me. I used to catch holy hell from Connie over how fast I ate. Our four kids also all ate fast. Connie would put food on the plates, and the rest of us would be through with dinner before she even got to sit down.

One evening, as we were about to sit down to dinner on Alvah's boat, he turned to me and said, "Tony, please, would you say grace?" I mumbled a catchphrase or two that I remembered from compulsory chapel at St. Paul's. I don't remember hearing any Ridder ever say grace. Except for one. In 1967 my grandfather flew out to San Jose for the dedication of a new building that I had broken my back getting the company moved into. After we all took our places for lunch, Grandpa rose to his feet and intoned, "I would like to say grace, so would you please bow your heads ... Now let us pray." He paused for dramatic effect, then spelled out that last word as p-r-e-y. There was a lot of nervous laughter. (Upon becoming CEO in 1995, I put an end to the practice of having grace said before meals with the board—I considered these strictly working occasions. Alvah kind of griped when I pulled the plug on the praying, but he didn't fight me on it, thank God.)

Alvah was a figure to be reckoned with in the industry. He had apprenticed in every part of the business, beginning with a paper route as a youngster and progressing to counting out papers for carriers to becoming part owner, president, and publisher of the *Savannah Morning News*. When it was sold out from under him, he obtained the job of executive assistant to Jim Knight at the *Miami Herald*, rising to president of the newspaper in 1969 and then in '76 to CEO of Knight Ridder and six years later to chairman.

That first weekend with him in Miami, Alvah formally offered me the presidency of the newspaper division—I would be responsible for both the business and news sides of all the papers. He added that this was a job no one person had ever been entrusted with before (the division was run by a senior VP of operations in tandem with a senior VP of news). But then—in what was aggravatingly reminiscent of the Times Mirror offer from Bob Erburu—came the kicker: All the publishers would be reporting to me *except for one.* The outlier was Dick Capen, the publisher since 1983 of one of the company's most important papers, the *Miami Herald*—he would be reporting only to Alvah.

When I told Alvah I needed time to think about his offer, he looked crestfallen. He was widely believed to be grooming Jim Batten to be his successor as CEO and chairman, and Capen to be Batten's successor as president. Capen was a Navy man, with the kind of military background that Alvah set great store by. When Alvah was Regimental Commander of the Corps of Cadets at The Citadel Military College of South Carolina, he had had his classmate, Ernest "Fritz" Hollings, a future Democratic governor and senator of that state, suspended for a violation of the honor code (knowing where there was cheating going on and failing to report it). Alvah had gone self-righteously on to be a much-decorated B-17 bomber pilot and squadron commander in the Army Air Corps' European Theater and would often hold forth on the various kinds of planes he had flown in combat.

That Capen was adept at spinning military stories of his own gave him a big leg up with his boss. Before joining Knight Ridder, he had served in a number of high-level posts in the Department of Defense and been awarded its Distinguished Service Medal. He fit Alvah's mold to a tee in that he was as good-looking as he was smooth-talking.

Alvah was consumed with how Knight Ridder would function after he stepped down. Batten, he pointed out, had come up on the news side, rising to be top editor of the *Charlotte Observer,* but had no business background. Alvah confided to me that he didn't feel comfortable turning the company over to him and Capen, who also came up short in newspaper-operating experience. He said he hoped that was where I would come in. (Capen never did become president. The highest position he ever achieved in the company was a vice chairmanship, with responsibility for its non-newspaper interests, including retrieval systems for technical and financial information. In 1992 President George H. W. Bush named him ambassador to Spain. I would hear from various people that, a chip off the old Alvah block, Capen pressed his dinner guests at the embassy in Madrid to hold hands while he said grace.)

What *would* it take, I asked myself, to give up being the publisher of the *San Jose Mercury News*? To blow my own horn, I had been voted California Publisher of the Year in 1983, and we were far and away the best paper in northern California—thanks to our comprehensive business coverage, we were hailed as the *Wall Street Journal* of Silicon Valley. There was also Connie's career to consider. Following graduation from Santa Clara Law School, she had landed a job with the leading firm in the state, Gibson, Dunn & Crutcher, and if we were to move to Miami, she would have to take the Florida bar and then go through the process of joining a local firm.

And what about our son, Par? We would be most reluctant to disrupt his senior year in high school. On top of any of that, Miami held little appeal for us. It had the ocean, sure, but San Francisco, where I spent a considerable amount of time serving on nonprofit boards, had the bay. The whole issue, as far as we were concerned, was water under the bridge.

Dad was against my accepting Alvah's offer. "It's awfully political down there," he advised, adding, "Be very wary of the sixth floor" (the code name for corporate, which occupied the top floor of the Miami Herald Building downtown on Biscayne Bay).

Another consideration: going to corporate would mean I would be working in an environment where the top five executives were strongly religious. They were all the same denomination, too—Presbyterian or maybe Methodist, whatever it was—and they worshiped at the same church. One of the first things Alvah had asked me was what denomination I was. Connie and I didn't really go to church, and when we did, it might be only on Easter Sunday or Christmas Eve, and it was to an Episcopal church, or for a funeral or wedding—it meant little more to us than the performance of a social function.

A more coercive reason not to take the job was that I didn't much care for Alvah personally. He was rigid and regimental (Uncle Joe's apt sobriquet for him was *martinet*) and took himself super-seriously—not a whit of humor there. Plus, he had the reputation of being an overly deliberative executive. Gannett's Al Neuharth coined the epithet "Pray and Delay" for him because Alvah overthought everything—he took too long to come to a decision.

Alvah's ability to judge people was limited. Competence aside, the deciding factors for him were invariably: were the candidates good-looking? Had they served in the military? And did they have religion? That there was this God-fearing, military-minded culture at the pinnacle of the company helped make the job I was up for one that I really wasn't all *that* up for.

I went back to San Jose and took a couple of weeks to mull things over. What finally persuaded me to take the job was the hope, if not the conviction, that I could incrementally overhaul certain aspects of corporate decision-making that I had been unhappy with for years. For instance, one of KR's diehard rules was that each newspaper had to contribute toward the shortfall of the underperforming ones, such as Philadelphia, one of our biggest and least profitable papers. I wanted each paper to begin carrying its own weight, to stand and fall on its own.

The *Mercury News*, for instance, was the fastest growing newspaper not only in the company but in the country, and I objected to having our growth slowed just because Philadelphia, let's say (again), was not doing the job it should have been. If a publisher was making his budget, he shouldn't have to cut back. It didn't seem fair that the winners should sacrifice for the slackers. Alvah had promised that if I came to Miami, I could run the newspapers the way I saw fit. One thing I knew I wanted right out of the box was to impose company-wide performance-measuring statistics—benchmarking—so I would be able to compare newspaper to newspaper. In San Jose I had devised a five-year plan that hit all our profit targets.

Connie and I made the move to Miami on the first of February 1986. We had arranged for Par to stay in Saratoga for his senior year and live with our closest friends, Don Lucas, who owned some of the top car dealerships in the West, and his wife, Sally. Par was over the moon—he figured that his hosts would be spending most of their time in their house in Hawaii, where Don also had dealerships, and that he would have the Saratoga place all to himself and could come and go as he pleased. But then Sally contracted Epstein-Barr disease and was bedridden at home in California, and Par ended up cooking a lot of the Lucas's meals and not having anywhere near the free time he had counted on.

We went native, Connie and I, and bought a two-story stucco 1940s house on one of the inlets off Biscayne Bay. It had a dock, so we went and bought a forty-foot speedboat. I developed kind of a routine for our visitors: I would take them on a ride to Government Cut, the shipping canal between Miami Beach and Fisher Island where the cruise ships were docked and you could get a bird's eye view of all the showplaces. Then we would travel a little further south to a uniquely picturesque place called Stiltsville where the wood shacks were built on poles in the middle of Biscayne Bay.

Miami was a great newspaper town because there was nonstop corruption. Where we lived, on Sunset Island Two, our neighbor on one side was a rough-looking Hispanic guy who I became

The Miami Herald Building, One Herald Plaza, directly on Biscayne Bay. KR corporate headquarters occupied the sixth (top) floor, the Miami Herald newsroom the fifth and the advertising department the fourth, and so on. The building was demolished in 2014.
Photo by Marc Averette

increasingly convinced was a drug dealer. Stretch limos were pulling up at all hours of the day and night, and the hombres piling out of them didn't exactly strike me as Miami's leading citizens, and as for their lady friends, they likely were hookers. Our dodgy neighbor had a dock also, and we would hear boats coming in till the early hours of the morning. *Miami Vice* rented that house for shoots multiple times—it checked all the boxes in that it was white and had a lot of glass.

When I told the editor of the *Miami Herald* that there was suspicious activity going on right next door to me, he gave me a so-what-else-is-new, in-Miami-there's-suspicious-activity-going-on-everywhere kind of look. In the end, it turned out my suspicions were accurate, and the guy ended up in the pokey.

One of the first things I said to Connie after we moved to Miami was "Where's the gun, we're probably going to need it." She had never wanted me to have one—she didn't like the idea at all. I had hunted, growing up, before going off to St. Paul's. Mainly partridge—the season around Duluth was September through November. I had also shot pheasant with my mother and father. And later when I went out to work in Aberdeen after college for about a year, I borrowed guns to go pheasant and duck and goose hunting with friends on weekends. And later in California I went duck hunting a few times with a shotgun. That was the extent of it, really.

Two weeks after Patty Hearst was kidnapped by the Symbionese Liberation Army in 1974, a family living in the Santa Cruz mountains, only ten miles from us in Saratoga—a doctor and his wife and children—were savagely slaughtered. The chief of police in San Jose came to my office at the *Mercury News* to inquire if I owned a firearm. When I said no, he told me to go out and get one. Then he arranged for Connie and me to take lessons at the police shooting range on the outskirts of town. They handed us pistols, and we went at it for about an hour, boom boom boom.

On the way home in the car, I said to Connie, "My ears are ringing—*loudly*. Are yours?" Hers weren't, but mine went on ringing 24/7 for two weeks. Connie remained adamantly opposed to having a pistol in the house, even though we lived in kind of an isolated situation—an old farmhouse on several acres. Our son was only six at the time, so I would have to put the gun in a brown paper bag and hide it—I'd move it around between various closets and chests of drawers. But one or another of our kids would sometimes find it. Another problem was the gun would be in one place and the bullets in another. Every time we heard a strange noise downstairs that sounded like somebody was trying to break in—our dogs would be barking like mad—I would say to Connie, "I can't find the damn gun, do you remember where we put the thing?" and she would say, "I don't know—you keep moving it." And then, me: "I found the damn gun, but I can't find the damn bullets." It was like the Keystone Kops. So, when we moved to Florida and I asked her where the gun was, she confessed that she had thrown the blasted thing away.

One of the petty things that frustrated me no end about Miami was that if I called a community-related meeting for three o'clock there would often be no one there. The city operated on Cuban time—folks thought nothing of walking in fifteen minutes to half an hour late. And at fundraising events, dinner would be served around 11:00 p.m., which didn't do a whole lot for my digestive system.

The *Miami Herald* had a section called *El Herald*, which consisted of various stories from the paper translated into Spanish (there was no independent reporting). When Connie was interviewing for a job with the Greenberg Traurig law firm, which she ultimately joined, the Cuban American partners made a point of mentioning that Knight Ridder was not well regarded or even respected by the Cuban community in Miami. When she brought up this issue to Alvah at the "Welcome to Miami" party he threw for us, he told her, coldly, "You have been misinformed—that's just not true." Not long afterward, however, the Cuban American Foundation, where one of Alvah's closest friends, Armando Codina, was a force, voted to boycott the newspaper. So, clearly, we did have a problem.

We subsequently created a full-fledged Spanish newspaper called *El Nuevo Herald* to be delivered to subscribers along with the *Miami Herald*—a newspaper within a newspaper, in other words. It had a staff of its own and its own editorials and news coverage, and it quickly achieved and then surpassed its goal. In fact, it got to the point where people were picking up the stand-alone *El Nuevo Herald* and tossing the *Miami Herald*. At that point, we decided to sell it separately. It vastly improved our relationship with the Hispanic community, which was huge, amounting to seventy-five percent of the population of Miami, with Cubans constituting sixty percent of that. *El Nuevo* went on to win the highest prize in Spanish-language journalism, the Ortega y Gasset Award.

When Connie and I first got to town, the only friends we had were people in the company. Connie had had a slew of friends in San Jose, but now she didn't have time to even think about making new ones—she was working six days a week, all hours. She had a difficult boss, and when she began having problems with him, I advised her to get out of there, if for no other reason than that she was making *me* unhappy listening to how unhappy *she* was. I arranged an interview for her with the co-founder of the big national law firm Holland & Knight, Chesterfield Smith—oddly, he had no nickname. He was president of the American Bar Association during the Watergate scandal and called for Nixon's impeachment. Anyway, Holland & Knight hired Connie and by 1992 she made partner. She began as a corporate attorney and ended up one of only two trust-and-estate attorneys in the Miami office. In my opinion, she was too conscientious for her own good—she wouldn't begin billing clients for all the hours she put in until she had gotten fully up to speed on their cases.

Chesterfield always fondly referred to Connie, as well as the firm's two Black female partners, as "my girls." He wouldn't have been able to get away with that today, but he was around eighty at the time, and the world was a hugely different place. When the firm started putting pressure on Connie to try and get me to give Holland & Knight some Knight Ridder business, I told her that the only way that could happen would be if she quit.

As president of the newspaper division, I traveled out from Miami to our various newspapers at least once a week, and I would also regularly have to call on institutional investors and attend analyst meetings—I was spending an awful lot of time on the road. I found myself missing certain aspects of what I had been doing as publisher in San Jose, like visiting the newsroom and talking one-on-one to our reporters and columnists or dropping in on the mailroom or the distribution center or the circulation department. I had always made time to wander around the newspaper, and whenever anybody called me "Mr. Ridder," I would correct them with a "No, please call me Tony."

Now, of course, I had a very different job and had to follow another routine when I visited our newspapers. Typically, I would talk for ten or fifteen minutes about what was going on not only in the company but the industry—kind of a stump speech. I would make a point of thanking the employees for their good work and then I would take questions, of which there would always be plenty, some of them surprisingly hostile.

CHAPTER FOURTEEN

The Unprecedented Price of Total Autonomy

For my first few years as newspaper division president, I had to live with a living nightmare. Long before I moved to corporate, Knight Ridder was sued for libel. It was by leaps and bounds the biggest lawsuit the company had ever faced and one of the biggest ever brought against any newspaper.

In the early 1960s, the namesake son of Pennsylvania's state police commissioner, Rocco Urella, and his LaSalle College pre-med classmate were involved, in some way never definitively determined, in the beating to death of a forty-eight-year-old General Electric company clerk in the latter's apartment after he had made some sort of "improper suggestion" or advance. The chief of the homicide division in the Philadelphia district attorney's office, Richard Sprague, declined to prosecute and ultimately had the case discharged.

A full decade later, our *Philadelphia Inquirer* majorly revisited the case in the form of six articles and four editorials. They left the reader with the impression that Sprague may have engaged in, at best, favoritism toward the son of an admittedly "exceedingly close" friend and professional associate and, at worst, a cover-up. To make matters substantially worse, one of the authors of the series turned out to have been convicted by Sprague the year before for illegally recording phone interviews for the *Philadelphia Bulletin*, which had then promptly fired him, after which, inexplicably, he was hired by the *Inquirer*. This reporter was now presumed to have had a vendetta against Sprague.

The more we dug into it, the greater our realization of just how weak our case was. There was no whitewashing the fact that there were serious mistakes and inaccuracies in the reporting, including the improper use of hearsay evidence. Whether any of this was intentional or not was the question, because you can't be successfully sued for negligence, carelessness, or oversight.

The company turned down a chance to settle the case for a couple of million. Again, this was before I got involved—I would have accepted that offer in a Miami minute. Gene Roberts, the *Inquirer*'s executive editor since 1972, made the decision to reject it. That he had been granted the power to make a call like that on his own can only be explained by the fact that he was winning us all these Pulitzers—an astonishing seventeen in as many years. The joke among the editors of our other papers was that, until Tony Ridder came along, Gene Roberts had an unlimited remit and exceeded it.

During an eight-week trial in 1983, the prosecution succeeded in proving the reporter had indeed acted with malicious intent and a reckless disregard of the truth that "violated the right of a public official to his good name." The court awarded Sprague $1.5 million in compensatory damages and a further $3 million in punitive.

The company appealed, naturally. For the retrial in 1990, I replaced the lawyer who had lost the case for us with Dechert Price, one of the leading Philadelphia firms. Roberts spent a grueling seventeen days on the stand under withering cross-examination. For all that, Sprague was awarded $2.5 million in compensatory damages and a staggering $31.5 million in punitive—the largest sum ever awarded in a libel case against a news organization. The State Superior Court ultimately reduced the amount of punitive to $24 million, and we wound up settling for considerably less, though still a sum that seemed excessive in relation to any actual harm that could conceivably have been done Sprague.

We always had lawsuits going in Philadelphia, a city that *Philadelphia Magazine* described as "the most dangerous in America in which to practice journalism." We had more issues there than anywhere else. (It was our largest newspaper city: we owned both papers, the tabloid *Philadelphia Daily News* as well as the *Inquirer*. They reached very different parts of the market. A third Philadelphia paper, the *Bulletin*, went out of business in the early 1980s.) It's important to note, however, that the *Inquirer* won all forty-six other libel suits filed against it over the years by public officials.

The *Inquirer* was the only one of our newspapers where the top editor was not required to report to an on-site publisher. In 1990 I finally laid down the law to Gene Roberts that he would no longer be exempted. He maintained that the company was breaking its word to him, that in the early '70s, Jack Knight, Lee Hills, and Alvah Chapman had all promised him virtually permanent autonomy. Ever since, he had been holding sway—lording it—over a newsroom numbering 560 at one point, not to mention seven national bureaus and six foreign bureaus. I conceded that most of the time Gene exercised autonomy, it was a good thing. But I held that nobody at KR was entitled to *total* autonomy. God knows *I* never had it—I was responsible to a board of directors. Anyway, his answer to my ultimatum was to quit.

Gene never admitted publicly that the reason for his departure was his refusal to report to anyone other than corporate—rather, he told the staff that he was leaving because of the general differences he was having. The facts were, the newspaper under him was first-rate editorially but drastically underperforming in ad revenue and circulation. We were constantly having to tamper with what we called the zoning. Philadelphia was in decline, all the growth was in the suburbs, and we needed to attack the circulation weaknesses there and cater to that market. Our suburban readers were complaining that there was too much Philadelphia news. Yes, they appreciated the enhanced sports and business sections we had given them, but they also wanted to know what was going on in their own neck of the woods, which had led to our introducing weekday zoned sections called "Neighbors."

Gene ended up going to work for the *New York Times*, where he had been national editor back in 1972 when the *Inquirer* hired him. His new job was the *Times*'s number-two editorial position, where he would be responsible not to the publisher but rather to the editor-in-chief. Shortly afterward, I happened to run into the publisher, "Punch" Sulzberger, and the first thing he said was, "Tony, have I made a terrible mistake?" I hedged my bets. I told him, "Gene's a terrific editor."

CHAPTER FIFTEEN

Filling My Own Shoes

One of the things I missed the most when I moved to corporate was that I could no longer sit on any of our papers' editorial boards, helping to decide which politicians to endorse and which positions we should adopt. At the *Mercury* News, that process had not been, to be perfectly honest, purely democratic—mine counted for a lot more than one vote. But I never imposed or overruled—I would always simply try to persuade. One issue I felt particularly strongly about was a tendency on the part of the newsroom to take a pro-union stand, and to that end I worked with the editorial page editor to modulate any editorial I felt was too biased. (Some of our newspapers had both unionized and non-unionized departments. The unionized ones tended to have lower morale, which made sense—the job of the union leadership, after all, was to foment dissatisfaction and create discontent to, if nothing else, prove their own worth.)

As soon as I took the job in Miami, I notified all our unionized newspapers that in the event of a strike they would have to be prepared to publish, no matter what, because the minute you stop, you've lost. They needed to right away begin training their people in how to print the paper without union support. I was convinced that if the unions could be made to understand that Knight Ridder was determined to publish at all costs, we wouldn't *have* any strikes.

Knight had had various strikes in the past and not been sufficiently aggressive with the unions. To me, this was not acceptable.

Ridder had had strikes as well. There was a doozy of a one at the *Mercury News* in 1959, five years before I started work there. Uncle Joe made no effort to try to publish, and that strike lasted 129 days and the three unions involved ended up getting everything they wanted. To his credit, Uncle Joe had kept employees' health insurance in force and even allowed them to borrow from the money he personally had in the company credit union.

In San Jose I had gotten along generally very well with the heads of the unions. The newspaper had a full-time labor negotiator, and he and I worked together. But after I was promoted from business manager to general manager in 1975, I no longer sat in on labor negotiations.

After Connie and I moved to Miami, we would have lunch with my parents—I won't say religiously but certainly most Sundays—in nearby Ocean Ridge during the six months a year they spent there. If there was a football game on, we watched it with them. Dad's best friend, Tom Hoak, had retired to Ocean Ridge from Minneapolis, where he'd been an executive in his family's lumber company. He lived only a couple of miles away, but the two of them, instead of just watching the game together, would be on the phone analyzing every play—you know, a running commentary—while Connie, my mother, and I would just be sitting around. The phone rang every five minutes, and if it didn't, it was because Dad was busy calling Tom. I used to say, "Why don't you just invite him over and you can sit in those two chairs over there?" And Dad would go, "Tom wants to be at home with Mary." "Well then, Dad, you could go over to Tom and Mary's." Anyway, that was the way they wanted it, those two. And Dad had a similar routine going with another close friend who wintered nearby, Leo Spooner, who owned the highest-end clothing store in Duluth—Allenfall's.

Both Tom and Leo were exceptionally good golfers, even better than Dad. If Dad won the Northland Invitational twice, Tom won it four times and Leo fifteen. And Leo had gone on to play in the National Amateur ten times, to Tom's five and Dad's only once.

In 1989, Pete Rozelle, the NFL commissioner for going on thirty years, announced his retirement. One of the old-guard team owners, the founder of the Buffalo Bills, Ralph Wilson, got it into his head that I would make a good commissioner, given my media, marketing, and labor experience. He was on the six-member search committee, along with Wellington Mara of the Giants and Art Rooney of the Pittsburgh Steelers, and he wanted to know if I had any objection to his putting my name forward for the job.

The committee was seriously considering the New Orleans Saints president, Jim Finks, who I knew and admired—he had been the longtime general manager of the Vikings. When Dad, who had stayed in touch with him, mentioned that Ralph Wilson was prepared to recommend *me*, Jim, gentleman that he was, called me to say that if I wanted it, he would withdraw his name. I told him he had nothing to worry about on that score—I mean, how many times was I going to have to repeat to people that I loved the job I had? (The commissioner's job ultimately went to the NFL's Washington counsel, Paul Tagliabue.)

I did truly love my job. My immediate boss, Jim Batten, and I were on the same page. We did pretty much everything together, although he was always happy to have me take on the more challenging business tasks. When there was a downturn in 1991 and we were going to have to cut back on expenses throughout the company, he and I visited most of the newspapers together to stress that budgets were a reality and costs had to be slashed. But I was always the one who did the talking and who was left to take the flak for saying the tough things that needed to be said: the bad cop, the protector of shareholder value, the bearer of bad news.

The staff of the *Philadelphia Inquirer* came up with a nickname for Jim—"Mister Rogers," because he was fundamentally a friendly, soothing kind of guy. For me they thought up "Darth Ridder." Nobody called me that to my face, of course. But it followed me—that nickname stuck, it kept appearing in stories about me. If somebody was going to write something negative, I could count on them to employ the *Star Wars* epithet. Meanwhile, Wall Street was busy singing my praises for my willingness to "take the hard steps" necessary to ensure the success of the business.

The biggest natural disaster on my watch as company president was Hurricane Andrew in August 1992. The *Miami Herald* ended up winning a Pulitzer for its coverage. Connie and I had just left for a long-planned bicycle trip in France, and we were in Paris when the storm picked up speed and was barreling toward Miami as a Category 5. I turned around in my tracks but wasn't able to reach the city until twenty-four hours after Andrew hit. It would end up as the costliest and most destructive hurricane not only in Florida's history but the nation's (until Katrina came calling).

Several of our employees spent the night in the Herald building, which had been constructed to withstand off-the-charts wind speeds. ATM machines had stopped working, but I came equipped with around $10,000 of company cash and handed it out to those in need. There were emergency workers converging on Miami from all parts of the state and from neighboring states, whether to cut down trees and clear off branches and other debris or repair structural damage, and the only way you could get anyone to do anything for you was by paying upfront.

I arranged for the publisher of the *Miami Herald*, who was none other than my old speed-eating competitor Dave Lawrence, to meet me at the newspaper the next morning with a company van and driver and stacks of newspapers. We got driven slowly around the hardest-hit areas of the city, with Dave and me standing on top of the van tossing papers to all the houses—he threw them to one side of the street and I to the other.

I eventually made it home. My house felt like a furnace—large swaths of Greater Miami were without electricity. In short order, President Bush, George H. W., reached out to Alvah, who set the standard for good works in the state, to spearhead a private-sector relief effort. It got tagged "We Will Rebuild," and rebuild they did, I have to hand it to them.

The year after Andrew, I received one of the more gratifying surprises of my life. The former mayor of San Jose, my old friend Tom McEnery, called to inform me that the city had voted to set aside a section of Guadalupe River Park, in the middle of the downtown area, to be named Ridder Plaza in my honor. I was floored. True, I had had real longevity in San Jose—I had lived there for twenty-two years, from December 1, 1964, through February 1, 1986, to

Running in the *San Jose Mercury News* race, 1984.

be exact. Over that period, I had gotten to know a good many of Knight Ridder's 2,000 local employees, not just through work but through company picnics, golf tournaments, Christmas parties, and the *Mercury News* race I started. And that's not counting all the folks I met through my various community endeavors (I had been chairman of the museum, the chamber of commerce, and the county United Way). But people have short memories—when you move on, they're quick to forget you—and by this time I had been gone seven long years (when I *had* been back, it was in my capacity as president of the newspaper division and I would be in town for a day or two only).

Tom added that my contributions to the civic, cultural, and social life of the city were going to be commemorated with a statue of me. I was touched and humbled, but before it could go to my head, he had explained that the statue would be only of my feet. Or not even (but enough already)—it would consist of a pair of oversized brass-plated running shoes, which would, however, be a considerable step up from the beat-up ones I wore. Tom read me what was going to be etched on the plaque: "These shoes symbolize the long run that Tony Ridder made to support and improve San Jose. They are big shoes to fill. If others fill them by following his example of strength, selflessness, and dedication, Tony Ridder will be happy indeed. They will further serve to give children something to aspire to, filling his shoes with their own strength. People of San Jose, 1993."

Connie and I flew out for the dedication ceremony, and in keeping with my "long run," I sprinted to the podium to acknowledge the honor. Then I proceeded to cut the ribbon on the statue and, following that, to lead a crowd on a nature walk through the park. People continue to tell me that when their kids stream out of the adjacent Children's Discovery Museum, they make a beeline for my shoes and take turns stepping into them. I couldn't wait to step into them myself—to fill my own shoes, as it were.

It was around this time that I learned from Jim Batten I could be filling *his* shoes sooner than I had anticipated. One afternoon he

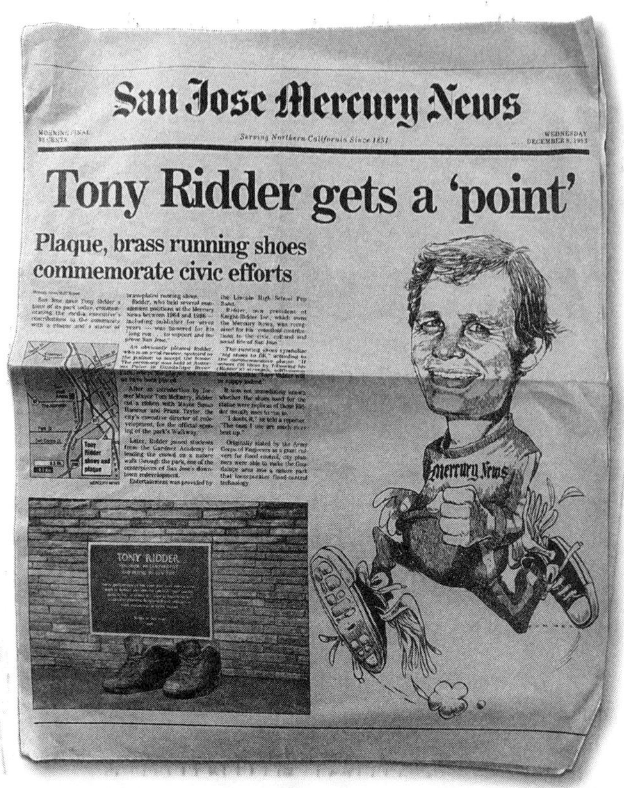

San Jose Mercury News

Serving Northern California Since 1851

Tony Ridder gets a 'point'

Plaque, brass running shoes commemorate civic efforts

took me aside and said, "Tony, I'm fifty-eight and if I stay on till I'm sixty-five and have to step down, that would leave you only five years as CEO until *you* reached sixty-five. I think it only right and fair that we split the difference so each of us is CEO for around the same amount of time." If fate had permitted it to play out this way, Jim would have retired in 1997, three years early, to make way for me.

That October, 1993, he was driving home to Coral Gables from the Miami airport (he'd been on a short trip to buy a second home, in the mountains of North Carolina). Around four in the afternoon, he blacked out for a few seconds and plowed into a steel utility post, hitting his head on the steering wheel. Within the hour I got a call saying that he had been helicoptered to the hospital and was in the ICU, on a ventilator, and might well die. I rushed to the hospital and kept vigil there for four or five hours. When I got home, I had to pour myself a stiff cognac. I lay awake all night—Jim was a whole lot more to me than just my boss. The next day we found out he was going to make it.

After six weeks he returned to work, seemingly none the worse for his brush with death. The only worrying thing was they weren't able to determine what had caused him to lose consciousness in the first place. About six months later he began getting terrible headaches. Connie and I had just arrived in Vail for the Fourth of July, which we celebrated there every year, when Jim called to let me know that they had discovered a brain tumor and were having to operate. I offered to come right back, but he wouldn't hear of it.

The diagnosis was a stage-four glioblastoma, where the patient normally lives for only about a year. The somewhat mitigating news was that the most advanced treatment was available right in Miami.

For a while, Jim managed to make it into the office occasionally, but within a few months I was running the company. He kept insisting he was going to "beat this thing," and he was determined to address the annual KR editors' meeting in January. He had painstakingly written down what he wanted to say but kept having trouble

With Connie, on board Malcolm Forbes's yacht, *Highlander,* sailing up the Hudson River to West Point for the Army-Rice game, early 1990s.

finding his place. It was heartbreaking. Everybody loved Jim. He was a revered leader. He had such great personal and professional values.

He lasted another five months. I would go out to his house every other day or so to fill him in on things, and he would say, "Tony, I sometimes have a little difficulty following what you're saying, but I deeply appreciate your trying to keep me in the loop." When Alvah and the board made me CEO that March, Jim said, "Tony, you deserve it, you're already doing the job—only now that I'm no longer CEO, I don't know what I'm going to do with all my time."

Only much later on did I learn that, at an early point in his illness, Jim had written to reassure the board about me: "Tony is deeply versed in the details of our business and deeply committed to the fundamental importance of editorial quality for KR's successful economic future. He is acutely aware of the obligations of the free press in a free society to provide the free flow of honest, illuminating information that allows it to function successfully. And finally, Tony has a genuine appetite for understanding and, where appropriate, adopting new ways of delivering news and information. He fully understands that we are both a journalistic enterprise and a business."

Jim died that June, leaving behind a loving wife, two sons, and a daughter, not to mention a thriving company (KR had posted almost $3 billion in revenue that year). That same month, the board gave me the additional title of chairman.

On July 13, 1995, just four months from when I was named CEO, approximately 2,500 members of all six labor unions, including the Newspaper Guild and the Brotherhood of Teamsters, at the *Detroit Free Press* and the *Detroit News* went on strike: journalists, pressmen, printers, truck drivers, and maintenance workers. The issue that triggered it was "featherbedding," a restrictive work practice requiring us to hire more people than we needed and to retain that excess staff. Knight Ridder, which owned the *Free Press*, and Gannett, which owned the *News*, were of one mind about publishing a combined edition. The unions were just as determined to do everything in their considerable power to prevent us from publishing.

It was the only strike I was ever personally involved in, and it was visceral and violent. The violence initially took the form of rocks being thrown through the company's windows and at its trucks but soon escalated to steel auto parts (stolen from a local plant) being hurled at the police who were themselves in riot gear and firing pepper spray at the picketers. The strikers' tactics progressed to the illegal blockading of the exits to our production facilities to prevent the trucks from leaving. We, in turn, rented helicopters to take the newspapers over the picket line. During these demonstrations, hundreds of strikers and other protesters were arrested on various criminal charges, which ran the gamut from unlawful assembly and disorderly conduct, to resisting arrest and inciting a riot.

Mitch Albom, author of the mega-bestseller *Tuesdays with Morrie*, was the most popular columnist on the *Detroit Free Press*. When he called to ask my advice on whether he should cross the picket line, I told him that that was up to him. He went ahead and crossed it (along with about forty percent of our editorial staff). It was a big blow to the unions when the paper's biggest-name writer reported to work, and Mitch caught a lot of flak from his unionized colleagues. I need to add how surprised and disappointed I was when he was quoted in the press as saying, "Tony Ridder told me to go back to work."

Each time I visited Detroit I had to arrange to be picked up at the airport by a blacked-out van driven by an armed undercover policeman. During the strike, we held our annual meeting in Philadelphia. As the unions there were supportive of the Detroit unions, we had to have a police escort to the hotel where the meeting was taking place. Accompanied by heavy-duty security, we walked into the room to chants of "Tony Ridder hires scabs."

Early in 1997 I was invited by the University of Michigan to moderate a panel of four distinguished speakers marking the forty-fifth anniversary of the founding of the Marshall Scholars program. The subject was a popular one—how technology was changing the media—and there were hundreds of people in attendance. The provost handily introduced me, but when I looked out over the audience, my eye was drawn to the Teamsters massed in the back of the room. They immediately began shouting me down. The provost made an attempt to quiet them, but they were already too unruly. She then announced a short break during which she disappeared offstage to summon the campus police. Before restarting the program and turning it over to the panelists, she helpfully suggested I exit the building by the back door. My sister Laura and her husband were in the audience, and she later told me that the moment she saw me leave, she became frightened not only for my safety but, somewhat unaccountably, for her own.

I made my way to the lot where I had parked my rental car, then headed for the freeway and the airport. Suddenly a van pulled up behind me, then alongside me; its blacked-out windows rolled down, and stones were thrown. This persisted all the way to the next two exits, where they turned off. I was badly shaken. I had naively believed that this time, because I was in Detroit on non-newspaper business, I could get away with having no security.

February 14, 1997, was the day we finally settled—after nineteen months—one of the most bitterly fought labor battles of the 1990s. A fortuitous offshoot of my previous labor-negotiating experience in San Jose was a friendship with Chuck Dale, the international president of the Newspaper Guild, which was the largest union in Detroit, representing as it did the newsrooms of the two papers, including the clerical people. Working now with Chuck and the Gannett labor negotiator, we huddled with the Guild in a session that lasted until seven in the morning, at the Marriott Hotel at Dulles Airport (the Guild headquarters were in D.C.), thus paving the way for the five other unions to fall into place.

When KR refused to fire any of the replacement workers who had showed up every day during the strike, the National Labor Relations Board ruled that we were engaging in unfair labor practices. We appealed, and the ruling was reversed by federal courts in 2000.

Although we lost at least $100 million (in advertising, circulation, and related expenses), we set a record in the American newspaper business for the first time a big-city unionized newspaper was successfully published and distributed in the face—in the teeth—of a strike.

CHAPTER SIXTEEN

Embracing and Enforcing Inclusivity

JIM BATTEN HAD believed deeply in the importance—the necessity—of diversity. I couldn't have agreed more—our newsroom and sales staff needed to reflect the community we served. I redoubled the company's commitment to diversity at all levels, from the top down. As CEO, I increased considerably the percentage of women editors, publishers, and officers. One of our five senior VPs was a woman, as were seven or eight of our twenty other corporate officers. And we put three women on the board.

We had come a long way from how Ridder Publications looked when we merged with Knight in 1974. In those benighted days, white males—most of them Ridders—held all the publisher jobs, and there were no women serving as top editors. My great-uncles had all been "violently opposed" to what they called "skirt control." There's a letter in the company archives from one of them vowing that "as long as I have anything to say about it, our business will be run by men."

I also thought it a good idea to have a Hispanic or two on our board since we were headquartered in a community where they predominated. My first appointee was the head of Barclays Bank for Latin America. I also put a highly qualified African American on the board—a professor at the Harvard Business School, Jim Cash.

We already had three Black publishers and several Black editors.

Soon after I became president of KR, I plucked Jay Harris out of the *Philadelphia Daily News,* where he was executive editor, to be my executive assistant (a position I continued to use as a training ground to develop outstanding newspaper leaders). A year later, I elevated him to VP of operations, with responsibility for nine of our smaller newspapers: with that promotion, he became the highest-ranking African American not only in the company but in the entire industry—the most influential minority newspaper executive in the country. And when Larry Jinks retired from the *Mercury News* in 1994 (he had relinquished the executive editorship of the newspaper in 1981 to become senior VP for news and operations in Miami and then returned to San Jose in 1989 as publisher), I replaced him with Jay.

In 2004, the year I was president of ANPA, I pushed through a program to train minorities (a classification that at the time included women, believe it or not) for newspaper management. These were all people who already occupied management positions but needed additional training in order to maintain them. We set up weeklong sessions at Northwestern and at Harvard where we used the facilities of their Nieman Foundation for Journalism.

I came down especially hard on sexual harassment. One of our key people in San Jose—he ran the circulation and advertising departments and was also someone I played golf with every now and then—was reliably accused of making suggestive comments to women in general and, specifically, of badgering a woman who worked under him to go out with him. His wife worked for us as well, in a different department (they had gotten together when they were both already at the paper). I had no choice but to let him go. Knight Ridder meant business when it came to what's now known as Me Too, and we made that known publicly.

I mandated training throughout the company, including for our corporate and news executives. People had to be educated to understand that sexual harassment could consist of having nude photographs on display at work or of even just embodying—projecting—the wrong attitude. I attended the sessions myself.

We had gay people throughout our company—one of our senior VPs lived openly with another woman and brought her to board dinners. One of the early inclusionary advances I authorized when I became CEO was healthcare benefits for same-sex partners. There was pushback—some of our publishers balked, I regret to say. I remember the publisher in Wichita having a tough time with that. Look, it's not like we were the first public company to do it—Disney had done it, for example—but I believe we were the first newspaper company.

Uncle Joe, once he got to Hawaii, lived out in the open with another man for years. A genuinely nice guy, too: Ted Sheridan, a Stanford grad, and a good influence on him. At some point after I moved to San Jose in the mid-'60s I had gone to Dad and said, "I think Uncle Joe might be gay." He said, "Oh, I know, Tony," and that was all there was to it, ever.

Another thing I did when I became CEO was make it company policy that our newspapers each contribute a minimum of two percent of their pretax profit to their community organizations—I had that built into their budgets. I believed that, when you owned a newspaper, the journalism you provided was not the only way you should serve. I considered the communities where we had papers to be among our constituencies, along with our advertisers, employees, and shareholders. Along with D for Diversity, E for Equity, and I for Inclusion, I was a cheerleader for C for Community.

CHAPTER SEVENTEEN

Enmeshed in the Web

I HAD BEEN saving for the proverbial rainy day, systematically unloading our relatively unprofitable cable interests and information-services operations such as Knight Ridder Financial. Now that the time had come to establish the company as an online media business as well as a newspaper enterprise, we had the wherewithal to do it.

As far back as the mid-1970s when I was not yet publisher of the *Mercury News*, I had become friendly with many tech innovators and avatars—Andy Grove, Bill Hewlett, Dave Packard, Gordon Moore ... I was struck by how many of these founding fathers had started out working for other companies. Take Gene Amdahl, who was working for IBM when he came up with the idea of building a giant mainframe computer and said to himself, "Wait a second, why don't I go out on my own?" Ergo, Amdahl "plug-compatible" computers. That was Silicon Valley for you in a nutshell, and that's what it still is, if to a lesser extent: someone gets a lightbulb idea when they're working for somebody else and runs with it—or runs off with it, depending on your point of view. Newly minted billionaires are practically a dime a dozen these days. There have been plenty of lawsuits, of course, with IBM and other mega-companies suing former employees for supposedly stealing their intellectual property. To be a patent lawyer in Silicon Valley can be a very lucrative little gig.

Starting in the early 1990s, by which time I was president of KR, I devoted a good deal of time and money to the internet space and worked diligently to grow that part of our business. I was good at reading the signals, though I wouldn't go as far as to claim I was any kind of visionary. I simply recognized the potential of digital as the agent of fundamental product reinvention and the gateway to a brave new world of computing. Our efforts in crossing the electronic frontier were gratifyingly validated by the price of our stock.

Along the way, I endured a lot of criticism for my advocacy of digital. Instead of support, I encountered resistance from the business side and the sales and marketing staff, as well as consternation and dissension in the newsroom. People were worried that I was undercutting our core business and pressed me to stay focused on revenue-producing print. Intellectually, they understood why I was doing what I was doing, but at the same time they felt it wasn't the best use of the company's resources. It was certainly true that developing and evolving digital was going to entail stinting print. It was one of those short-term-vs-long-term propositions—you're trying to build a business by diverting resources from an existing one, you're stealing from Peter to pay Paul. To mix the metaphor, you have to eat your seed corn. Over my dead body were we going to wind up like the buggy whip company of yesteryear that became obsolete without even knowing what hit it, because it hadn't seen the "horseless carriage" coming—that is, the dawning of the auto age. We needed to get right on top of this coming thing.

In 1992 I appointed Bob Ingle, the executive editor of the *Mercury News*, someone who had had experience with electronic systems, the company point man to develop a business plan and create a platform to get the newspaper digitized ASAP. By early the next year, we were able to launch what we were calling Mercury Center, the first news site that was accessible online. This version of our newspaper was made available to subscribers through a dial-up service provided by AOL, which we were the first newspaper to use. In 1995 we switched to Netscape—we were *their* first paying customer, too—which enabled us to deliver the paper on the World Wide Web, complete with a search feature called Newshound.

We made the decision to offer access for free to maximize the size of our audience, which was, after all, what we were selling to advertisers. It worked like a charm: Mercury Center proceeded to draw 1.2 million unique visitors monthly and, in 1996, was ranked the country's best Web newspaper by *Editor & Publisher.* The *Mercury News*, for its part, was acclaimed the most internet-savvy paper in the country by *Time* magazine, and Knight Ridder was rated by *InformationWeek* the most innovative newspaper-company user of technology (out of 1,200 surveyed). We were on a roll.

1995 was also the year we joined forces with other leading newspaper publishers, including the New York Times Company, the Tribune Company, and the Washington Post Company. Each of us contributed a million dollars to set up an aggregate website called New Century Networks (NCN): a platform that would offer the most comprehensive package of advertising services and news content. With this venture, there turned out to be too many cooks in the kitchen—the Times had their idea of how to do things, we had ours, and so forth—and by 1997 it was toast.

At a meeting with Knight Ridder editors from across the country soon after I became CEO, I had been asked what kept me up at night. I replied, "Electronic classifieds," and that was used time and again to disparage me. But it was all too true. Electronic classified did pose the biggest threat to high-quality journalism. To that end, we concentrated on the largest category in electronic classified—employment. We started CareerPath.com with eight other companies, including Times Mirror and the New York Times. Same old problem—too many decision-makers at the table. We were never able to function as enough of a unit to get things cooking on all four burners.

In 1997 we hit on something that did go places. With fewer other companies involved, we started ClassicVentures.com, which consisted of Cars.com for people looking for a new or used auto, and Apartments.com for those looking to sell, buy, or rent. Cars.com turned out to be the more lucrative category by far.

In 2000 we took another run at classified employment. This time, we teamed up with only one partner, the Tribune company, to acquire an already going business, one with competent management, the Chicago-based recruitment site CareerBuilder.com, for $200 million. It was a good fit with our respective newspapers (the Trib had just purchased Times Mirror), and one of the first things we did was integrate all our "help wanted" sections. And a year later, in pursuit of even greater dominance in the electronic employment category, we paid another $200 million for the Atlanta-based job-recruiting site Headhunter.net and combined it with CareerBuilder. In 2002 we brought in Gannett, with its ninety newspapers, as a one-third partner. CareerBuilder was a real winner for us. It eventually muscled out its chief competitor, Monster.com, to become the biggest and most successful employment site on the web.

So: Homes, cars, jobs—we had all those categories covered.

This big push to build up our internet interests depended on the support of not only management but our publishers, editors, and ad directors as well. I was getting a lot of pushback that Bob Ingle was short-tempered, rude, and otherwise impossible to deal with. I must confess that I had always had trouble picturing him selling sweet corn door to door in his native Iowa, which was something he would tell people he had once done. He never understood that being the boss didn't mean just ordering everyone around. That doesn't work nearly as well as trying to convince them that what you want done—what you should be asking, not ordering, them to do—is the right thing. *That's* what leadership is.

We could no longer put up with Bob alienating the very people whose cooperation was essential to our success (and doing it in the face of the best efforts of his number two, Kathy Yates, a very capable Stanford Business School graduate who had been general manager of the *Mercury News).* In 1999 I moved him out of KR Digital to our internet-investing arm. He could now spend all day by himself figuring out which start-ups to recommend we provide seed money for in our role as quasi-venture capitalists.

Bob did an excellent job there on the whole. He brought Elon Musk to my office. I had no idea who he was—actually, he *wasn't* anybody, or at least anybody to speak of, at the time. He had a company called Zip2, his first company, kind of an online Yellow Pages—a searchable directory for local businesses that came with mapping software. I remember how nervous he was when he pitched me. He struck me as a rather strange individual, and I recall commenting to that effect the minute he left the room. We wound up buying about twenty percent of his company. It wasn't what I would call a home run, but we made money. Bob had also recommended that we invest in Netscape when it was just starting up, and we joined with Hearst, Adobe, and Times Mirror to buy an eleven percent stake. It went public about a year and a half later, the stock skyrocketed, and we realized a windfall.

We dropped the internet ball spectacularly only once. In the mid-1990s, Bob came to me with an auction startup he said we could have around twenty percent of for around $25 million. I was hesitant because, still believing strongly in the future of print journalism, I had just finalized the biggest and most expensive newspaper acquisition in history, paying Disney $1.65 billion for a package of four newspapers: *The Kansas City Star*, the *Fort Worth Star-Telegram*, the *Wilkes-Barre* [Pennsylvania] *Times Leader*, and the *Belleville* [Illinois] *News-Democrat.* That same year, I had traded the [Boulder] *Daily Camera* to Scripps for their *Monterey County Herald* and *San Luis Obispo Tribune.* And two years before, we had purchased the Bay Area's *Contra Costa Times* for around $365 million. Newspapers were still very much our bread and butter, accounting for eighty-five percent of our revenue and nearly all our profit.

I told Bob we could invest *either* in this auction thing *or* in a company that he'd been talking up for a long time, Golf.com, a news site that also sold merchandise. "We can't do both," I reiterated. "You choose." He said, "Let's do the golf." But later he went around telling people, "I brought eBay to Tony and he turned it down." I called him on that. I said, "Goddamn it, Bob, why don't you tell the whole story? That I gave you the choice. That you're the one who picked Golf.com, and where the hell is *that* today."

Anybody who reported to me, if and when the time came for them to be let go, I always personally fired. I believed that if there was unwelcome news to be delivered, I should be the one delivering it. I continue to be amazed at how many chief executives have other people do the dirty work for them.

Bob I fired only after discovering that behind my back, and not only on company time but using company resources and coopting company employees, he was attempting to put together some sort of internet startup of his own. He was abusing his position, the position I had given him, to raise money for his own purposes, and from some of the same people we were investing in. All in all, it amounted to a direct conflict of interest—gross misconduct, in fact. He even had the gall to solicit one of my closest friends, Don Lucas. Don called me and said, "Tony, I feel awkward about this, but I feel you should know ..."

I had our general counsel do a little spadework—make that a lot of forensic investigating. She accessed Bob's KR emails, and the evidence she assembled was so egregious that both she and our top HR person concluded it was tantamount to stealing. At Knight Ridder, unlike many other Fortune 500 companies, we allowed employees who'd been terminated to leave with their dignity intact. The only circumstance where we would demand that someone vacate the building immediately was if we had caught them red-handed. I called Bob in and laid it all out. I said, "That's it, you're out of here." And I walked him to the elevator and showed him the proverbial door.

CHAPTER EIGHTEEN

Entering the Arena

You would be right to think I had more than enough on my plate in February 1996, what with engineering KR's journey into digital, in addition to overseeing thirty-two newspapers and coping with the growing demands of institutional shareholders. But I was also a concerned citizen of Miami and was avidly following the travails and tribulations of the CEO and chairman of the biggest company in town (KR, not incidentally, was number two), the Carnival Corporation, the world's largest cruise operator. Micky Arison was also the sole owner of the NBA Miami Heat expansion team and, as such, was deeply entangled in trying to convince the city to build him a new arena downtown.

The Heat was playing in an arena that had been built (with public money, a then stupendous $53 million) in Miami's Liberty City neighborhood just eight years before. This facility was out of date practically from the day it opened, thanks to inadequate revenue-producing extras such as skyboxes and premium seating. It lacked adequate seating capacity at all levels, as a matter of fact. Micky now had his eye on a choice thirty-acre parcel a few blocks from the arena. Because it was land that had been purchased by the county in the early '70s for a projected park, there was, shall we say, heated opposition.

The day the *Miami Herald* ran a story that the new arena was dead in the water, I hastily arranged a meeting with Micky. He told me outright that he was giving serious thought to teaming up with his fellow Florida billionaire Wayne Huizenga, the rough-around-the-edges Waste Management, Blockbuster Video, and AutoNation mogul, on an arena to be built twenty-five miles away, on the edge of the Everglades. Wayne, whose ice hockey team, the NHL's Florida Panthers, had been sharing the Miami Arena with the Heat since 1993, had recently obtained construction approval from Broward County and was predicting that the new facility would be up and running by 1998, loaded with revenue-producing prerequisites: seventy skyboxes and 2,600 club seats.

I could see that Micky was all but reconciled to the idea of an arena on the outskirts, his hard-won rationale being that, when push came to shove, season holders would be willing to venture as far as West Broward County for the Heat's home games. The team was almost certainly headed there till I got into the middle of the muddle, and, frankly, had I not come along, that's where they would undoubtedly be playing today.

What business was this of mine, you might well ask. The question of an upgraded arena for a professional sports team was of major economic significance to Miami—it would create scores of new jobs, provide additional tax revenue, and altogether help to promote a big-league image for the city. And what was good for Miami was good for the *Miami Herald* and, by extension, Knight Ridder.

Micky gave me forty days to come up with a feasible plan. I worked the phones to put together an ad hoc committee of leading citizens, then called a meeting for 3:00 p.m. a couple of days later in our corporate headquarters on the top floor of the Herald Building. My fifteen committee members didn't begin drifting into our conference room till a quarter past, or even later, and during the meeting I noticed several of them either talking on their phones or looking at their watches. Better to do it all on my own, I felt, and I disbanded the committee.

This wasn't my first foray into public advocacy, mind you. I had put my foot in once before. Way back in 1972, when I was business manager of the *Mercury News*, I had led the effort to build a badly needed sports and entertainment arena in San Jose. The newsroom took a dim view of my involvement, snidely referring to it as "Tony's toy," but I persisted because—again—the arena would be a good thing for the city and—again—what was good for the city was good for the newspaper and the company as a whole. The proposition was approved two to one by the city, but a year later, the state passed a law requiring approval by the voters of the county. We were in a recession by that time, and folks were understandably nervous about extra spending, so we lost. The effort was revived in the late '80s, and the San Jose arena got built, and it's been a roaring success.

Anyway, back—or rather, forward—to the Miami arena. I met regularly with the county manager and board of supervisors, the mayor of Miami, and the heads of the port authority, the Dade County Commission, the Miami City Commission, and the Miami Sports and Exhibition Authority. The *Herald* published several editorials, news stories, and columns in favor of the new arena. None of them were my doing: I did not direct the news coverage of *any* of our papers—our people were at liberty to criticize my plan, and even me personally, with impunity. But, as was the case with the San Jose endeavor, the feeling on the part of the newsroom was that the top executive should ideally not be making news that they would then be required to cover impartially.

I was lauded and lambasted in just about equal measure in the general press. I laughed when I saw myself described as a "veritable Shaquille O'Neal in downtown Miami's corridors of power." But I was anything but amused when my critics got together and placed an ad in the *Herald* featuring a cartoon of Micky and me disparaging the public as "chumps"—a sentiment that I have never subscribed to and a word that, in any case, I would never have used.

In concert with the board of supervisors, I hired a well-respected deal-making consultant and set him up with an office in KR's corporate department. With Micky's deadline coercively in mind, we structured a plan for me to present in person to the city council and county board. And once it was in hand, I was able to persuade them to vote in favor of the proposal to construct an arena on the aforementioned parcel bordering Biscayne Bay and to put their money where their mouths were. We quickly settled on the amount of their respective contributions.

Micky was my last stop. The day I was scheduled to run the numbers by him he happened to be hosting a grand opening for one of his 100,000-ton Carnival Cruise bruisers, so the meeting was held on board ship. I outlined the terms, to all of which he was readily agreeable. Late that afternoon when Connie and I were driving to Ocean Ridge for dinner with my parents, we turned the radio on and all the talk on all the talk shows was of the arena.

A prominent member of the Dade County board of commissioners—Alex Penelas, who would shortly be elected the first Cuban American mayor of Miami-Dade County—had been vehemently opposed to the arena and was outvoted. He didn't take his defeat lying down: rather, he upped and joined forces with a high-profile environmental and First Amendment lawyer named Dan Paul, who in 1974, as the *Miami Herald*'s legal counsel, had won a decisive victory for Knight Ridder in the U.S. Supreme Court in an important freedom-of-the-press case (the company was challenging a Florida law that required newspapers to give equal space to the opponents of political candidates they endorsed). Paul and Panelas formed a "Stop New Arena Committee," which mounted a petition drive to gather enough signatures to put the issue to the county electorate.

I didn't think they could pull it off, but they did. By claiming, among other things, that voting against the arena would save taxpayers money, they were able to gather some 48,000 signatures, more than enough to have a referendum placed on the ballot. At that point, in order to gain the support of Panelas and Paul, Micky increased his contribution.

When this political issue went what today would be called viral, it would have been inappropriate for me, as the CEO of the company that owned the *Miami Herald*, to continue being directly involved and I stepped down—bowed out, withdrew to the sidelines. To my bemusement, in 2015, at the behest of various activist groups, the county-owned five-acre waterfront parcel directly behind the arena that Dan Paul had fought so hard to prevent being built was turned into a park posthumously named for him.

Speaking of naming, the mayor of Miami amazed me by announcing his intention to move to have the new arena named for *me*. There was a history, a tradition, in Miami of calling streets after civic leaders and prominent politicians but, to my knowledge, stadiums and arenas were almost always named for the companies that underwrote them—the only exceptions I could think of were Madison Square Garden and Yankee Stadium. I declined the tribute, because the naming rights needed to be sold to the highest corporate bidder.

Ground for the new arena was broken in late January 1998. Designed and constructed at a cost of $213 million by the world-renowned Miami-based architectural firm Arquitectonica, it opened on New Year's Eve 1999 with a concert by Gloria Estefan (Wayne Huizenga had beat us to the punch—his arena in Broward County for the Florida Panthers had opened the previous year with a concert by Celine Dion, followed the next day by a performance by Elton John). Named the American Airlines Arena, aka Triple-A or A3 (cubed), it boasted a jumbo aircraft with an AA logo painted on its solar reflecting roof. The sleek, dynamic building had a seating capacity of 20,000, including 2,100 club seats and eighty skyboxes. Two days later, the Heat played its first game in the new arena, triumphing over the Orlando Magic.

I had done more than my bit for the city of Miami—little knowing that in no time I would be moving Knight Ridder out.

CHAPTER NINETEEN

Disaster in Alaska

My sister Robin, my junior by nine years, was happily, not to say ecstatically, married to a debonair Swiss gent by the name of Alain Resor.

She had had a previous husband, our mother having pushed her, at twenty-two, into marriage to the young man she was living with in what Mummy considered sin. He was, like Robin, a graduate of the University of California at Santa Barbara—a sunny guy who never really did very much other than surf. They bummed around Europe for a couple of years, then bought an old thirty-five-foot wooden boat to sail the Mediterranean. They finally got around to sailing it home, across the Atlantic and through the canal and up the coast of California, ultimately arriving in Long Beach, her husband's home port. At that point, Robin decided that her marriage of four years had come full circle—to naught.

In the wake of her divorce, she came to live with Connie and me and our kids in Saratoga, but half a year into her stay she startled me by saying, "Tony, I'm starting to feel like I'm your oldest child—I'm out of here." She moved to Berkeley for a year of trying to find herself. Then, still at something of a loss, she found her way to Alaska and put down stakes in a quaint little village called Halibut Cove (picture boardwalks and, if you can, a floating post office). It was accessible only by boat, water taxi, float plane, or helicopter, and its population was only around sixty at the time. But it was just twelve miles from the halibut-fishing capital of the world, Homer, which had been settled in the first decades of the twentieth century by Scandinavians following a rich herring run there.

Herring *and* halibut be damned, Robin plunged into salmon fishing. It was just the kind of life she aspired to, and she loved every minute of it. At some point, she decided to take a break from the fishing and took a trip to Indonesia, which is where she caught Alain's eye.

From then on, Robin's routine consisted of spending winters with her new husband in Bern, where he owned and ran a contracting business that had been started by his father, and summers with him in Alaska. She and a business partner owned a salmon-fishing boat, and during the season they took turns going out with the nets. It was an around-the-clock endeavor, and one of them would sleep while the other fished. They then iced their catch, which was mostly king, or Chinook, the biggest and choicest (thanks to its buttery texture) of the Pacific salmon, and sold it to a wholesaler to prepare and distribute to, first, the Last Frontier State and then the lower forty-eight.

On visits to Robin and Alain, Connie and I would stay in this very rudimentary house she had. She served us, as you might expect, a lot of salmon fresh from the water that was out-of-this-world. She had all sorts of ways of fixing it—grilled, broiled, fried, fileted, pan-seared, baked, you name it. I would go as far as to say that Robin's king salmon dishes were regal.

The only problem in the marriage was that, when she and Alain were in Halibut Cove, she was working and he was at loose ends. In refreshing contrast to her first husband, Alain got bored doing nothing. One day out of the wild blue yonder, he announced that he wanted to become a bush pilot—a particularly high-risk profession, requiring, as it did, training well beyond standard private piloting. He persevered and succeeded in obtaining his license.

Halibut Cove, the fishing village in Alaska where my sister Robin put down roots in the 1990s.

Alain had a brother who lived in Switzerland, and the brother and his girlfriend made an annual pilgrimage to Halibut Cove. They decided to spend the first part of their visit in 1997 camping out on a lake three or four miles from town, where the scenery was particularly salient. Alain dropped them off in his plane and a few days later returned to pick them up.

Taking off with his two passengers, he taxied down the lake, but as he approached the end of it, he must have realized he was going to have a problem clearing the trees, despite the wings of his bush plane being mounted on top of the fuselage to ensure adequate ground clearance. Not getting the lift he needed and with precious little margin for error, he must have desperately attempted to turn the plane around when what he should have done was kill the engine. He wasn't all that far above the surface—the plane would simply have sunk slowly into the water with its wings up, and they would probably all have survived. Instead—Alain's downfall, along with his two passengers'—the plane lost altitude suddenly, dropping like a rock to the bottom, and they all drowned.

Robin, obliviously, was out fishing for her vaunted king salmon when her husband became a statistic (occupational bush-plane pilot deaths run on average two to four times higher in Alaska than anywhere else in the U.S., amounting to some forty fatalities a year).

Our family left immediately for Alaska: Connie and I and our daughter Susie, my brother Peter, my sisters Jill and Laura and Laura's husband Ned, and Mummy and Dad. By the time we arrived, the three bodies, and all the personal effects, had been recovered by the sheriff's department and helicoptered to the funeral home in Homer. I went with Robin to the mortuary to collect Alain's wallet and watch. That was a gulp moment, to be sure, but Robin, more power to her, has always been an extraordinarily strong person—much as she loved Alain, there were no waterworks, or any other kind of carrying on.

On a previous visit to Alaska, Connie and I and our daughter Linda experienced what could safely be described as a near-death experience. One evening, we set out with Robin from Halibut Cove on her skiff, a twenty-foot rowboat with an outboard engine. When we reached Homer, we piled into her beat-up old pickup to drive an hour or so north to the marina where her commercial-fishing boat was docked alongside a slew of others. The idea was for us to get to see her boat and then have a general look around—to take the measure of Robin in her element, the element she had literally thrown herself into.

When the fishing opened at midnight, we said so long to Robin and drove back to the skiff, confident we would be able to find our way home to Halibut Cove over the open water (the gaping forty-mile-long Kachemak Bay). But the water was choppy and there turned out to be no visible marker of any sort, not even a sliver of moon. About halfway there, we ran into big trouble, and I mean big: a mega-ton freighter bearing down on us. We were only just able to maneuver ourselves out of harm's way.

Reversing course, we headed straight back to Homer and checked into the nearest motel. The three of us flopped down on the king-size bed—we just lay on top of it, drained of the energy it would take to slip under the covers. The sun rises early in Alaska, and at first light—the dawning of the legendary reddish-pink alpenglow—we were out of there. Later that day, Robin confessed that immediately after we left, she had realized her mistake in letting us try to make it to Halibut Cove by ourselves. It's hard not to look at this narrow-miss adventure as some kind of prelude to the full-blown tragedy that lay ahead of us, on the far horizon.

A couple of days after Alain's accident, we were notified that a married couple who lived in a house on the island in the middle of that infernal lake had witnessed it. We decided to visit the site as a family and get their first-hand account. Dad was in no shape to make the trek, the last part of which would be on foot through taxing terrain, we were cautioned. Despite having been a champion squash player in his youth, he had shunned all forms of exercise since around the end of World War II. From the minute the golf cart was invented, which was when he was pushing forty, he never walked on the green if he could help it, whereas *I* always walked all eighteen holes, and Mummy always walked. When Connie and I lived in Miami, we would play golf with my parents at Gulf Stream, and Dad never failed to take the cart. He got out willingly only to hit a ball, at which point Mummy got in and drove away down the fairway so he'd be forced to walk to at least where his shot was. He grumbled all the livelong way.

Robin, understandably, chose not to accompany us to the scene of the disaster but enlisted a friend to serve as our guide. I tried to talk my then nearly-eighty-year-old mother out of going on what was sure to shape up as an exhausting hike. But she had retained her Delano gumption and wasn't about to let *us* go and fill her in afterward—she wanted to see, and hear, for herself.

Alain's brother's grown children had meanwhile arrived. The funeral service, conducted by a local priest, unfolded on Robin's deck. Alain's best friend, a retired investment banker by the name of Vincent Stecht, a pleasant, outgoing type of guy, was also on deck that afternoon, and Robin ended up marrying him.

She's kept Ridder as her name through all three marriages. She and Vincent spend most of every year at the small farm Robin owns in Healdsburg, seventy miles north of San Francisco, in the middle of Sonoma County wine-growing country, and a month or so in her snug house in Halibut Cove. She's long since given up catching fish. But not, thank heaven, cooking it.

CHAPTER TWENTY

Moving Coast to Coast

AT VARIOUS TIMES since becoming CEO, I had asked myself a rhetorical question: What was KR doing in a backwater like Miami where the economy was mostly just trade and tourism? Aside from us and Carnival Cruise Lines, the largest companies in South Florida were Royal Caribbean, Ryder System (rental trucks), Latin American banks, and multinational companies that had their American headquarters there because it was an easy commute to Bogotá, Caracas, Buenos Aires, and so forth.

We needed to be more in the mainstream, and I had given serious consideration to relocating the company to New York, Washington, D.C., or Philadelphia. But it wasn't until 1998, when we were having a terrible time luring high-caliber talent to our digital division because the most desirable candidates were averse to working out of Miami, that I began pressing strenuously for a move.

I called a meeting of my top twelve corporate people, and to my surprise they unanimously agreed that it would indeed be in the best interests of KR to move. I charged our CFO with estimating the likely cost of such a move. He came up with the doable figure of $25 million, which included severance, transportation, and the rental and refurbishing of new headquarters. I then put the $64,000 question to the group, "*Where* do you think we should move?" Again to my surprise, there was unanimity: San Jose. Several of my colleagues admitted it would hardly be their first choice of a place to live, but added that if we *were* going to relocate, how could it *not* be to Silicon Valley, where our senior employees could be strategically exposed to a dynamic new business culture? (Once we were firmly established there, I arranged for on-site visits with senior managers at a host of high-tech companies.)

Largely as a courtesy, I previewed the idea of the move to Alvah a month before bringing it up to the full board. He really let me have it: "You can't do that, Tony! San Jose is a *Ridder* city, and Knight Ridder needs to stay in a *Knight* city." I was stunned to hear him, of all people, come out with something like that. Alvah had been proclaiming, from the minute the ink was signed on the merger contract in 1974, that there were no Ridder or Knight cities anymore, that they were all Knight Ridder cities, and that we were one big happy integrated family. He had always been the chief mouthpiece for how united we were. Well, that turned out to be just a line, didn't it?

When I did finally ask the board for approval of the move, only Alvah objected. "You're moving way too fast, Tony," he rebuked me. "This is not a decision that should be made today. I move that we postpone it until the next board meeting." That was three months away: clearly—transparently—he was playing for time to lobby board members, and maybe even the Greater Miami community, against the move. His motion was denied, and I announced, "There's a motion and a second to move the company." As expected, everybody else voted in favor.

Around this time, I came to the realization that we should really have an age limit for board members. This was somewhat controversial—a lot of boards had no age limits. George Shultz, for example, was continued on Chuck Schwab's board well into his eighties. I proposed that the age limit be set at seventy and that we grandfather those who were older so they could finish out their terms. Alvah had a couple of years to go.

Directly after the board meeting, I put in calls to the governor of Florida, the mayor of Miami-Dade County, the chairman of the county board of supervisors, the president of the Greater Miami Chamber of Commerce, and the CEOs of Carnival Cruise Lines and Royal Caribbean. I informed them, one after the other, that we would be leaving town—I wanted them to hear the news directly from me. Knight Ridder's defection was certain to be experienced as not only an economic but a symbolic blow to the city. I gave each of them my word that we would continue to play an active role in Miami's civic affairs and contribute to South Florida causes.

Alvah came out publicly against the move, playing the tired old hardship-on-employees card. But when I convened the entire KR corporate staff to announce it, I had stated that the financial arrangements would include generous relocation expenses to what was, after all, the state with the highest income tax in the country. I had also made clear we weren't going to have to lay anybody off, since we were keeping some corporate functions in Miami (it went without saying that the combined workforce of the *Miami Herald* and *El Nuevo Herald*, which numbered around 2,000, would stay in place). Gratifyingly, more than sixty out of 150 accepted the offer to move.

Subsequently, somebody mentioned to me that the bestselling novelist Carl Hiaasen, whose column ran in the *Miami Herald* a couple of times a week, had based a character in his then latest book on me. It was a detective story-cum-satire called *Basket Case*, about the downscaling and diminishing of American newspapers. My character, Race Maggad III, was described as a "greedy, profit-hungry, soulless guy who ran a newspaper empire ... a money-grubbing yupster twit." And not unlike me, he liked to drive fast cars—thus his name, "Race." When he moved his company headquarters to California, "a corporate press release claimed that the reason was to capitalize on the dynamic, high-tech workforce in California. The truth is more banal. Race Maggad wanted to live in a climate where he could drive his German sports car year-round, far from the ravages of winter. The salt damage to his Carrera alone was rumored to be in the five figures."

Hiaasen was taking a page from longtime GE chairman Jack Welch who had had the nerve to say to one of our KR board members, who was also on *his* board, that my moving Knight Ridder to San Jose was a personal life-style choice—to enable me to play more golf at Cypress Point. Jack was a smart aleck—that remark fit with his personality. He meant less than nothing to me, he was just someone I knew from golf. In fact, the last time I ever saw him was in the locker room of the Sankaty Head Golf Club on Nantucket, which, remember, was where my father and mother first met, and he made another smart-ass remark—it rolled off me, and I walked away.

I ran into Hiaasen about ten years ago in the clubhouse at Cypress Point—he was just a guest whereas I was president of the club, so technically he was *my* guest. We had the opposite of a run in—a very friendly conversation, in fact. I brought up the novel, saying something jocular like, "How come I've only made it into *one* of your books?" He laughed and said, "Do you want me to put you in more books? I'd be happy to." So, he was being as good a sport about it as I was.

What I had always admired about his column in the *Herald* was how he would poke fun at certain leading citizens of Miami—often deservedly, in my opinion. He was provocative but not, I didn't think, irresponsible. Take his skewering of one of the biggest home-construction companies in the country, Lennar. It had built thousands of houses in South Florida, maybe tens of thousands, but a lot of them were shoddily constructed, by which I mean their roofs were flying off. The founder of Lennar, Len Miller, was a friend of Jim Batten's and Alvah's—didn't matter, Hiaasen was not a columnist who could be reined in. Not for nothing was one of his three volumes of selected columns titled *Kick Ass*.

Dave Barry wrote a nationally syndicated column for the *Herald* for about twenty years and even won a Pulitzer for his use of humor in serious commentary, but he would never single anybody out—he had a softer edge than Hiaasen. I would regularly invite him to speak at KR publisher meetings, and when I was chairman of the NAA, I featured him at an executive-committee meeting up at Napa. He always went over in a big way.

Even after moving the company to San Jose, I made it a point to hold the January meeting of the board in Miami, as a gesture of friendship and solidarity with the city. And I always invited Alvah and Betty to the dinner we customarily held the night before the meeting, in a private room at Joe's Stone Crab, the most famous restaurant in that part of the world. At some point between courses, I would get up and say a few words about KR's continuing financial support of Miami causes and I would give a shout out to Alvah just to make him feel good—nobody I would ever know had more of an appetite for adulation.

I was in Hawaii when he died in 2008—on Christmas Day, wouldn't you know it? Without the slightest hesitation I abandoned a good game of golf to fly from Kona to Honolulu, where there was a layover, and then on to Dallas, where there was another layover, and finally to Miami. With no time to spare, I went straight from the airport to the church for the service. There were a lot of old KR and especially *Miami Herald* people milling around, and they all seemed glad enough to see me.

Alvah's best friend, Armando Codina, delivered one of the eulogies. He was a grandstanding Cuban who had come to the U.S. and made good as a Coral Gables real-estate developer, and he sat on a lot of important boards such as General Motors, BellSouth, American Airlines, and Home Depot. His effort made the case for Alvah as "Mr. Miami"—how he loved the city and how the city loved him back. There was certainly no denying that: Alvah had been, at various times, chairman of the Florida Philharmonic, president of the Greater Miami Chamber of Commerce, president of Goodwill Industries of South Florida, head of the Orange Bowl Committee and of Miami Citizens Against Crime and of the Miami

Coalition for a Drug-Free Partnership and of the committee to build the Miami Performing Arts Center, need I go on? And after stepping down from KR, he took on the leadership of the Community Partnership for the Homeless, where he tried mightily to inspire visitors with his oft-stated belief that "Jesus would have spent much more time here at our homeless assistance center than at the Indian Creek Country Club or a Knight Ridder board meeting."

All well and good, but then the eulogy took a steep dive as far as I was concerned. Codina stated baldly that the biggest disappointment in Alvah's long professional life was that a certain CEO of Knight Ridder, and everybody knew exactly who was being referred to, moved the company headquarters from Miami to San Jose—that that was the one thing Alvah had never been able to get over. I was blindsided that Codina would bring that up on such an occasion.

As I left the church, I found myself replaying in my mind the unpleasant conversation I had with Alvah's wife in 1998, shortly before I went to the board for approval of the move. Betty was a gentle, kind, softspoken, all-around-wonderful southern lady, and she started off by saying, "Tony, bear with me—I just think you should know that I'm every bit as upset about the move as Alvah is. For the life of me, I can't understand why Knight Ridder needs to be in Silicon Valley—the internet is everywhere." I tried explaining that if this were the early part of the twentieth century and Knight Ridder were an automobile company, we would be moving to Detroit because that was where the action was, and that only if we were a cruise-line company instead of an information company under serious threat from the internet, would it make sense for us to stay in Miami. I pointed out that we already had a couple of hundred people in San Jose, working in KR Digital.

Betty then drew herself up and accused me outright of personally betraying her husband: "Alvah is so hurt and disappointed you're doing this to him, Tony. We're both praying you'll see fit to reconsider." It was now a full decade later, and I went on to have a nice conversation with her at the reception at the Biltmore in Coral Gables after Alvah's service.

With the move to San Jose in the works, Connie and I listed our Miami house for $2.5 million—a not excessive price for 1998. Right away a broker called to say that she represented Barry Diller and he wanted to buy it. I was incredulous—I said, "He hasn't even seen it, so how can he know he wants it?" She said she had shown him photos, the location was perfect for him, and he was prepared to pay the asking price—provided I agreed to take the house off the market, in which case he would be down to look at it that Saturday. I thought, Great, and it's Barry Diller and all that.

Typically, when you're selling a house, you make yourself scarce when a prospective buyer is coming. But Diller and the broker showed up early—Connie and I were just pulling out of the driveway. I stopped the car to talk to him, because we were sort of in the same business, and we exchanged a few words. When I didn't hear back from the broker for a couple of days, I called her, and she said, "It wasn't at all what he was looking for." I said, "I took it off the market for the better part of a week, including the long Memorial Day weekend, because you told us it was *exactly* what he was looking for, and that hiatus might have cost us a sale." She said, "It's the exact *opposite* of what he's looking for. Your house faces in the wrong direction for him—north. He wants south." I came out okay on it in the end—I had paid a million two and it sold for two million two. And as for Diller, I read that he had recently bought a waterfront plot of land in Miami Beach for an "eyewatering $45 million."

When I started the protracted process of should I move the company or not, Connie had said, "Please don't raise this subject with me again, I can't afford to get my hopes up that maybe we can go back and live in California." She had given Miami her all—she was active in the Fairchild Tropical Botanic Garden in Coral Gables, among other nonprofits—but her heart remained in San Jose. We had moved there when we were both only twenty-four, the time of life when you're making the best friends you'll ever have, and when we moved to Miami we were in our mid-forties. I was busy traveling around the country to all our newspapers and going to endless meetings with analysts and shareholders, and Connie was working ten-hour days at the law firm, including Saturdays, so we never got to have much of a social life. The moment the decision was made to relocate the company headquarters to San Jose, Connie began looking for a house in earnest.

I was busy scouting places all over Santa Clara County for our offices. I settled on the tallest and, thanks to its marble façade, the most impressive-looking building in downtown San Jose, 50 West San Fernando Street, which had been put up in the early 1990s. Although we were leasing only three of the seventeen floors, it would quickly come to be referred to as the Knight Ridder Building. I had made it part of the deal to have two chrome signs that said "Knight Ridder" installed on the roof—one of them facing east, the other, west; and both lit up at night. I wanted them not only to dominate the downtown skyline but to be visible for miles around so when you were flying west, once you passed Denver you could make them out clearly, and then when you landed at the San Jose airport, wow, they would be in your face. I should add that those signs were larger than the city had anticipated and it later passed an ordinance prohibiting similar-size ones.

Connie found a house and property that she really loved. It was in Woodside, midway (thirty miles or so) between San Jose and San Francisco (she would be driving north to work, and I would be driving south). Being so close to Silicon Valley, the town was home to such tech all-stars as John Doerr, Gordon Moore, Larry Ellison, and Steve Jobs. The 6,000-square-foot house was sorely in need of remodeling, which was just about the last thing I wanted to deal with, having recently weathered a year and a half of that in Miami. But Connie and our daughters talked me into it. There was a dismal staff apartment above the detached garage that we could camp out in during the year the work was going on.

The Knight Ridder Building, San Jose, 1998. You can't miss that sign.
Photo by John Pozniak

The biggest attraction for Connie was the grounds: two acres of formal gardens complete with three greenhouses. The woman whose estate we purchased the place from had been head of the Woodside Atherton Garden Club, and her own garden had been designed by the renowned landscape architect Thomas Church. In Florida, Connie had been new to the law—associates get worked like dogs, and she was conscientious to a fault, which didn't leave her with a whole lot of time to root around in the soil. In Woodside, on the other hand, she lost no time digging in, and she got our garden up to where it qualified for tours.

The house had been designed in the mid-'50s by a famous modernist architect, Joseph Esherick, to fit into the natural landscape. Just as she had with our place in Miami, Katie worked on the Woodside project in tandem with her architect husband, Peter. Connie had two major requests: additional windows in the kitchen to furnish more expansive views of her garden, and walls painted to reflect the flora. Katie and Peter created an environment for us that was both cultivated and comfortable, and the home was prominently featured in *House Beautiful*.

There was a brief downside in Woodside. We had to tolerate security outside our gate for about a month, thanks to a credible death threat I'd received in the mail pertaining to the Detroit strike (its bitterness, sadly, had persisted). Over the years, death threats would come in all different forms. Most of them I didn't take seriously. Together with the FBI, I determined what to do about each one, weighing the gain in protection against the loss of privacy.

Just a year after we renewed residence in California, Connie decided to wind down her law career with an eye to soon retiring. She rationalized it this way: "For the past twenty-five years I've been raising our children and going to school and then working nonstop. My mother died in her late fifties. I'm fifty-nine now myself, and I want more out of life, and the two things I want the most are to work in my garden and play more golf." As we already belonged to three clubs in California (in addition to Cypress Point, we were members of the Burlingame Country Club and the San Francisco Golf Club), I couldn't have supported her second sentiment more wholeheartedly.

Or should I say *hole*heartedly. Connie was determined to improve her game. As Linda put it, "My mother didn't do anything light-heartedly—she was the definition of tenacious." Katie described Connie as a "student of golf," forever consulting magazines and videotapes, "analyzing everything." Little wonder that she ended up the head of Cypress Point's Ladies Golf Committee.

CHAPTER TWENTY-ONE

Projecting "The Tech"

WITHIN A FEW months of our moving back to California, one of my most ambitious nonprofit projects was finally realized. On October 31, 1998, the San Jose Tech Museum, which I had been instrumental in literally getting off the ground, held its official opening—its truly grand opening.

The idea for it originated in the late '70s—with the Palo Alto Junior League, to give credit where credit is due. Silicon Valley was already established as the high-tech mecca, and folks from the Bay Area were impatient to see what was happening in their own backyard. The problem was there wasn't really a "there" there: all you had were all these companies, but no designated place where you could demonstrate, for instance, how a Silicon chip wafer was made. The museum was envisioned as a tool to decipher technology and, at least the hope was, inspire the innovator in everyone.

A board was formed in 1981, and as the publisher of the *Mercury News* I was invited to join. A year later I was elected chairman—chairman, bear in mind, of a museum that was still only an idea. We didn't have a building, we were going to have to raise the money to build one, and we didn't even have a place to put it. We were looking for a donation of land as well as cash.

My first challenge was figuring out the most propitious place to launch such an undertaking. Among the fifteen cities in Santa Clara County, a vigorous competition developed between San Jose and Mountain View. To our surprise and delight, they went on outbidding each other indefinitely. In 1984 we accepted San Jose's offer of $41 million plus a parcel of land downtown on South Market Street that bordered the Plaza de Caesar Chavez (across from what would one day come to be known as the Knight Ridder Building). The city also made available to us rent-free space next door in a former convention center.

We were already leaning heavily in the direction of the trailblazing architect Ricardo Legoretta. That he was a Mexican was a happy coincidence: at one time, Mexico owned all of California, and there were now probably more Mexican Americans (that is, Americans of Mexican descent, both legal and undocumented)—nearly a third of the state's population of around forty million—living there than anyplace else on earth. The Mexican American makeup of San Jose alone was roughly thirty percent.

In June 1985, I firmed up plans to fly to Mexico City and poke around in some Legoretta buildings, along with HP co-founder Dave Packard's wife Lucile, who was on our board. At this point, the story got personal—it would literally hit home. Connie was about to graduate from Santa Clara Law School, which, since she was also a hands-on mother and an active corporate wife, she had had to attend part-time. This marked the end of four years of drudgery for her. She was expecting me to stick around after the ceremony to socialize with her professors and hobnob with her classmates and then take the proud new graduate out to dinner. But I had to skip the reception in order to meet Lucile at the airport. Connie never quite forgave me for not having planned things better. She was not easily moved to anger, but twenty-five years later, if anybody ever mentioned her graduation, she would say, "I'm still so mad at Tony for taking off right at the moment I was handed my diploma."

The Mexico mission, poorly conceived as it was, as far as Connie was concerned, was a success: Legoretta was clearly the one to bring the project to fruition. Meanwhile, I was having trouble finding somebody to succeed me as the Tech chairman when I moved to Miami to head KR's newspaper division. In the event, not having a number two, I had no choice but to continue in the role—trying to keep things on track from halfway across the country at a time when I had more than a full-time job.

At some point that year—what I think of as a day of deliverance, it was just such a relief—I was able to persuade the president of the Silicon Valley Manufacturing Group, Peter Giles, to take the job of paid president and CEO of the Tech (miracle of miracles, he stayed for almost twenty years). I presently stepped down as chairman in favor of Ed Zschau, an erstwhile Silicon Valley CEO and a onetime U.S. representative from California who, thanks to his skill on the ukulele, was known as "the singing congressman."

Ed certainly sang for his supper when it came to the Tech. He, Peter, and board member John Warnock (the co-founder and CEO of Adobe and a board member of Netscape and, later, of Knight Ridder) worked together to raise the money for the building. One hundred and ten million dollars later, there rose a mind-blowing 132,000-square-foot three-story horizontal domed edifice reminiscent—to the eye of disparate beholders—of pueblo settlements, Egyptian pyramids, and Inca palaces. Legorreta has been described as a veritable "scholar of color," and the hues he chose for the façade, mango and azure, make his building positively sing. It became an instant landmark in the cityscape.

Connie stood proudly at my side that October 31st at the inauguration—the "plugging in"—of an institution that for the previous eight years had been operating faute de mieux out of a smallish space on West San Carlos Street known as "The Garage." It had originally been designated the Tech Museum of Innovation, but later some focus group or other advised that the word "museum" was alienating, with its intimations of the past, and recommended the name be changed to the Tech Interactive. Shortly after the opening of the building, John Warnock, who was by then board chairman,

The stunning Ricardo Legoretta-designed Tech Museum in San Jose whose board I chaired for several years.

With Connie at a Tech dinner, 2000.
Photo by Doorstep Photography

inveigled me into succeeding him. I thought to myself, Here I go again, but there I went. I held the position for a couple of more years.

In early April 2000, President Bill Clinton descended on the Bay Area to fundraise in Silicon Valley and affirm his commitment to high tech. He was all set to deliver the keynote address, "Meeting the Challenges of the New Economy," at a symposium to be held at the Tech. His people, for security reasons, had him driven into the building adjacent to the museum and had asked if I could be there to welcome him—it was just him and me.

The president had been briefed that I was the CEO of KR, and the first thing he said to me was, "The *Miami Herald*—that's one of yours, isn't it?" He then began to talk about the dilemma he was facing: whether the five-year-old boy who on Thanksgiving Day had been found clinging to an inner tube off the coast of Fort Lauderdale by two fishermen and handed over to the U.S. Coast Guard, his mother having drowned during their attempt to flee communist Cuba, should be permitted to stay with relatives in Miami or be returned to his father in Havana. Clinton told me he was under tremendous pressure to allow him to remain in the U.S. About ten minutes into our conversation, his press secretary came to get him, saying, "Mr. President, everyone is waiting." Clinton couldn't have cared less. He said, "Tell them to wait, I need to talk to Tony some more."

I told him I felt he should try to figure out a way to let the poor kid stay with whatever family he had in Miami, that that was the right thing to do. The *Miami Herald* was naturally all over the story. It was *the* story, worldwide—that little boy had become a geopolitical football. (About three weeks later, Clinton would announce that he concurred with Attorney General Janet Reno that the rules of the U.S. Immigration and Naturalization Service and the precepts of international law must be upheld and Elian repatriated; and sure enough, in late June, after all the various legal appeals had been exhausted, he was sent home to his dad.)

I accompanied the president to the hall of the Tech where practically every dignitary in California was champing at the bit to shake his hand. I said hi to Governor Gray Davis and then faded, stage right or stage left, into the maw of the—pardon the expression—museum.

I must add that I have visited more than my share of science centers and never encountered one as comprehensive as ours. It enables people of all ages to not only explore but participate in the technologies that impact their lives. And the Tech is not only educational, it's fun, it's exciting—one exhibition had visitors designing and building their own robots.

The museum itself is a spatial experience, what with its spectacular skylit atriums and its Imax theater that boasts the world's first dome laser projector—the gigantic wraparound screen makes you feel like part of the action. In a word, it's a trip. And it's certainly been a hit—ten million visitors and counting.

CHAPTER TWENTY-TWO

Addressing and Redressing 9/11

WHERE WAS I—where was everybody—on September 11, 2001, when the world turned topsy-turvy, wrong-side-up? I was in my office in San Jose, and just as soon as planes resumed flying after the FAA had "shut down the sky," I convened the head of our D.C. bureau and the top editors of our six largest newspapers and told them, "We've always allowed each Knight Ridder paper to chase and report a story in its own way, but this one is too big for any of you to try to cover alone. We need to pool our resources, mount a coordinated effort under the guidance of our Washington bureau, and attack the story on a company-wide basis." Although we were in the depths of the dot-com bust, I assured them we would spare no expense in covering an event that had exponentially extended the meaning of the word *catastrophe*.

Our subsequent reporting on the country's response to 9/11—the invasion of Iraq—would amount to some of our most fulfilling moments as journalists. The *Wall Street Journal*, the *New York Times*, the *Washington Post*, and the *Los Angeles Times*, plus the major networks, had better Rolodexes than we did and had already gotten to Bush, Cheney, Rumsfeld, Colin Powell, and Condoleezza Rice, for what that would turn out to be worth. The print-and-broadcast mainstream media swallowed the weapons-of-mass-destruction justification fabricated by the administration as a pretext to invade. Our reporters burrowed deeper, talking off the record to people at the next level down—Pentagon and intelligence underlings who proved to be invaluable sources. As a result, we were able to confidently report that there was no verifiable information—no hard evidence—of WMDs, and that, on top of that, there was no game plan in place for running the country if and when the U.S. toppled the regime.

One of our papers, the *Philadelphia Inquirer*, always insisted on covering a major story on its own, something that was resented by the editors and publishers of our other papers. In this case, mostly using *New York Times* stories, it functioned as a cheerleader for Bush, toeing the administration's line that Saddam was in bed with Al Qaeda and on the cusp of obtaining nukes.

Knight Ridder was virtually the only outfit to declare that any war Bush preemptively waged against Iraq would be based on a lie. We should have won a Pulitzer. I believe to this day that the only reason we didn't is that Pulitzer decisions were sometimes made for political reasons, and a nod by the Pulitzer board to KR would have embarrassed the *Wall Street Journal*, the *New York Times*, the *Washington Post*, and all those other untouchable icons of quality journalism.

In 2007 the PBS program "Bill Moyers Journal" produced a ninety-minute documentary, *Buying the War: How Big Media Failed Us*, based on KR's coverage during the run-up to the invasion and featuring interviews with the four members of our foreign-affairs and national-security reporting team and our D.C. bureau chief. A decade later, the actor and filmmaker Rob Reiner directed and produced a movie also based on our coverage—*Shock and Awe*—starring Woody Harrelson and Tommy Lee Jones. Reiner himself played our D.C. bureau chief John Walcott. John contacted me during the filming to say that Reiner had asked him to find out if I had ever been pressured by "W.," Cheney, or Rumsfeld, to lay off—to call off our reporters. Granted, that would have added a nice dramatic flourish, with its echoes of Nixon trying to intimidate Kay Graham to not publish the Pentagon Papers. But it never happened.

Speaking of Kay, I enjoyed and admired her Pulitzer Prize-winning autobiography, but the recent movie about the *Washington Post* didn't sit so well with me. Its central theme was that when she made the decision to go ahead, she was putting the whole company on the line. The mundane truth is that all the *Post* did was trot along behind the *New York Times* which had already published the material—which makes them copycats. At the time the injunction was filed, the Washington Post Company was about to issue an IPO, a traditional way to generate money, but the movie would have you believe that if Kay published against Nixon's will, the offering would be jeopardized, when in fact it wouldn't have added up to anything more than the shares going for a little less. It was never going to lead to disaster. But that's the movies for you.

When Kay came out to San Jose in the early '70s for a dinner honoring Janet Gray Hayes, who was not only the first woman to be elected the city's mayor but the first woman ever elected mayor of any major U.S. city, she mentioned to me that her son, Don, was just coming into the business and would I look after him a bit. As it turned out, Don didn't need my help, or anybody else's, and he and I later worked together on some internet ventures, such as New Century Networks.

As for Janet Hayes, when Knight bought Ridder in 1974, I was business manager of the *Mercury News*, and she said to me, "Tony, I'm worried this might mean you're going to lose your job." A quarter of a century later, just after I had moved our headquarters to San Jose, she invited Connie and me to lunch at her home. She was long out of politics by then, and I was the CEO of Knight Ridder. I took the occasion to good-naturedly remind her of what she had said. "Did I really say that? I couldn't have," she said. I said, "You said it, all right."

CHAPTER TWENTY-THREE

Stormy Weather

AD REVENUE ACROSS the industry was swooning—no newspaper was immune, including the *Wall Street Journal* and the *New York Times*. Knight Ridder, for its part, continued to place a premium on topnotch journalism across all its newspapers. As luck and/or ill luck would have it, one of our finest hours lay just ahead, delivered by one of our smaller papers. Thirty-four hours after Hurricane Katrina made landfall on August 23, 2005, devastating New Orleans and the Mississippi coast, it bashed into Biloxi where we owned the *Sun Herald*. I was at home in San Jose, glued to the TV and considering ways we could help.

I arranged for the head of KR's diversity efforts, Larry Olmstead, to meet me at the airport the next morning, then commandeered Connie's station wagon and drove to the grocery store to load up on food and bottled water. Larry and I flew on the company plane to the nearest open airport—Mobile, Alabama. We rented an SUV there and hit the road—Highway 10, to be exact, which runs north of the coast. We hadn't progressed more than a few miles when we saw a sign that said the road up ahead was partially closed. As there was nobody around to stop us, we just kept going. When water started seriously sloshing all around us, we turned off the freeway in search of a less precarious way into Biloxi.

All the trees were down, and the terrain had taken on the trappings of post-apocalyptic nightmare. Don't ask me how, but we managed to get there—only to find the city practically leveled. The winds were remorseless and had flattened building after building.

The interesting thing to me is that the closest the president of the United States, George W. Bush, who was on his Texas ranch when the hurricane hit, ever succeeded in getting to the cataclysm was that infamous flyover—witness that famous photo of him looking helplessly out the window of Air Force One. He claimed there was no way he could get in there because the airport was shut. Well, a mere civilian from California by the name of Tony Ridder was on the scene within twenty-four hours.

We ran into trouble finding our way to the newspaper, though I had driven there on previous occasions to help during less severe storms. I was relieved to find the building still standing. I soon discovered that many of our employees had spent the night at the paper rather than risk trying to make it home in one piece. Others had rushed from home *to* the shelter of the paper. A good many of our people had lost nearly everything. I quickly distributed the supplies that Larry and I had brought, and I talked to the employees as a group and then to as many as I could one-to-one. Their stories were agonizingly similar: "My house is completely gone … I couldn't save a thing; the water was coming in so fast … I was lucky to get out with the clothes on my back." This litany was a very emotional thing to hear.

I stayed at the paper till all hours. The edition we were struggling to get out was going to have to be printed in Columbus, Georgia, and transported back to Biloxi. I got a room on a high floor of the Beau Rivage Resort & Casino (Biloxi was the third biggest gambling center in America, after Atlantic City and Las Vegas). All the casinos downtown, very sturdy structures, were badly damaged by storm surges—the barges had come unmoored from the docks and been catapulted onto land where they acted as battering rams. I spent two nights in that casino, and believe me, there was no gambling going on.

The *Sun Herald* shared the Pulitzer public-service prize with the *New Orleans Times-Picayune* for its "valorous and comprehensive coverage of Hurricane Katrina, providing a lifeline for devastated readers, in print and online, during their time of greatest need." I joined the editor and publisher at the prize-giving ceremony up at Columbia University. That should have been an unadulterated happy occasion, but that morning the *New York Times* ran an item in its media column that, at a newsroom meeting of the *Philadelphia Inquirer* in 1987, I had quipped that there should be a Pulitzer Prize awarded for cost-cutting because I would win it hands-down. It was a bold-faced lie, and I was livid.

The first person I ran into at the reception before the ceremony was *Times* publisher Arthur Sulzberger, Jr., and I read him the riot act. He was flustered and said, "Let me go get my managing editor." He returned with Bill Keller, who sputtered that he would look into the matter.

Immediately after lunch, I put in calls to Gene Roberts, the *Inquirer*'s top editor at the time I was alleged to have made that unbelievable remark, and to his deputy, Gene Forman. Each of them backed me up: they had never heard anything remotely like that issue from my lips at any newsroom meeting or in any other context.

A week later, the *Times*' media column reported that I denied making the remark in question, but then went on to name the source—an editor of the *Columbia Journalism Review* who had previously worked at the *Inquirer.* I had never met this guy but his name rang a faint bell and I remembered having been told he was a great complainer in the newsroom. The *Times* added that this constitutionally disgruntled former employee of mine was standing by his story and never even bothered to check with Roberts or Foreman. Let it be stated for the record that that's not my idea of responsible journalism.

CHAPTER TWENTY-FOUR

Stormier Weather: D-Day for KR

MY LOVE AFFAIR with print journalism waned as well as waxed. By 2004 I was thoroughly fed up with our partnership with Gannett on the two Detroit papers, the *Free Press* and the *News*. The 100-year Joint Operating Agreement entered into by Alvah Chapman and Gannett's Al Neuharth stipulated that business operations be combined, separate editorial staffs maintained, and profits equally divided. Gannett, however, had come out on top, with three to two on the management committee, so if we disagreed on something, they would just go ahead and do it anyway.

It was past time for us to get out from under. Our Detroit paper was not particularly profitable for its size and, in my estimation, didn't have much of a future. I proposed to Gannett's CEO Doug McCorkindale that he give us their *Indianapolis Star* in exchange for our *Free Press*. He proposed alternative deals, including trading us Reno and Salem, Oregon. Negotiations dragged on for a year or more. Finally in August 2005, we agreed to give Gannett the *Free Press* plus the *Tallahassee Democrat* in exchange for the *Idaho Statesman* plus two papers in Washington State, the *Bellingham Herald* and the *Olympian*—and $262 million in cash.

I flew to Detroit to deliver the news to the staff myself, because that's what you do—you have to show leadership at times like those, especially when you know people are going to be angry. Nobody had seen this coming, and I knew that nobody but nobody would want to work for Gannett if they could help it.

Greater tremors lay in store. Our internal-analysis projections, once we broke out the figures separately, showed that print was essentially flat and that ad revenue increases were all coming from our internet interests. Upwards of ninety-five percent of Knight Ridder stock was held by institutional investors, and our single largest shareholder—Private Capital Management (PCM), which held a nineteen percent stake worth roughly $1 billion—began pressuring us to sell. PCM's co-founder and owner, Bruce Sherman, went as far as to write me a bullying letter and release it to the press. Our third largest shareholder, Harris Associates, followed suit, demanding that we "aggressively" pursue a sale, and sent a letter to that effect to the U.S. Securities and Exchange Commission.

Our second largest shareholder, the hedge fund Southeastern Asset Management, preferred that we do a recap—borrow two or three billion to buy back a substantial amount of our own stock. Shareholders are typically happy when you're buying back stock: the number of shares outstanding generally gets reduced, and your earnings per share go up. But eventually, even Southeastern pushed for a sale, and together these three dreadnoughts controlled thirty-six percent of the company's outstanding shares.

I unequivocally declared that we were not for sale, fully realizing that to be able to maintain that position I would need to make a coercive case to our other shareholders to stick with us. I would have to convince them that the future looked rosy when in fact it looked anything but.

Sherman was threatening to run a campaign to elect a rival slate of Knight Ridder directors. But under our bylaws we had a staggered board, with only three directors elected each year, and it would have taken Sherman three years to gain control that way. Unfortunately, KR had a single-tier stock structure which left it exposed.

The die had been cast thirty-two years before, when Knight merged with Ridder. To be eligible for trading on the New York Stock Exchange, the so-called Big Board, the company was required to issue only one class of stock. None of the principals were worried about this, including Dad who led the negotiations with Knight on behalf of Ridder—they simply assumed that since they owned so much of the company themselves nobody could ever take it away from them. (In 1969, shortly after Knight went public, Jack Knight had addressed a group of Wall Street analysts. "Ladies and gentlemen," he asserted, "I do not intend to become your prisoner." He could get away with that because, at the time, he and his brother controlled the lion's share of the stock.)

Had we had a dual-class structure in place—which is what newspaper families such as the Sulzbergers, the *Wall Street Journal*'s Bancrofts, the *Washington Post*'s Grahams, and the California-based McClatchy family all had, with their tightly controlled super-voting Class B shares—we would have been better protected. What the Knight Ridder board *had* taken care to enact in the early 1980s was a number of strong poison-pill measures to discourage hostile takeovers by activist shareholders like Sherman, and, if they persevered, to severely restrict their ability to succeed.

My decision to sell the company was arrived at with no small degree of anguish. I'm normally someone who's calm under pressure. Connie would always marvel, "How can you possibly sleep after what you went through today and what you're facing tomorrow? *I* can't sleep." The question was, of course, rhetorical. She knew better than anyone that the more I had going on, the happier I was—I would hit the pillow and be gone. Not this time, though—sleep was beyond easy reach. I tossed and turned, as if literally wrestling with which way to go. Then one night in November—actually, it was between four and five in the morning—I made up my mind that it was in the company's best interests to sell. I told Connie at breakfast that as soon as I got to the office, I was going to convene a meeting of my five senior managers.

I was surprised when not a one of them tried to get me to change my mind. I called a board meeting for a week from that Sunday and included two partners from Goldman Sachs, our principal investment bankers. The board unanimously agreed that we should sell, and I went ahead and made the public announcement that we were "exploring our strategic alternatives" (corporate speak for "the company is up for sale"). Goldman then proceeded to contact potential buyers.

In January and February, we made presentations to around twenty interested parties: newspaper companies and private-equity firms, including Bain Capital and KKR. (George Roberts, the "R" in KKR, had come to me in 2002 looking to form a partnership to acquire newspaper properties, but KR had either traded or purchased outright seven newspapers in the previous five years and we were done for the time being.) We set a date in mid-March for the final offers.

In the end, there was only one—everybody else passed up the opportunity to bid on what was, after all, the nation's second largest newspaper company in terms of footprint and circulation. Not even Gannett kicked the tires. The sole suitor, represented by Credit Suisse, was the McClatchy newspaper company of Sacramento, founded in 1857, around the time of the California Gold Rush. Its biggest acquisition to date had been the purchase of the Minneapolis *Star-Tribune* from the Cowles family for $1.2 billion in 1998. For all that, the company's revenue remained half the size of ours, and one information industry analyst summed up the prospective deal as a dolphin swallowing a whale.

I was comfortable with the thought of our newspapers ending up with McClatchy. The company had a culture of quality: they were as devoted to independent reporting as we were and had also won a string of Pulitzers. And they had not only the same solid journalistic values but similar ethical standards: fairness to their employees and service to their communities. I knew McClatchy's chairman and CEO, Gary Pruitt—he was someone I had once tried to hire, with the idea of grooming him to be my successor. I had also known his two predecessors. The late "C. K." McClatchy, who was, like Uncle Joe, not a day-to-day kind of guy, had poached the general manager of our Charlotte paper to come in and run the business for him, and he in turn had groomed Pruitt to be *his* successor (Pruitt, for his part, would go on to become president and CEO of the Associated Press).

When we had met with Pruitt in February, he informed us that he planned to sell approximately five of our newspapers to help reduce the debt that McClatchy would be taking on to finance the deal. Knowing that he was bound to have misgivings about strongly unionized papers, I expected that the *Akron Beacon Journal* and both our Philadelphia papers would be on his to-sell list; and I was sure the *Pioneer Press* would be, since retaining it, given McClatchy's ownership of its competitor, the Minneapolis *Star-Tribune*, might well trigger an anti-trust challenge.

On a Friday in mid-March, Goldman brought me and my five senior VPs McClatchy's formal offer: $67.25 per KR share at closing, amounting to some $6.5 billion: $4.5 of it payable sixty percent in cash, and the rest in McClatchy stock, plus the assumption of our $2 billion debt. I also learned, to my shock and utter dismay, that McClatchy was intending to sell *twelve*—nearly a third—of the newspapers they would be acquiring from us and, to add insult to injury, to unload them the very day the deal closed. The bitterest disappointment for me personally—a heartbreak, really—was that the *San Jose Mercury News* was on the list. As one of its columnists would despairingly put it to me, "It's as if the paper had been orphaned and then told its replacement parent didn't even want it."

I directed Goldman to have Credit Suisse lean on McClatchy to reduce the number of papers they were planning to sell, to in any case refrain from selling the *Mercury* News, and finally to sweeten the deal financially. Overnight, McClatchy agreed to up their offer by seventy-five cents per share, which amounted to between $60 and $70 million, but on the other two issues they would not budge.

I outlined and explained the final offer to the board at a meeting in New York two days later. Several of our directors protested that we were selling too cheap. I responded forcefully that McClatchy would be paying nine and a half times our cash flow, plus a premium over what our shares were selling at; that there were no other bidders; and that it was clear to me there was never going to be a better time to sell, that this was the best we were ever going to do. With that, the board fell in line and authorized me to recommend to our shareholders that they vote in favor of the offer.

A month or so after the announcement of the sale, I asked Pruitt point blank if he had made any deals with anyone in advance to buy any of the papers. He denied it, but I wasn't buying that. And it would turn out that he had had at least one buyer lined up: William Dean Singleton, chief executive of MediaNews Group, which owned the *Denver Post* and the *Salt Lake Tribune*. Our *San Jose Mercury News*, *Monterey Herald*, and *Contra Costa Times* were perfect fits for him geographically, since he already owned all the newspapers between Contra Costa and San Jose, as well as other, smaller papers in Alameda County, not to mention the *Los Angeles Daily News*. Singleton's thing was "clustering," and, clearly, he was aiming for a clean sweep here. Pruitt was quoted in the *New York Times* as saying, "We care who we sell to." Well, I happened to know this Singleton (from both the NAA board, where he had been my predecessor as chairman, and the AP board, of which he eventually became chairman), and he struck me as one slick operator.

Had McClatchy committed to keeping all of our newspapers, the shareholder approval required for the sale would have been just a majority vote. However, one of the poison-pill provisions entrenched in the Knight Ridder bylaws stipulated that any company seeking to purchase us had to meet a certain standard of journalism as certified by a panel of three experts selected by us. A sale to any entity that failed to meet that high standard would require eighty percent approval. That provision had now been activated, not because McClatchy's standards weren't in line with ours but, rather, because they would be scattering a full twelve of our papers to the winds, leaving them in danger of falling into the hands of owners who did not measure up.

Like Dean Singleton, not to name names. With some difficulty he was able to raise the billion dollars it took to obtain four of our newspapers from McClatchy (part of the deal for the three California papers entailed his taking on the *St. Paul Pioneer Press* as well). The task of introducing him to the *Mercury News* staff as the paper's new owner fell miserably to me. The employees there, as well as at the other papers Pruitt sold Singleton, were never very happy. (Four months after the sale, the *Mercury News* announced it was laying off 101 people, including forty from the newsroom, and within four short years Singleton would be filing for bankruptcy.)

To achieve that eighty percent approval was going to be an uphill battle. April, famously "the cruelest month," and May, in this case no less cruel, brought turmoil. While I was working around the clock to convince enough shareholders to vote our way, there were forces at large campaigning against us. Not only did the Newspaper Guild, a force in our unionized newspapers, vigorously oppose the sale, but some of our employees, including editors and reporters, formed an anti-sale committee. Then the bygone Bob Ingle crawled out of the woodwork and did his vindictive bit to try to block the sale. These were all very public efforts, extensively covered in the general press.

Some of the attacks were ad hominem, with liberal use made of the "Darth Ridder" sobriquet I abhorred. The most potentially damaging of the campaigns was orchestrated and led by the one-time managing editor of our *Philadelphia Inquirer*, Jim Naughton. Back story: in 1990 I had gone and rented three rooms in a hotel out by the Philadelphia airport so that our CEO Jim Batten, our senior news executive Jenny Buckner, and I could separately vet the four candidates for the paper's top editor's job. We passed over Naughton, the preferred candidate of the departing editor Gene Roberts, in favor of the number-four editor, Maxwell King, and Naughton was always openly antagonistic toward me after that. Now, sixteen years later, he was still carrying that grudge and using the much-trafficked website of the Poynter Institute for Media Studies, the Florida-based nonprofit school for journalists of which he was the recently retired president, to try and screw up the sale for me.

In mid-May, I noticed a rash on my chest, which I assumed was nothing more than an allergic reaction to something. My dermatologist failed to identify it but succeeded in alarming me when he said he thought I might have a "bit of a cancer problem." He referred me to an oncologist, who couldn't put his finger on it, either. "We're going to have to consult on this one," he said, and proceeded to take a bone-marrow sample to send to the Stanford lab for analysis. He really drilled in, and it hurt like hell.

On June 10, I was told it looked like I had the beginnings of something called mantle cell lymphoma. I said, "What does that mean in plain English?" The doctor then put it plainly enough: "The average life expectancy is three years." And when I blurted out, "*What?*" he put it even more plainly: "If you have it, you have only around three years to live."

I drifted home in a daze. I do remember sitting on our bed with Connie and both of us despairing. In the morning, I went to work as usual—I had to finish the job. I said nothing about the medical news to any of my colleagues because the last thing they needed to hear at that point was that I had this potentially deadly cancer issue. We were in the home stretch with McClatchy, but there were still issues to be resolved.

June 26 was D-Day for KR, and I was anxiously making calls to institutional shareholders right up to the last minute. By the end of the workday on the twenty-fifth, we weren't yet at the eighty percent we needed, and we had done all we could in the U.S. I went home with a list of shareholders to call in London just as soon as the financial district there opened, and at 1:00 a.m. California time I was on the phone trying to persuade the English contingent to cast their votes for us.

In the event, of the sixty-eight million shares voted, 54.4 were in favor—80.1 percent, to be exact. So, just over the threshold. Whew. A pacifying irony of the sale was that Bruce Sherman's gain on his Knight Ridder shares was modest and later offset by the downturn in the McClatchy holdings he had.

That I had acted coolly and calmly as a professional manager didn't for a minute mean I didn't feel an emotional tie to the Ridder family legacy. My mother and sisters were present at the final shareholders meeting (Dad had died four years before), and I choked up. I had tears in my eyes when they, along with the corporate officers, gave me a standing ovation. There's no escaping the fact that I was the Ridder who brought down the curtain on five generations of the family that had made major contributions to American journalism and to the communities where they owned newspapers.

When we sold to Knight in 1974, it had been with the provision that the merged company would include the Ridder name (much remarked on at the time was the coincidence that in German the word "ridder" *means* "knight"). The difference now was that I was representing neither the Ridders nor the Knights—I was representing the Knight Ridder shareholders and protecting shareholder value. And when all was said and done, the transaction was a tremendous outcome for them. Indeed, it would go down as the last great deal in the newspaper industry.

By the time of the sale, there were only two other family members working in the company who carried the name Ridder. My brother Peter had begun his career in Duluth and moved on up to become the publisher of four of our newspapers—Fort Wayne, Indiana; Long Beach; St. Paul; and Charlotte, North Carolina. And my son Par, from the day he embarked on his paper route in Saratoga, had known he wanted to make his life in the newspaper industry. Both he and Peter, if they could reasonably have done so, would probably have changed their last name. I worked things out so neither of them ever had to report to me directly.

I need to add for the record that when a publisher's job opened up in the company, four or five of us at the senior corporate level would

Opening the final Knight Ridder shareholders' meeting, San Jose, June 26, 2006. One of the worst days of my life.
Photo by Len Vaughn-Lahman/*San Jose Mercury News*/KRT/abacapress.com

put on our thinking caps, but that whenever my son or brother was in the running, I recused myself. It was senior people other than I who picked Par to be president and publisher of our paper in San Luis Obispo, which in 2003 was voted Knight Ridder Newspaper of the Year, based on overall business performance. Not only was it the fastest growing newspaper in California, it was the second fastest growing in the nation, and it had also won a raft of awards for outstanding journalism. The next year, Par was posted to the St. Paul *Pioneer Press* as president and publisher, becoming the sixth Ridder to hold those positions, following in the footsteps of his great-grandfather Ben, his grandfather Bernie, his great uncles Hank and Dan, and his uncle Peter.

Today Par is a leader in what's left of the newspaper industry. He's general manager of the Chicago Tribune Media Group and Senior VP of the Tribune Publishing Company, with overall responsibility for the news, opinion, and business pages of the company's flagship *Chicago Tribune* (both the newsroom and the publisher report to him). Also on his plate are *Chicago Magazine*, six dailies, and thirty-three suburban weeklies across the Greater Chicago area, plus the Trib's newspapers in Norfolk and Newport News, Virginia.

The day after the sale to McClatchy was approved by KR shareholders, I repaired to the Stanford clinic—to a new doctor, by reputation the best there was at this thing. She, at least, wasn't counting me out. She told me, "Everybody thinks you have mantle cell lymphoma, but I'm not so sure—it may only be a case of elevated proteins." Once a month, she would run tests, the results of which were uniformly reassuring: whatever it was, it wasn't progressing. The diagnosis in the end was *pre*-mantle cell lymphoma, which wouldn't necessarily ever become full-fledged. After about nine months of going back and forth on this, I gratefully accepted that the odds were in my favor.

The KR board's compensation committee, citing the usual practice of rewarding a CEO who advantageously sells a company, raised the subject of a special commission for me. I ended the conversation by stating that I had simply been doing my job and would not accept anything extra. I was a great believer in balanced remuneration, which was a staple of the company culture that had existed under my noble predecessor, Jim Batten, and that I was determined to adhere to at all costs—now, literally, at my own expense.

There was expeditious affirmation of my having sold at the optimal time. In the fourth quarter of 2006, ad revenue across the industry, both internet and print, began an irreversible decline. The price of McClatchy stock at that time was $308 a share, and two years later it was $6.50.

I had agreed to serve two years on the McClatchy board, to assist with the transition, because without me they would not have had the necessary institutional knowledge. The directors met every two months (my old KR colleague Larry Jinks was also on the board), most often at the company headquarters in Sacramento, where McClatchy owned the *Bee*.

I spoke my mind at those meetings. There were two things McClatchy did, or didn't do, that I thought were dead wrong. Although they had retained our publishers on the papers they kept, they drew the line at hiring anybody from corporate—not a single KR executive made the cut. On another front, I didn't think they had taken the whole internet thing as far as they could and should have. They certainly failed miserably to avail themselves of our proven expertise. KR, along with the Trib, was universally recognized as the most aggressive and successful newspaper company in tackling the internet space. But McClatchy shut down KR Digital overnight. They did take on our investment in CareerBuilder, but our partners in that venture, the Trib and Gannett, refused to allow them our full third, diluting it down to fifteen percent. McClatchy also held on to our stake in Classified Ventures, but that also amounted to relatively small potatoes.

The minute I went on their board, I was enjoined from selling any of my stock for a period of at least sixty days. It wasn't until October/November that I was free to dispose of any of it. But then McClatchy made the decision to put the Minneapolis *Star Tribune* up for sale and not announce it, and their general counsel advised me to immediately stop selling, since as a board member I would have had prior knowledge of the deal. If I hadn't gone on the board, I most likely would have sold all my stock the day we sold the company. Believe me, if I could do it over again, I would never have gone on. It wound up costing me a considerable amount of money, aside from which they didn't make nearly enough use of me.

I couldn't wait to get off that board for personal as well as financial reasons. With the acquisition of Knight Ridder, McClatchy became the second largest newspaper company in the U.S., yet the market continued to punish them for overpaying for us. It became increasingly awkward, almost physically uncomfortable, for me to be around while the stock was taking such a beating. My fellow directors must have been feeling like patsies, and the man who had, in their eyes, taken them to the cleaners—the guilty party, so to speak—was sitting right there beside them in the boardroom. But never in my wildest nightmares had I foreseen the business tanking on such a scale and with such velocity. That said, McClatchy worked hard to reduce their debt (they had borrowed $3.75 billion from JPMorganChase and Banc of America Securities to buy us), but it was all for naught. On February 13, 2020, a date that will live in newspaper-industry infamy, they were forced to file for bankruptcy.

CHAPTER TWENTY-FIVE

Lost

SUDDENLY I WAS a CEO no longer, but I don't remember feeling any particular sense of rejection or neglect. Nothing like what Robert Frost foreshadowed in a poem about the harsh realities of later life: "No memory of having starred / Atones for later disregard, / Or keeps the end from being hard."

I can't say it had never crossed my mind that retirement might be a problem, but that's not how it turned out. In addition to serving on the McClatchy board, I was elected a director of Sun Microsystems. Not only did it produce computers, workstations, servers, and software, but it had pioneered the Java computer-programming language, the Solaris operating system, the Network File System, and SPARC microprocessors. The company operated out of a large campus in Silicon Valley's Menlo Park, the so-called "Capital of Venture Capital." Today, Facebook is located on the former Sun site.

I was one of the board members who pushed for a sale in 2010. IBM made a bid of $7 billion, which we turned down. Two weeks later, we sold to Oracle, whose chairman Larry Ellison was a friend of Sun's dynamic co-founder Scott McNealy. Scott, by the way, was known almost as widely as an enthusiastic golfer, a gene he passed down to his son Maverick McNealy, a Stanford graduate who went on to become a topnotch golf professional. In retirement I was now free to become more active in the sport off the course as well as on. I served as admissions committee chairman of Cypress Point (2006–2010 and 2014–2018) and as club president (2010–2014).

I was also active—you might even say busily employed—on the real estate front. One of the first things that went through my mind, after that first oncologist told me I could easily be dead within three years, was that the three-bedroom condominium in Hualalai on Hawaii's Big Island, which I'd purchased in the summer of 2004, wouldn't be sufficient to accommodate all of my family at the same time (the previous couple of Christmases we had had to rent a condominium to house the overflow). My personal Doomsday Clock might have been ticking overtime—dare I say in dead earnest—and I was seized with the need to provide a place where my future widow and our four children and *their* children (each of my children now had three—two girls and a boy each) could be comfortable when they gathered to grieve for me.

Having sold the company, I had more money at my disposal, and in August 2006 I bought a 10,000-square-foot single-story wood-and-stucco house in Kukio, on the Big Island's Kona-Kohala coast. It had belonged to Sidney Frank, who made his billion developing Grey Goose Vodka and who had spent a total of only four nights there. The house had four large bedrooms plus a huge area that Connie and I turned into a dormitory where the kids and grandkids could all camp on mattresses, if need be. We called that space the chicken coop, which was what, growing up, my siblings and I called the converted dormitory on my parents' farm in St. Paul where we slept when they hosted big family reunions (the difference was it had been a real chicken coop). A lot of the Silicon Valley hotshots had places in Kukio or next door at Hualalai—Michael Dell, Chuck Schwab, George Roberts … . Anyhow, I didn't die, I went right on living. And not only living but living it up—getting to spend about six weeks a year in Hawaii, which Mark Twain perfectly described as "the loveliest fleet of islands that lies anchored in any ocean."

How Connie and I ended up with a place of our own there is

With Susie, Linda, Katie, and Par in Hawaii, 2012.

a little dizzy making. We had been going to Vail for vacations, but Connie developed some lung-capacity issues and was prone to altitude sickness. At its onset, she would have to drive to a lower elevation, Glenwood Springs, and sit in the lobby of the hotel there and read for three or four hours until she had recovered enough equilibrium to drive back up to us. It finally reached the point where this was happening all the time, so, clearly, we had to find someplace else to ski.

I found a good-size house in Sun Valley. Connie had once been Central U.S. ski champion and skied in the Nationals, but as she got older, she slowed down—and I didn't. I was able to keep up with our kids, who all wanted to ski fast. Even when it was just the two of us on the slopes and we took off together, she would get frustrated when I surged ahead. I would always wait for her to catch up, but then I would take off again. After four years of this, she said to me, "Skiing with you is no fun—you are never not going to want to just keep going. Why do we even need to ski anymore? Why don't we just get a place somewhere like Hawaii for the winters?"

A couple of years after taking on the big house in Kukio, I sold our place in Woodside. We had made the major lifestyle decision to make Pebble Beach our principal residence and purchased a beautiful property there from the estate of Charles de Bretteville, president of Spreckels Sugar and CEO and chairman of the Bank of California. As the longtime president of Cypress Point, he had sponsored me for the club in 1975, making me its youngest member. In World War II Charlie had served on the *USS Bunker Hill* aircraft carrier with Dad, who later put him on the board of Ridder Publications where he served from 1969, when we went public, until '74 when we merged with Knight. In the end, everything connects.

The easygoing indoor-outdoor ranch-style house had been built in 1960 by Gardner Dailey, a St. Paul native who went on to become one of the leading purveyors of modernism in the Bay Area. The second of eleven houses ultimately built on the Cypress Point golf course, it had a priceless view of the second hole—all dunes and fairways—and, in the distance, of glittering Fanshell Beach along the famous 17-Mile Drive. We renovated the wood-and-stucco main building, which was a mere 2,500 square feet, with the help of our architect son-in-law. Connie and Katie then collaborated on the interiors, not stinting on my preferred palate of blue and green. This was the sixth house of ours that Katie had contributed her artistry to, and it merited a six-page feature in *Town & Country*. There were also two small outbuildings on the property, and those we simply painted and spruced up a tad.

I was up to my eyeballs with all this un-settling and resettling in the span of a handful of years. In 2010 we also sold an apartment we had in San Francisco, above the Four Seasons Hotel. The couple who bought it owned three luxury condominiums on the world's first residential cruise ship, called, in fact, "The World"—twelve-deck vessel that continuously circumnavigated the globe. "Be our guests," they said, and followed up by sending us the ship's itinerary.

Connie and I opted for a trip for that June and invited Linda and Susie to join us. We boarded in Venice and sailed lightheartedly down the Croatian coast for a week or so. The girls left us—split—in Split. By the time we docked at Syracuse, on the Ionian coast of Sicily, Connie was feeling unwell—increasingly so. She was convinced there was something really wrong, and she wanted to get home. There was an airport in nearby Catania, and we flew from there to Munich and then nonstop to San Francisco.

Connie went right to her doctor. They did a series of tests, and it turned out she was right: there *was* something wrong. *Seriously* wrong. The diagnosis was bile duct cancer—a rare disease afflicting only about eight thousand people a year in the U.S., and even more challenging than the normally lethal pancreatic cancer. The statistics were massed against her.

The doctors recommended a complex but possibly life-saving operation called a Whipple procedure. She was operated on in Monterey. All four of our kids were there with her. While she was in surgery, I received a call from George Shultz saying he had just heard the news from our mutual friend Helen Schwab, Chuck's wife, and wanted me to know that he had undergone the same operation at the hands of the same doctor ten years back and was not only still alive but kicking. He went on to live, by the way, to the age of a hundred.

Connie's surgeon was optimistic: he assured us she had "clean margins," that, in effect, he had "got it all." But for whatever reason, she remained unconvinced.

We were referred for chemotherapy consultation to the head of gastrointestinal oncology at the University of California at San Francisco, one of the world's leading medical institutions. The doctor was a big deal with a fancy title—a nationally known specialist. She prescribed a six-month course "just to be on the safe side. Connie tolerated the treatments pretty well. Each session lasted about three hours. We were in an enormous room with around twenty-five other patients—the only distraction was there always seemed to be at least one person who was being guarded by police.

We had a routine: we would drive up from Pebble Beach on Monday afternoons, spend the night at the Huntington Hotel, then report to the UCSF hospital at 8:00 a.m. And on our way home we would always stop at the Burlingame Country Club in Hillsborough for lunch.

In January we had our final meeting with the doctor. We had just begun to thank her profusely when she said, "I've just received the latest test results and I'm afraid I have bad news for you—it's spread to the liver." Once we heard that, we knew it was all over.

Connie, who had never stopped suspecting that the surgeon had *not* "got it all," took the news stoically. But *I* was shocked—shocked almost in the sense of electricity.

That day, she told me she didn't want to stop for lunch at Burlingame and have to face people. It happened to be Ladies Golf Day, and all her girlfriends were sure to be there and they would be asking how she was doing. We went to a restaurant in San Francisco instead—not that either of us felt much like eating. Then we drove home to Pebble Beach, not speaking much, and called the children.

Connie continued with chemo—this time administered by an oncologist in Monterey. We were determined to lead as normal a life as possible for as long as possible.

In late April we flew to Hawaii for what we knew would be our final time there together. The loss of our sweeping ocean view—a casualty of a neighboring couple's soaring palms—made Connie miserable. When we bought the house, those trees were not an issue, but in the space of five years they had grown to become one. Our respective houses were on the grounds of the Kukio Club, which had added a requirement to their homeowners association agreement that tree height could not exceed roofline. The couple countered that their trees were grandfathered.

Connie and Susie on paddleboards a few weeks before Connie died.

On one of our previous brief visits, when things were still looking hopeful for Connie, I had appealed to the wife, explaining that Connie possibly didn't have long to live. The woman maintained that it was up to her husband, which was hogwash—they were in it together. I pleaded with them to have their trees trimmed in compliance with the rule—a plea that fell on deaf ears. At this point, our dear friend, Sally Lucas (she and Don had a house at the Kukio Club) got involved. She marched right over there and gave the couple a piece of her mind, but her tirade also went unheard. At that point, the majority of homeowners went to bat for us. The couple's response: "So sue us."

Our children made regular visits to Pebble Beach. During one of them, Connie came up with a plan for impartially distributing her jewelry to the three girls. I was delegated to draw numbers out of a hat. First up was Susie, so she got first choice. Connie had all the items neatly laid out on our dining room table: necklaces, bracelets, earrings, rings, and some keepsake Delano items that my mother had given her.

One of the rings was an emerald surrounded by small diamonds that none other than Uncle Joe had had specially designed for Connie. He had made a big thing of presenting it to her—it was the one and only time we were ever invited up to that apartment he maintained in San Francisco. Connie wore that ring out to dinner a lot—it was definitely not the kind of thing you would wear around the house.

The other ring of note was simply of sentimental value: the $200 engagement ring I'd bought in Traverse City in 1960. One day years later, I noticed that she had stopped wearing it and was wearing only the band, but I said nothing. Sometime after I sold the company, she told me that she had always wanted an important diamond ring. No sooner said than done: a couple of our California friends recommended an artisan in New York who designed high-quality rings, and when we were next in the city, we picked out a beautiful one with the help of Katie and her tutored eye. Susie has it now.

The one thing Connie expressed a wish to hold onto until her last breath was her wedding band.

She had told me emphatically that she did not want her older brother Jerry showing up at her funeral. She had a fixation about him. I asked her about it many times, and she would never tell me. The interesting thing is that this was the *only* thing she never told me—at least that I know of. One thing about Connie: she was great at keeping secrets—she was very lawyerly that way. She did confide that it was something that had happened when she was a little girl. But Connie being Connie, she hadn't totally cut Jerry off: we had attended his daughter's wedding in Detroit five years earlier. Knowing that his sister basically had no use for him, Jerry had the decency not to bother her when she was battling cancer—he checked in with me instead. I finally said to her, "He's your brother, I think he should be allowed to come to your funeral, and I'm not going to be the one to tell him he can't." So she asked her younger brother Steve, who she'd stayed close to, to let Jerry know, when the time came, that he wouldn't be welcome.

The morning of August 5, I was at Cypress Point conducting a meeting as president. One of the items on our agenda was a vote on the admission of spouses of members who had gotten remarried. Connie's and my close friend, Glenn Charles, the co-writer and -producer of the TV series *Cheers* and *Taxi*, had lost his wife and later remarried, and now this second wife, Angela, the widow of Ernest Hemingway's son Jack, was up for approval, and that was always a tricky business.

My focus was shattered by a panicky call from Katie from our house saying that Connie was slipping away. My first thought as I bolted from the room was to try and find a plane to fly Susie and Linda from Seattle to her bedside.

Katie was waiting for me at the front door with Par. She said that Connie had been told that the other two were on their way and was refusing medication, wanting to be awake when they arrived. The minute I walked into her room, she said, "Tony, did they approve Angela?" I nodded affirmatively.

Those were her last words. She died as she had lived—always following up, wondering how things had gone, always thinking of others. Katie, Par, and I were holding her close.

Connie's funeral service took place the following Tuesday, on a classic Pebble Beach afternoon. The church, which held 400, was packed to overflowing, and there were plenty of people lined up outside. Each of our four children spoke (our twelve grandchildren were also fully present). Par feelingly evoked his mother sitting in the bleachers during his football practices reading her law school books. Linda, for her part, recalled how fair and consistent Connie always was as a mother. Sally Lucas also spoke, making the salient point that Connie was a person who always wanted to work in order to earn what she already had.

We requested that, in lieu of flowers, donations be made to Filoli in Woodside, a property of the National Trust for Historic Preservation, where Connie had served as the first female president of the governing board. The estate's formal gardens and nature

The memorial to Connie that I commissioned, adjacent to the ocean she loved, and with a view of the sixteenth green at Cypress Point, arguably the most famous hole in all of golf, where she was the Ladies' Golf Captain.

preserve are renowned, and the mansion is frequently recognized by visitors of a certain age, owing to its appearance in the opening credits and assorted scenes in the 1980s television soap opera "Dynasty." In the words of Filoli's executive director, Connie was the essence of "wisdom coupled with grace."

As she had also been an active trustee of the Carmel chapter (we had had a small house there, too, for a time) of the Garden Club of America, I thought to honor her work there by commissioning a rejuvenation of the rundown, overgrown garden in front of City

Hall—the very city hall that Clint Eastwood had famously presided over as mayor in the 1980s. In partnership with the club, I hired a talented landscape architect, who went on to labor for a year on both softscape and hardscape. The garden was unveiled in all its lush new greenery at a municipal ceremony where the mayor, the landscape architect, and I all spoke. My mother came down from San Mateo, and my sister Robin, from Healdsburg; and all four of our children were there. Our three daughters went on to honor Connie's legacy by becoming avid gardeners in their own right.

The day after the funeral, the kids all went home. I was utterly at a loss. Literally, in fact: my wife of fifty-one years was lost to me, and I was lost without her.

One of the last things Connie did in all her all-too-short life—she was just seventy when she died—was line up a woman to come in and cook for me a couple of times a week.

CHAPTER TWENTY-SIX

Found

THE FALL AFTER Connie died, I kept pretty much to myself. It wasn't until December that I began going out some. The children, God bless them, were urging me to date. Registering on an online dating site or visiting a singles bar were completely out of the question. In time, friends began suggesting women for me to meet. The Schwabs fixed me up with an attractive friend of theirs—a prominent woman, a widow. We had dinner a couple of times, but it didn't go anywhere. I went out for lunches or dinners with various other women, but I would hesitate to call what I was doing "dating," which, in any case, I would have been sorely out of practice in, after half a century.

Every five years or so, a friend from the newspaper industry—he owned the *Arkansas Democrat-Gazette* in Little Rock—would host a three-day-long bash, in festive places like Palm Beach and New Orleans, and the 2011 venue was Pebble Beach. At cocktails before the final event of the whole enchilada—dinner at the beach club—a woman I barely knew asked if I was beginning to go out and mentioned that she had an attractive friend who lived next door—meaning, it turned out, Carmel. She invited me to lunch with this woman the next day at the Lodge, the main hotel in town. First thing in the morning, she called to say she had just received word that a relative had died during the night and she had to leave immediately for

Napa, but why don't I have lunch with her friend anyway.

This fluky, circuitous way was how I came to meet "Dede," the woman with whom I continue to enjoy a domestic happiness that I had not believed life would have twice for giving. First impression: very pretty; blond hair worn long, and totally charming. Second impression: high-energy. During lunch, and thereafter, because almost immediately we started to—time to use the "d" word—date, I learned that she was sixty (no problem—I had promised myself never to date anyone close to my daughters' ages); hailed from Jacksonville, Florida; had majored in music at Sweet Briar; did graduate work at Harvard; was twice divorced; had a daughter by the name of Mallory who was off at college; and was a highly sought-after decorator based in Carmel who had earlier practiced her trade in Atlanta, San Francisco, and Washington, D.C. She had

Dede, 2015.

also, she mentioned, dabbled in California real estate and done well. So, no fortune hunter.

I couldn't help noticing she was wearing a cross, and she confessed she was an Anglican Episcopalian and a strong Christian. She turned out to have political passions as well, but, like Connie, to be more conservative than I was.

She also confessed to not being much of a golfer. Oh well ... We were already off and running.

Dede owned an adorable black pug called Roxanne. I'm an early riser, so it normally fell to me to feed and walk her, and for the first time in my life I found myself falling in love with a dog (one often learns the simplest things last). Roxy soon died, of old age, and Dede and I acquired a pug together, which I suggested we name "Polly" after my fabulous great-aunt Laura Delano, a notable dog breeder

Lounging with Polly and Bitsy, 2021.

In front of the church in South Kona, Hawaii, where we were just married—August 16, 2014.

and national dog show judge. A year later we got ourselves another pug, which Dede named Bitsy because she was so tiny when she came to us. They are both gone now, alas, and we have another enchanting pair of pugs, Eloise and Olivia.

Dede and I were married quietly in Hawaii on August 16, 2014, with only Sally and Don Lucas in attendance. The ceremony took place in a small Anglican chapel in the Captain Cook community of South Kona, on the west coast of the Big Island. While Dede and I were dating, Katie had continued decorating for me, but once we were married, my daughter decorously ceded her professional role to my new wife, who began adding her own decorative touches to the main house in Pebble Beach.

A couple of years later, we consulted my son-in-law on ways to enhance the two other buildings on our property. He sized them up unsparingly as good for nothing, or rather, for one thing only—teardowns. He then let slip that he and Katie, not to mention her brother and sisters, had hated staying in the guest house all those years. I "got" it: if I wanted my four kids and their spouses to go on visiting, I needed to class things up. We wound up razing both buildings, then putting up a new guest house on the footprint of the old. And when we replaced the other structure, we enlarged and repurposed it, creating a spacious new master bedroom and a second living room. That building we connected to the main house by a glass-enclosed breezeway.

In 2016 a friend from Cypress Point, John McCoy, the former chairman and CEO of Bank One (at one time the sixth largest in America), invited me to Florida to play in the member-guest tournament at Gulf Stream, with its beautiful Mediterranean Revival, Addison Mizner clubhouse which I knew from when Dad was a member. Dede and I stayed in the McCoys' house, in a gated enclave in Ocean Ridge. At dinner that first night, John said, "Why not move down here—live half the year in Florida instead of Hawaii." I demurred; for one thing, I had no appetite for going through the hassle of joining yet another golf club with a long waiting list. John

Delano Family Reunion: with my siblings Laura, Robin, Peter, and Jill—2015.

said, "If you promise to move to Florida I promise to get you into Gulf Stream within a few months." That sounded next to impossible, but he proved to be as good as his word. (Later, incorrigibly, I also joined Seminole, north of Palm Beach.) As I was leaving the McCoys in Ocean Ridge, I found myself wondering, what on earth do we need that big house in Hawaii for? Circumstances had changed, life was different, the grandchildren had grown up and all gone off to college ... And Dede, for her part, was losing interest in Hawaii because there was so little to do there if you didn't play golf. I mean, if you weren't on the green, or on the beach, or at the gym, or eating, or ... There were none of the cultural, and especially musical, events that were meat and drink for her (she had maintained her strong interest in classical music, and have I mentioned that she plays the violin and the piano?).

I put Hawaii house on the market. It was scooped up by Jay Y.

With Dede in Beijing, 2018.

Lee, the executive chairman of Samsung and the wealthiest man in South Korea, for his mother who already owned a smaller house on the island. He was an acquaintance I had played golf with at Cypress Point, and the two of us sat down in my living room in Pebble Beach and negotiated the deal. He explained that his government paid rapt attention to where its highest-profile citizens owned property outside South Korea, and thus, for political reasons, his mother couldn't afford to own two houses in Hawaii. God knows I didn't want her house—or, for that matter, any other house in Hawaii—but for the deal to work I had to take it as partial payment. I couldn't dispose of it fast enough, but it took a full year.

A few months later, when Dede and I and my brother, Peter, and his wife, Cathy, were about to leave for a cruise in Asia, I let Jay Lee know that we would be stopping in Seoul, and he said, "Let's get together." He arranged for his mother herself to give us a private

Dede and I with my children and grandchildren at a family reunion on the shore of Lake Tahoe, 2020. Katie took the photo.

tour of the spectacular art museum that she had founded with his late father. The three buildings in the complex were designed by world-famous architects—Mario Botta, Jean Nouvel, and Rem Koolhaas—to showcase work by both traditional and contemporary Korean artists. Just as comprehensive and compelling was the collection of Korean artifacts on display: daggers, swords, crowns, ancient manuscripts, jewelry, ceramics, stoneware …

Jay joined us on the tour, then gave us a tour of his own commanding house above the museum, and then of his mother's house, and finally of the house, half a mile or so away, that had belonged to his late grandfather, the founder of Samsung. It was a full day—a crash course in Korean culture.

With Hawaii now behind us, Dede and I were on the same wavelength when it came to relocating to Florida. We purchased a 3,500-square-foot single-story stucco house on the ocean in the same gated community as the McCoys. This move to Ocean Ridge can be counted Tony Ridder's version of Old Home Week. Or, more accurately, Old *Second*-Home Week. Mummy and Dad, for four decades, had spent half the year in their Ocean Club condominium, and my sister Laura, for the past quarter century, has been spending several months a year nearby. The same Laura who was so dreadfully embarrassed at having to share a cabin with her brother on the *SS America* on that European grand tour with our parents in 1960. A lifetime ago.

I've noticed that lives do tend to curve back on themselves—to re-mark their territory. It seems that's just par for the course.

CHAPTER TWENTY-SEVEN

Still in Full Swing

THE ODDS OF a nonprofessional golfer shooting a hole-in-one have been calculated at approximately 12,500 to one. Many above-average players over the course of an entire golfing lifetime never get a hole-in-one. I consider myself damn lucky—I hesitate to say truly blessed—to have scored five, because, believe me, there's a lot of luck involved.

My first hole-in-one was at Cypress Point in 1976 on the fifteenth hole. I was ecstatic.

My second was in 1983, in a member-guest tournament at La Rinconada Country Club in Los Gatos, with its beautiful tree-lined fairways and views over the Silicon Valley to the mountains of Santa Cruz. Every year the club prevailed on a local auto dealer to donate a car as a prize to whoever scored a hole-in-one on the eleventh hole, and that year the car was an expensive Pontiac. I was hitting a golf ball from 160 yards away that had to travel over water, land on the green, and then roll into a cup—exceptionally long odds to the finish line. The auto dealer also dealt in Hondas and let me exchange the Pontiac for two of them, one red and the other blue. I gave them to Susie and Linda, who were both in college at the time.

My third hole-in-one was at Cypress Point in 2004 on the third hole, in the back right position—the most difficult spot on the green.

My fourth hole-in-one was at Gulf Stream, in Florida, four years ago, and that was on the eleventh hole. I was playing with the same person who had been my partner at the member-guest at La Rinconada when I won that car—those cars. What were the odds of *that*?

And what were the odds of my ever getting yet *another* hole-in-one?

My fifth was back at Cypress Point. The Fourth of July 2024 tournament. The ball landed on the left fringe of the seventh green and rolled down to the cup. It was a blind shot—I couldn't see the hole. But when we reached the green and my caddy went over to look, there it was! He shouted, "You got a hole-in-one!" and everybody yelled and screamed. There are four par 3s on Cypress Point, and to have made a hole-in-one on three of them was a once-in-a-lifetime thing—it had never been done before.

Dad never even got one hole-in-one.

The greatest aspirational golf feat aside from the hole-in-one is something that fewer than one percent of us avid golfers ever manage to bring off—shooting our age. Shooting my age had always been on my bucket list, and last year I finally did it, and I did it twice. And this year I did it twice again. So, two years running! (Longevity kicks in. The oldest guy to ever shoot his age was 103.)

Plato said that life must be lived as play. (We tend to remember the quotes we agree with.) Never having lost my competitive edge, I intend to go on playing the ball as it lies.

I'm dead set on keeping my game alive.